Schema Therapy

Step by Step

A Contemporary Guide to
Schema Therapy Concepts and Techniques

Marjolein van Wijk-Herbrink and
Remco van der Wijngaart

Schema Therapy Approaches & Resources

Schema Therapy, Step by Step

A Contemporary Guide to Schema Therapy Concepts and Techniques

Published by:

Pavilion Publishing and Media Ltd
Blue Sky Offices, 25 Cecil Pashley Way
Shoreham by Sea, West Sussex, BN43 5FF

Tel: +44 (0) 1273 434 943
Email: info@pavpub.com
Web: www.pavpub.com

A catalogue record for this book is available from the British Library.

ISBN: 978-1-80388-512-4

Pavilion Publishing and Media is a leading publisher of books, training materials and digital content in mental health, social care and allied fields. Pavilion and its imprints offer must-have knowledge and innovative learning solutions underpinned by sound research and professional values.

First published in Dutch under the title:

Schematherapie, stap voor stap, Marjolein van Wijk-Herbrink & Remco van der Wijngaart en Hannie van Genderen, edition: 1., ISBN 978-90-368-3169-7

Authors: Marjolein van Wijk-Herbrink and Remco van der Wijngaart
Cover design: Emma Dawe, Pavilion Publishing and Media Ltd
Page layout and typesetting: Anthony Pitt, Pavilion Publishing and Media Ltd
Printing: Independent Publishers Group (IPG)

Contents

Preface and Acknowledgements

After several years of brainstorming about the content of this book, we are delighted with the result! Our collaboration began while teaching schema therapy, where we noticed that therapists appreciate guidance in designing individual treatment plans and implementing methods and techniques. The first result of our collaboration is the audiovisual production 'Schema Therapy for Children and Adolescents: Step by Step', in which we show how schema therapy can be applied to young people. This production builds on 'Schema Therapy: Step by Step', which shows all the steps of schema therapy with an adult client with borderline personality disorder.

We discussed the guidelines provided in this book at length. We often agreed, but sometimes we did not. In those cases, we engaged in dialogue, consulted the (scientific) literature and conducted research with colleagues and clients. Based on these findings, we were always able to reach agreement, further refining the guidelines and learning a great deal from each other and our research.

We are grateful to our clients and colleagues for the insights and inspiration to do our work and write this book. Special thanks go to Hélène Bögels, Hannie van Genderen and Marrit Elzinga, who contributed to this book by proofreading chapters and providing commentary. Finally, we would like to thank our partners and children for putting up with our many video calls on early Sunday mornings, the constant messages we have been sending back and forth, and for their support and patience when we were completely absorbed in writing this book.

Marjolein van Wijk-Herbrink and Remco van der Wijngaart

December 2025

Foreword

This book, *Schema Therapy, Step by Step,* is being published in an anniversary year. It probably offers the most comprehensive overview of all possible interventions that a schema therapist can use to shape schema therapy.

It is exactly thirty years since the introduction of schema therapy in the Netherlands and twenty-five years since the first Dutch-language book on this subject (Arntz and Bögels, 2000). It has been twenty years since the Dutch Register for Schema Therapy was established, of which Remco van der Wijngaart is now chairman. It is also twenty years since the first major study demonstrating the effectiveness of schema therapy in borderline personality disorder and the publication of the first audiovisual production on this subject, edited by Marjon Nadort.

Over the past two decades, schema therapy has taken off enormously. About fifteen years ago, Marjolein van Wijk-Herbrink was one of the first to investigate, in theory and practice, how schema therapy could be applied to adolescents. In 2018, she obtained her PhD on the application of schema therapy to adolescents with externalizing behaviour problems.

A great deal of scientific research has also been conducted into the effectiveness of schema therapy for other types of problems and other target groups. The range of audiovisual material has grown spectacularly since 2018, partly due to the efforts of Remco van der Wijngaart. The first production was Schema Therapy: Step by Step (2018), and the most recent, on its application to children and young people, was made in collaboration with Marjolein van Wijk-Herbrink: Schema Therapy: Step by Step (2025). It is therefore not surprising that this book has been given the title *Schema Therapy, Step by Step*.

The book clearly describes for the (novice) schema therapist how to carry out each intervention as successfully as possible, step by step, with both adults and youth. The advice is based not only on scientific knowledge, but also on experience gained in practice and in training as a schema therapist. Each intervention is accompanied by a well-developed case description based on three clients. Two clients are adults with cluster C or cluster B personality problems. It is mainly the third client, an adolescent with conduct disorder and low motivation for therapy, that makes it particularly interesting. In addition, it is very helpful for novice therapists that each chapter answers the questions of what to do if things do not go smoothly and what the possible variations are.

This allows novice schema therapists to choose from a large number of 'recipes' to put together a suitable treatment for each client. It is made clear that you must take into account the different phases of schema therapy. For each mode, it explains that you first need to do thorough preparation (assessment phase) and then use other 'recipes' for the starter (initial phase of treatment), the main course (middle phase of treatment) and the dessert (final phase of treatment). For each phase, it is clearly described how the role of the therapist changes: from being more caring and supportive, via jointly addressing problems, to coaching and encouraging from the sidelines. Ultimately, the client should be able to prepare the recipes themselves; in other words, their own Healthy Adult mode will have become so strong that they become the head chef in their own life.

The authors indicate that this book is intended as a reference work to help you shape and substantiate your treatment with schema therapy. Although they emphasize that the book does not provide a complete overview of all possible techniques within schema therapy, after reading all fifty-four chapters, you can conclude that they have nevertheless succeeded in being as comprehensive as possible.

Hannie van Genderen

December 2025

PART I: General Overview

Chapter 1: Introduction

With this book, we hope to support (novice) schema therapists in providing schema therapy and applying various techniques. To this end, we describe guidelines for each technique to ensure that the intervention is as successful as possible. Providing guidelines may suggest that the technique must always be performed in that specific way. Nothing could be further from the truth: schema therapy is not a manualized treatment, and there is room for all kinds of variations in the implementation of interventions.

What is schema therapy?

Schema therapy is an integrative form of psychotherapy (Young et al., 2003; Young and Brown, 2005) that is indicated for clients with personality disorders or persistent/recurrent syndrome disorders, such as depression. Schema therapy is an intensive, person-centred, non-manualized treatment that takes one to several years. There is currently no evidence for the effectiveness of (individual) schema therapy with fewer than twenty-five sessions. In the initial phases of therapy, sessions are held at least once a week. Schema therapy differs from other forms of psychotherapy in the following three characteristic elements (Vereniging voor Schematherapie [Dutch Association for Schema Therapy], 2024).

The use of language in the form of concepts such as emotional needs, schemas and modes

The extent to which a child's core emotional needs are met determines the formation of schemas (expectations about oneself, others and the world). These may be early maladaptive schemas resulting from deficiencies in the fulfilment of emotional needs (hereinafter referred to as 'negative schemas' or 'schemas'), or positive schemas when those emotional needs are adequately met. When situations in the here and now trigger those schemas, a temporary state of mind is activated and determined by the triggered schemas and the coping response (resignation, avoidance or inversion). These states of mind are called the 'modes' or 'sides' of your client. See Chapter 2: Overview of Concepts for descriptions of the modes.

The nature of the therapeutic relationship in the form of limited reparenting

As a schema therapist, you act as a role model for a secure attachment figure who, within the boundaries of the professional relationship, provides for the fulfilment of core emotional needs that were not met in your client's life. In doing so, you offer your client corrective emotional experiences, which serve as an antidote to their negative schemas. You also model the Healthy Adult in your client with regard to recognizing and fulfilling emotional needs. See Chapter 2: Overview of Concepts for concrete examples of the limited reparenting approach.

The use of experiential, cognitive and behavioural techniques

These techniques follow three different paths: the paths of 'feeling', 'thinking' and 'doing'. There is no fixed order for using these techniques, and they are not manualized, but should be used flexibly to change patterns within your client's personality. The guidelines in this book are therefore intended as a supportive framework. If you know the goal and guidelines of an intervention, you can improvise better and deliver tailor-made solutions. For each of the interventions, there are countless variations that deviate from the steps as described, without compromising their effectiveness.

Example

When a client says they are greatly troubled by memories from the past, you do not first need to do the happy place exercise or use an affect bridge as described in the guideline (see, for example, Chapter 23: Imagery Rescripting – The Therapist Rescripts). In such a situation, it is also perfectly acceptable to ask your client to close their eyes and go directly to the memory as if they were there again. Although it may seem as if steps are being skipped, the essence of the imagery rescripting technique is retained, namely that meaningful experiences from the past are rewritten in such a way that emotional needs are met.

How to use this book

This book is intended as a reference work to help you shape and substantiate the implementation of schema therapy. In Part II of the book, you will find interventions that can help you and your client understand their presenting problems in the diagnostic phase from the perspective of unmet emotional needs, schemas and modes. These are techniques that contribute to the case conceptualization, without claiming to be exhaustive.

In Parts III–VI, you will find techniques that you can use as desired during the treatment phase (with initial, middle and final 'subphases' of therapy) to work on different modes and underlying schemas. Although in your treatment plan you will already have considered which techniques to use to help your client achieve their therapy goals, it is important to remain flexible during sessions. Here are some guidelines:

- Always keep in mind the overarching goal of schema therapy: validating unmet emotional needs in order to change dysfunctional personality patterns.
- Use your limited reparenting attitude and various techniques to bring about corrective emotional experiences. This requires some degree of schema activation, after which you can validate unmet emotional needs. These corrective emotional experiences need to be consolidated so that they can be used as building blocks to change patterns of thinking, feeling and behaving and anchor them in your client's Healthy Adult mode.
- Work with the mode(s) that is/are active in the therapy session. At the start of the session and in challenging situations during treatment, the guiding question is: 'Who am I hearing here? Is this a child, coping or inner critic mode, or is it the Healthy Adult?' Once you have recognized and become aware of the mode, you can choose an intervention that is appropriate for it considering the phase of therapy. Although the book is divided into different initial, middle and final phases of therapy, this does not mean that the interventions described there can only be applied in that phase: note that it is only a guideline.
- In each session, work towards establishing contact with the Vulnerable Child and strengthening the Healthy Adult. Research has shown that changes in these two modes correlate with more positive therapy outcomes six months later (Yakin et al., 2020). Both coping and inner critic modes can get in the way of bringing your client into the state of the Vulnerable Child. The guideline with regard to coping modes is to negotiate with them and move past them. This allows your client to learn to connect with the underlying feelings and needs of the Vulnerable Child. Inner critic modes, on the other hand, will have to be 'fought' in order to validate core emotional needs. As a therapist, you are a role model for the healthy messages that are internalized by your client. The way in which the inner critic mode is 'fought' depends on the subtype (Punitive Critic requires a more robust approach than Demanding Critic or Guilt-Inducing Critic), the phase of therapy (in the initial phase, the counter-arguments will be more dichotomous and in the final phase more nuanced) and the *window of tolerance* (Siegel, 2012). (Your client must still be able to tolerate the schema activation evoked by working on inner critic modes.)

- Take into account the phases of therapy. Therapy follows a developmental process that can be compared to the phases of a growing child: the initial phase of therapy can be compared to primary school age, the middle phase to puberty and the final phase to young adulthood (Farrell and Shaw, 2012; Reubsaet, 2018; Brockman et al., 2023). Each phase is approached differently, both in terms of the therapeutic relationship and the application of methods and techniques.
- Tailor your limited reparenting attitude to your client's relevant core emotional needs and the phase of therapy: Do you need to be a role model of a parent who primarily offers safe attachment to others, or sets limits? In addition, in the initial phase of therapy your approach is more directive, aiming to create awareness and offer corrective emotional experiences. In the middle phase, you adopt a coaching role, 'alongside the client', helping the Healthy Adult recognize and work on modes independently and learn to validate emotional needs. In the final phase of treatment, you step back further, coaching from the sidelines and encouraging your client to implement behavioural changes.
- For each session, choose a technique that suits your client's active mode, therapy goals and the phase of therapy. This book emphasizes experiential techniques, but that does not mean that we consider them more important than cognitive and behavioural techniques. However, the addition of experiential techniques is characteristic of schema therapy, and many books have already been published on cognitive and behavioural techniques. Once again, we would like to emphasize that this book does not provide a complete overview of all possible techniques within schema therapy. The integrative nature of schema therapy means that you can use a variety of techniques, including those from other therapeutic approaches, to achieve the goals of schema therapy.

Two experiential techniques that are frequently used in schema therapy are imagery rescripting and chairwork. We will briefly explain them below.

Imagery rescripting is an evidence-based technique (Morina et al., 2017; Kip et al., 2023, Kroener et al., 2023) and is frequently used in schema therapy (Young and Brown, 2005; Arntz and van Genderen, 2021; van der Wijngaart, 2021). Mental images can evoke emotions, and changing these images, or the visualized course of events, can lead to corrective emotional experiences. This technique can therefore be used for therapeutic purposes. The guideline is to let your client empathize with a schema-activating mental image and to validate their core emotional needs in as vivid and realistic a way as possible in order to arrive at corrective emotional experiences, which then need to be consolidated. How you arrive at those meaningful memories/images is less important. The step-by-step plan described in Chapters 23, 26 and 34 can help with this, but there are various other routes that can be envisaged.

The essence of *chairwork* in schema therapy is that chairs can be used as representations of the different modes. In schema therapy, other objects are also used to represent a mode, such as cards and dolls. The advantage of chairs is that your client, sitting in the chair, embodies the mode more, so that getting up from the chair is not only a physical movement, but also an emotional distancing from the mode in the chair. This distancing, or defusion, is an essential step in the process of becoming aware of and then being able to work on the different modes. Based on this principle, chairwork has many variations (see also van der Wijngaart, 2023). This book describes step-by-step plans that have a certain logic to them and can help you find your way around the technique. It remains important to emphasize that you can use the chairs in different ways and with different positions in the room, whereby you and your client can both sit in those different chairs to work on therapy goals. Ultimately, the objective is to make contact with the Vulnerable Child and to validate the emotional needs that have not been met. In summary: chairwork also aims to activate schemas so that corrective emotional experiences can be brought about by validating core emotional needs, whereby those corrective experiences must ultimately be consolidated.

Cases

We illustrate the various methods and techniques in this book using three case studies, which are described below. See Appendix 2: Case conceptualization – Sandra and Appendix 4: Case conceptualization – Tim.

Sandra, 32 years old

Sandra presents with anxiety symptoms, escalating arguments with her boyfriend, self-harm, mood swings and depressive episodes.

She lives independently and has a social network that includes one significant friend. She is in a relationship with a man who does not have a steady job and regularly uses drugs (often cannabis, sometimes ecstasy) and drinks alcohol. His behaviour is very inconsistent: sometimes insecure and sweet towards her but, especially when under the influence of alcohol, he can also be verbally aggressive and distant. Sandra's job involves cleaning people's homes for twenty-four hours per week.

Sandra grew up with her brother in an intact family with a strongly dominant and aggressive father. Her mother is a sweet, somewhat anxious woman who tried to ignore or excuse her father's behaviour. Sandra has always felt 'different' from her peers and had little connection with them.

Sandra has very low self-esteem and doubts her abilities. As a result of this insecurity, she can lose herself in avoiding social activities (which makes her feel lonely and depressed) or she tries to keep her head above water by acting tougher than she feels (which leaves her feeling exhausted and overwhelmed).

Tim, 15 years old

Tim is sent to therapy by his mother and youth probation officer because of rebellious and aggressive behaviour (at home and on the street). He has had run-ins with the police (for stealing and fighting) and smokes cannabis. He does not see the point of therapy, but is willing to attend the first few sessions.

Tim lives with his mother and his half-sister (eight years old). His father lived with the family until he was six years old and was violent towards Tim and his mother. His mother left him with the help of the Youth Care Agency, and his father is now in prison for other offences. There is no longer any contact with his father. Tim was severely bullied during his childhood until he fought back one day. Since then, he has used violence more often and other children are somewhat afraid of him. He hangs out with older boys and regularly skips school. His mother has little control over him anymore. On the one hand, Tim shows affection towards his mother, but he can also lose his temper when she tries to set limits or insists that he talks to her about their rules and manners.

Tim generally appears nonchalant, as if nothing affects him. Beneath his mask of indifference, he feels bad about the problems between him and his mother and does not want to be aggressive towards her anymore. However, he is inclined to rebel against her (and rules in general). He tends to shout down underlying feelings of incompetence, inadequacy and distrust by presenting himself as big, untouchable and aggressive. The reactions this elicits in others (rejection, disapproval, distancing) reinforce his loneliness and feeling of being different from others.

Mary, 62 years old

Mary is seeking help for extreme fatigue, depressed mood, anxiety and perfectionism.

She works as an HR employee and is currently in a reintegration programme after being off work for six months due to her symptoms. Before that, she worked long hours and tended to take on a lot of tasks and responsibilities. She is married and has two adult children who live on their own. Her husband is a quiet man who keeps to himself, but takes care of all the practical matters. Mary has two friends with whom she meets regularly; apart from that, she has few social contacts. She does chat with others at the tennis club or while walking her dog, but she feels inhibited by feelings of inferiority and social awkwardness. Her parents are elderly and place heavy demands on her for practical matters and companionship, which makes it difficult for Mary to set limits.

Mary tends to adapt to (the expectations of) others and not express her own emotions and needs, which makes her feel overburdened and misunderstood. She is not sure what she wants and tends not to think about it. She is very perfectionistic and feels responsible and guilty about work and the well-being of her family members, which exhausts her.

Chapter 2: Overview of Concepts

Core emotional needs

Schema therapy focuses on the concept of (unfulfilled) core emotional needs: if core emotional needs are not sufficiently met, schemas and modes develop, resulting in mental health problems. Schema therapy therefore aims to meet those core emotional needs within the therapeutic relationship, using various methods and techniques.

To be considered a core emotional need, three conditions must be met (Dweck, 2017):

- The need is unique, i.e., it cannot be reduced to other needs.
- The need is universal and of great value, i.e., deeply rooted that the pursuit of it can already be seen in the behaviour of young children.
- The need is crucial to well-being and optimal development, i.e., mental health problems arise if it is not met.

We focus on the core emotional needs formulated by Young et al. (2003), supplemented by two emotional needs proposed on the basis of scientific research (Arntz et al., 2021). The most primary emotional needs are those of *safety and nurturance (including safe attachment)*: a child must be able to grow up in a safe environment, where they receive warmth and security. A child must then feel *freedom* to *express needs, opinions and emotions*, so that they experience that what they think, feel and believe is important and that they are allowed to express this. A child will gradually enter the world, and there must be room for *autonomy, competence and sense of identity.* This allows the child to discover what they like and dislike and what they can and cannot do. In addition, the child must also learn to accept the *realistic limits* that exist, and exercise *self-control*: you cannot have or do everything you want. There must be a certain degree of *fairness*: sometimes you win and sometimes you lose, sometimes something is possible and sometimes it is not, sometimes someone else can or is allowed to do more than you, and sometimes it is the other way around. There must also be room for *spontaneity and play*, so that the child can relax, have fun and enjoy themselves. When all these emotional needs are met, a child learns to understand themselves and the world to some extent. *Self-coherence* develops: the child, and later the adult, experiences a grip on themselves and the world, can mentalize and understands what they encounter in their inner and outer worlds.

These emotional needs are explained in more detail below and supplemented with suggestions for implementing your limited reparenting attitude.

Safety and nurturance (including safe attachment): A child needs to receive love, attention and care in a safe, reliable environment, so that they feel protected, connected and appreciated. In your limited reparenting attitude, it is important that you do what you say and say what you do, listen attentively, show closeness and express your appreciation. Working with *transitional objects* is a way to consolidate these messages: give your client small objects that symbolize these messages and your therapeutic relationship, such as a stone, a shell, a doll, a cuddly toy or another object from your therapy room. Helpful phrases are: *I am here to help you. You are safe now. What you feel and need matters to me. You are good just the way you are.*

Freedom to express needs, opinions and emotions: A child should be allowed to express feelings and experiences so that they feel they can be who they are. Your limited reparenting attitude is characterized by asking specific questions about emotions, making plenty of room for this and encouraging your client to share what is going on inside them. Helpful phrases are: *What do you think about this? Your feelings and needs are important. Would you like to say something yourself? You are allowed to set your boundaries. Emotions are normal. I would like it if you told me how you experience something.*

Autonomy, competence and sense of identity: A child should be allowed to discover the world in their own way and in a manner appropriate to their age, so that they learn to make choices and gain experience. Your limited reparenting attitude consists of connecting with your client's competencies, encouraging them to take steps towards autonomy without asking too much of them, and focusing their attention on the things that are going well or that they are good at. Helpful phrases include: *It's OK to make mistakes, you learn from them. I have faith in you and your abilities.* Also, use open questions that promote autonomy, such as: *What could you do now to...? How do you think it should be done? Go ahead and try it!*

Realistic limits and self-control: Children need to be given boundaries when it comes to their own or other people's feelings and functioning in society, so that they learn to regulate their emotions and impulses. You provide guidance on healthy behaviour and set personal boundaries for disruptive or inappropriate behaviour. Helpful phrases are: *I know it's easier to be angry* *with someone else, but that doesn't help you deal with difficult situations. I know you want that, but what you really need is not always the same as what you want. I think it's important that you stop ... [undesirable behaviour] and that you ... [desirable behaviour].*

Fairness: A child should be taught about inevitable inequality and about rules. It is important that they experience that injustice is being corrected where possible, so that they come to see the world as generally fair. With your limited reparenting attitude, you offer compassion for experienced injustice, but you also pay attention to reality (things cannot always be weighed on a golden scale). Explain why something is not possible, for example, if your client has unrealistic expectations of you. Helpful phrases are: *It is not fair how you were treated. You have as much right as others to ... Unfortunately, that is not possible because ... I made a mistake and would like to rectify it with you.*

Spontaneity and play: A child must be given the opportunity to play, relax, experience, follow their intuition, and express spontaneous and creative ideas, so that they feel free and can enjoy themselves. To fulfil this need, organize your therapy session and space in such a way that there is also room for an element of play, use humour and make exercises 'fun' and creative where appropriate. Ask your client to shape one of their modes (or mode dynamic) in their own creative way (e.g., with clay or in a drawing). Helpful phrases are: *Everyone needs time to relax and have fun. Relaxation is not a luxury but a necessity; it is needed to recharge your batteries. What would you really like to do right now? What makes you happy? Let's have a competition to see who can knock over the figure representing your inner critic first with these balls!*

Self-coherence: A child needs help to understand what they encounter within themselves and in the outside world, so that they can see themselves and the world as coherent, feel psychologically healthy and feel that they are leading a meaningful life. In order to achieve this, other emotional needs must be met. With your limited reparenting attitude, you give language to contradictory or overwhelming issues or feelings, help your client to mentalize, use mode language, and help them to recognize their different (social) roles, and consider ways of self-perception and world perception. Helpful phrases are: *You can feel different things at the same time. That man was angry and behaved badly, but perhaps he was actually very shocked. No one is saying anything about it now, but what you are feeling is logical / justified. This is very confusing; sometimes we don't know what we are feeling or what we should do. Well, that sounds like that ... side of you wanted to take over for a moment; we know by now that it comes at times when you feel a lot of stress, right?*

Negative schemas

Below is an overview of the negative schemas with descriptions, your client's feelings when this schema is activated (and they resign themselves to it), possible statements from your client, example items from the Young Schema Questionnaire-Short Form 3 (YSQ-S3) and examples of a therapeutic, limited reparenting attitude.

Disconnection and rejection (in response to unmet need for safety and nurturance)

Emotional Deprivation

Your client expects that significant others will not be sensitive or available to their emotional needs. They feel alone, lonely, unseen, misunderstood and unimportant. This schema is not easily recognized at the beginning of therapy, because the lack of attention and care is so common that your client may not notice it. Statements from clients include: *No one understands me. I am not seen / heard.* Example items from the YSQ-S3 are: *I haven't had someone to nurture me, share him / herself with me, or care deeply about everything that happens to me. I haven't felt that I am special to someone.* As a therapeutic antidote, you are consistently warm, responsive and attuned, offering emotional support and explicitly acknowledging that your client's needs are legitimate.

Abandonment/Instability

Your client expects important relationships to be unstable and that others will eventually leave. They feel rejected, sad, anxious and abandoned. Statements from clients include: *In the end, I will be on my own again. I cannot trust anyone to stay. Eventually, people abandon me.* Example items from the YSQ-S3 are: *I need other people so much that I worry about losing them. When someone I care for seems to be pulling away or withdrawing from me, I feel desperate.* As a therapeutic antidote, you ensure predictability in your interactions and clarity about the boundaries of the therapeutic relationship and your availability.

Mistrust/Abuse

Your client expects others to be malicious, and to abuse, manipulate or hurt them. They are suspicious, tense and anxious. Statements from clients include: *People cannot be trusted* (ask further questions to check whether this is about Abandonment, Emotional Deprivation or Mistrust/Abuse). *People always have a hidden agenda.* Example items from the YSQ-S3 are: *It's only a matter of time before someone betrays me. I feel that people will take advantage of me.* As a therapeutic antidote, you are transparent about your therapeutic methods and clinical documentation, you slowly build trust, you avoid an authoritarian style and you acknowledge any mistakes you make, explaining that they were unintentional.

Social Isolation/Alienation

Your client expects that they are different from others or an outsider, that they don't fit in. They feel alienated, lonely and insecure. Statements from clients include: *I feel like I don't belong. I feel like an outsider.* Example items from the YSQ-S3 are: *I am fundamentally different from other people. I don't fit in.* As a therapeutic antidote, you normalize being different, emphasize uniqueness and authenticity, and work on connection and togetherness within the therapeutic relationship.

Defectiveness/Shame

Your client feels that they are bad, inferior or worthless inside and expects rejection as soon as people really get to know them. They feel shame and fear of being exposed. Statements from clients include: *I am worthless. If people really knew me, they would not like me. I am less [nice / loved / attractive / smart] than others.* Example items from the YSQ-S3 are: *I am unworthy of the love, attention and respect of others. No man / woman I desire could love me once he or she saw my defects or flaws.* As a therapeutic antidote, you show unconditional acceptance and compassion, counteract self-criticism and focus on your client's valuable characteristics.

Other-directedness (in the case of unfulfilled need for freedom to express needs, opinions and emotions)

Subjugation

Your client feels that they must suppress their own desires and obey in order to avoid conflict. They feel tension, fear of conflict and guilt when expressing themselves. Statements from clients include: *If I choose for myself, the other person gets angry. I have to adapt, otherwise I will get into trouble.* Example items from the YSQ-S3 are: *In relationships, I usually let the other person have the upper hand. If think that if I do what I want, I'm only asking for trouble.* As a therapeutic antidote, you encourage assertiveness, acknowledge your client's needs and are alert to excessive adaptation or 'obedience' on the part of your client during therapy sessions.

Self-Sacrifice

Your client feels responsible for the well-being of others at the expense of themselves. They feel pressure (to be responsible) and guilt when they choose for themselves. Statements from clients include: *It is my job to ... [call my mother every day so she doesn't feel lonely]. You should always put others first.* Example items from the YSQ-S3 are: *I am a good person because I think of others more than myself. I have always been the one who listens to everyone else's problems.* As a therapeutic antidote, you support your client in prioritizing their own needs and act as a role model for healthy personal boundaries.

Approval Seeking/recognition Seeking

Your client experiences that their self-image depends on external confirmation and appreciation from others. They are insecure and afraid of rejection. Statements from clients include: *I need appreciation to feel good about myself. I change myself depending on the people I am with, so that they will like me more. Even if I don't like someone, I still want them to like me.* Example items from the YSQ-S3 are: *Accomplishments are most valuable to me if other people notice them. Unless I get a lot of attention from others, I feel less important.* As a therapeutic antidote, focus on internal appreciation and pay attention to who your client is rather than what they do.

Impaired autonomy and performance (with unfulfilled need for autonomy, competence and sense of identity)

Failure

Your client does not expect to be able to perform like others or thinks they will fail. They feel incompetent, stupid and afraid of failure. Statements from clients include: *I can't do it. I fail at everything.* Example items from the YSQ-S3 are: *I am not as talented as most people are at their work. I'm incompetent when it comes to achievement.* As a therapeutic antidote, you try to reinforce successes step by step, give realistic feedback, focus on skills and growth, and avoid criticism that feels like proof of failure.

Dependence/Incompetence

Your client feels unable to make decisions independently or cope with life. They feel helpless and anxious when faced with choices. Statements from clients include: *I cannot do without advice from others. Others know better what is good for me.* Example items from the YSQ-S3 are: *I lack common sense.*

My judgement cannot be counted on in everyday situations. As a therapeutic antidote, you try to encourage your client to make their own choices, gradually give them back responsibility and validate their fear without taking over.

Vulnerability to Harm or Illness

Your client expects disasters, accidents or serious illness and experiences a strong sense of threat. They feel fear, panic and physical tension. Statements from clients include: *Something bad could happen at any moment. My stomach hurts, so I might have something serious wrong with me.* Example items from the YSQ-S3 are: *I can't seem to escape the feeling that something bad is about to happen. I worry that I'll lose all my money and become destitute or very poor.* As a therapeutic antidote, you show calmness, help your client distance themselves from catastrophic thoughts and engage in reality checking.

Enmeshment/Undeveloped Self

Your client is struggling with their own identity and feels overly connected to significant others. They feel lost inside and are unsure of who they are. Statements from clients include: *I don't really know who I am without ... [my partner]. My parents are so close to me that I don't really know what I think myself.* Example items from the YSQ-S3 are: *I often feel I do not have a separate identity from my parent(s) or partner. My parent(s) and I tend to be overinvolved in each other's lives and problems.* As a therapeutic antidote, you create space for your client to experiment with their own preferences and pay explicit attention to their own identity.

Impaired limits (in the case of an unfulfilled need for realistic limits and self-control)

Entitlement/Grandiosity

Your client feels superior and believes they have special rights. They feel entitled, impatient and possibly irritated when limits are set. Statements from clients include: *I am generally just better than others. I don't have to follow the rules.* Example items from the YSQ-S3 are: *I feel that what I have to offer is of greater value than the contributions of others. I have a lot of trouble accepting 'no' for an answer when I want something from other people.* As a therapeutic antidote, you set clear limits in a consistent, personal manner and emphasize your client's own responsibility.

Insufficient Self-Control/Self-Discipline

Your client has difficulty with impulses and frustration tolerance, and often fails to complete tasks. They feel a lack of motivation and irritation when frustrated. Statements from clients include: *If I don't feel like it, I don't do it. I don't have the concentration for boring tasks.* Example items from the YSQ-S3 are: *I can't seem to discipline myself to complete most routine or boring tasks. If I can't reach a goal, I become easily frustrated and give up.* As a therapeutic antidote, you offer structure, set mild but clear limits, and practice slowing down and bearing discomfort.

Overvigilance and inhibition (with unfulfilled need for spontaneity and play)

Emotional Inhibition

Your client feels they should inhibit emotions because expressing them would cause danger, shame or rejection. They are reserved and feel inhibited and tense. Statements from clients include: *I am not a very sensitive person. I never cry/get angry.* Example items from the YSQ-S3 are: *I find it hard to be free-spirited and spontaneous around other people. I control myself so much that other people think I am unemotional or unfeeling.* As a therapeutic antidote, you welcome all emotions, set an example of healthy expression and ensure exposure to emotions in small steps.

Unrelenting Standards/Hypercriticalness

Your client believes that everything must be perfect and experiences high internal pressure. They feel rushed and stressed, and are afraid of failing. Statements from clients include: *I still have to ... and I still have to ... I don't have time to relax.* Example items from the YSQ-S3 are: *I try to do my best; I can't settle for 'good enough'. I can't let myself off the hook easily or make excuses for my mistakes.* As a therapeutic antidote, you focus on slowing down, introducing gentleness and (self) compassion, and showing your own imperfection.

Negativity/Pessimism

Your client expects everything to turn out negatively and tends to ignore positive perspectives. They feel anger towards themselves or others and have little compassion and strict morals. Statements from clients include: *Things will go wrong, as always. Things always go wrong in my life.* Example items from the YSQ-S3 are: *Even when things seem to be going well, I feel that it is only temporary. You can't be too careful; something will almost always go wrong.* As a therapeutic antidote, try to find small rays of hope together and point out nuances to your client without trivializing them.

Punitiveness

Your client believes that their own and others' mistakes should be severely punished. Statements from clients include: *You have to pay for your mistakes. If you do something wrong, you have to be hard on yourself.* Example items from the YSQ-S3 are: *If I don't try my hardest, I should expect to lose out. If I don't do the job right, I should suffer the consequences.* As a therapeutic antidote, emphasize compassion, place growth above punishment and demonstrate how to be kind to yourself while still taking responsibility.

Newly proposed schemas

For an unmet need for fairness

Unfairness

Your client experiences the world as fundamentally unfair, expects that this will not be corrected in society and fears becoming a victim. They are indignant and angry, possibly also fearful, about social or personal injustice. Statements from clients include: *I really can't stand injustice. The authorities are just muddling through and no one is intervening, and I'm the one who suffers again.* As a therapeutic antidote, you acknowledge feelings of injustice without polarizing them, explain normal variations in inequality and teach your client to tolerate them, focus on personal influence and repair any of your own actions that cause injustice.

In the case of an unfulfilled need for self-coherence

Lack of a Coherent Identity

Your client experiences themselves as fragmented and changeable, without a clear sense of being an 'I'. as they are confused, uncertain and alienated from themselves. Statements from clients include: *I consist of separate parts and have no control over them. I don't understand who I am or why I exist. I am always so confused.* As a therapeutic antidote, you provide consistency, you subtitle your client's behaviour verbally and non-verbally (and translate this into their modes), you reflect on their feelings, thoughts and behaviour, and you help your client to form their identity.

Lack of a Meaningful World

Your client experiences the world as empty or meaningless and feels disconnected from it. They feel empty and that life lacks meaning. Statements from clients include: *I just don't understand how the world works. What's the point of it all?* As a therapeutic antidote, you subtitle verbal and non-verbal messages from others, explore important values of society and of your client, and focus on meaning.

Positive schemas

In recent years, there has been increasing attention for positive schemas, which develop when core emotional needs are met in childhood. Positive schemas can play an important role in the recovery process and should be reinforced in therapy so that they are integrated into healthy modes. Positive schemas can be measured using the Young Positive Schema Questionnaire (Louis et al., 2018) and are divided into four domains:

- Connectedness: Emotional Fulfilment, Emotional Openness and Spontaneity, Social Belonging and Success;
- Autonomy: Healthy Self-Control/Self-Discipline, Stable Attachment, Competence and Optimism;
- Healthy and realistic standards: Realistic Expectations, Self-Care and Self-Compassion;
- Realistic limits: Self-Direction, Self-Discipline and Consideration for Others.

Modes

This section is an overview of the modes with underlying schemas and coping responses (according to Arntz et al., 2021). We describe the possible feelings, thoughts and behaviours of your client when these modes are active, ideas for personalized names for the modes, the purpose of working with that mode, and commonly used therapeutic methods and techniques.

Child modes (resignation to schemas)

Vulnerable Child (including Lonely, Abandoned, Abused or Inferior Child)

In this mode, your client resigns themselves to the experiences of activated schemas. These can be many different schemas, such as Emotional Deprivation, Abandonment/Instability, Mistrust/Abuse or Defectiveness/Shame. Your client **feels** loneliness, fear, sadness, insecurity or inferiority (depending on the activated schemas). For example, they may **think**: *No one is really there for me. I am being abandoned. I am not safe. Others don't like me.* What they **do** is, for example, withdraw, cling to someone, cry. This varies depending on the type of problem: in a client with obsessive–compulsive personality disorder, the Vulnerable Child mode looks different to a client with borderline personality disorder. Commonly used personalized **names** are: Little … [client's name], Sad … [client's name] or Fearful … [client's name]. The **aim** of working with the Vulnerable Child is to create a safe attachment to others and validate other relevant emotional needs. Commonly used **methods and techniques** include imagery rescripting, in which the child is protected or has another emotional need met, challenging beliefs that keep the Vulnerable Child small and practicing asking for support.

Angry Child

Many different schemas can be activated in this mode. Your client **feels** intense frustration and anger because emotional needs are not being met. For example, they may **think**: *Nobody sees what I need! It's unfair! You don't understand anything!* They may **react** by lashing out angrily or stamping their feet. Common personalized **names** are: Angry … [client's name], Fussyfoot, Firecracker. The **aim** is to vent anger within realistic limits and to recognize anger as a signal of unmet emotional needs. Commonly used **methods and techniques** include letting the Angry Child rage, distinguishing between anger caused by the current situation and anger caused by activated schemas, and practicing assertiveness without escalation. If a client has too little contact with their anger, it is important to normalize anger and to encourage it.

Enraged Child

In this mode, many different schemas may be activated. Your client **feels** intense anger and loss of control. What they **think** depends not only on the activated schemas (see Angry Child), but also: *Look what you've done to me!* What they **do** includes shouting, swearing, hitting, breaking things and exhibiting explosive behaviour. Commonly used personalized **names** are: the Hurricane, Tornado- … [client's name], the Bursting Bomb. The **goal** is to learn how to deal with tension and anger appropriately and to stop escalation. Commonly used **methods and techniques** include limit setting in combination with venting anger, body-oriented techniques and training frustration tolerance.

Impulsive Child

In this mode, your client resigns themselves to the schema of Insufficient Self-Control/Self-Discipline. They **feel** inner urges, restlessness and strong impulses. They **think**: *I want it now! I have to do it right away!* What they **do** is act impulsively, take risks and immediately follow their needs. Personalized names are: YOLO (you only live once), Spring-in-the-Field, Fast … [client's name]. The **aim** is to strengthen impulse control and awareness of needs versus impulses. Commonly used **methods and techniques** include providing direction, limit setting, chairwork, cognitive delay, stop-think-do and exposure to discomfort.

Undisciplined Child

In this mode, your client resigns themselves to the Insufficient Self-Control/Self-Discipline schema. They **feel** resistance, laziness and frustration when faced with obligations. They **think**: *I don't want this. I'll decide for myself. I'll do it another time.* What they **do** is avoid, give up, refuse and complain. Personalized **names** are: Loose Leaf, the Rebel, the Chill One. The **aim** is to build task persistence. Commonly used **methods and techniques** are giving direction, limit setting, chairwork, behavioural experiments and training planning skills.

Dysfunctional inner critic modes (resignation to schemas)

Demanding Critic

In this mode, your client resigns themselves to the Unrelenting Standards/Hypercriticalness schema. They **feel** stress and constant pressure. They **think**: *I have to work better/harder. It's not good enough.* What they **do** is, for example, push themselves, exceed their own limits, strive for perfection and not allow themselves any rest. Personalized **names** are: the Strict One, the Drill Sergeant, the High Bar. The **aim** is to combat the demanding messages. Commonly used **methods and techniques** are imagery rescripting, chairwork, challenging cognitions related to high standards, practicing with play, relaxation and doing tasks at a 'good enough' level.

Punitive Critic (including Guilt-Inducing Critic)

In this mode, your client resigns themselves to the Punitiveness schema. They **feel** self-hatred, guilt and shame. They **think**: *I deserve punishment. I am bad.* What they **do** is belittle themselves, punish themselves and act self-destructively. Personalized **names** are: the Whip, the Inner Bully, the Accuser, the Prosecutor. The **aim** is to combat these messages. Commonly used **methods and techniques** include imagery rescripting, chairwork, challenging cognitions related to self-punishment and self-accusation, practicing self-compassion and learning to disappoint others (if necessary).

Dysfunctional coping modes (avoidance or inversion of schemas)

Compliant Surrenderer

This mode may be underpinned by almost all schemas, which your client avoids. They may **feel** fear of rejection, tension and/or suppressed anger. They **think**: *I have to do what others want, otherwise I'll get into trouble.* What they **do** is please, adapt, not set their own boundaries or blur them, and avoid conflict. Personalized **names** are: the Pleaser, the Chameleon, the Adapter. The **aim** is to endure friction or conflict and to train assertiveness. Commonly used **methods and techniques** are empathic confrontation, chairwork, challenging beliefs (*I have to adapt to others to prevent ... [schema]*), practicing setting and monitoring one's own boundaries and expressing one's own wishes.

Detached Protector

Almost all schemas may underlie this mode, and your client avoids them. They feel flat, empty and detached. They **think**, for example: *Feelings are dangerous, I must shut myself off.* What they **do** is put up a wall, dissociate, and avoid contact and intimacy. Personalized **names** are: the Wall, the Mask, the Robot. The **aim** is to reduce avoidance and restore contact with one's own emotions. Commonly used **methods and techniques** are empathic confrontation, chairwork, challenging beliefs (*I'd better not feel / express my emotions, because otherwise ... [schema]*) and exposure to emotions.

Angry Protector

Almost all schemas may underlie this mode, and your client avoids them. They **feel** anger, irritation and distrust. For example, they **think**: *Stay away from me, otherwise I will get hurt.* What they **do** is create distance through sullenness, cynicism or an angry, dismissive attitude. Personalized **names** are: the Gruff, the Grumpy, the Porcupine. The **aim** is to reduce (angry) avoidance and restore contact with one's own emotions. Commonly used **methods and techniques** include empathic confrontation, chairwork, challenging beliefs associated with the schemas (e.g., *I will not be understood. I never get what I need.*), exposure to emotions and practicing allowing closeness with others.

Detached Self-Soother

This mode may be underpinned by almost all schemas, and your client avoids them. They **feel** tension, restlessness or emotional pain that needs to be numbed. They **think**: *I don't want this feeling, I'll numb myself or seek distraction.* What they **do** is excessive gaming, working, exercising, phone scrolling or watching TV series; use substances; overeat; or self-harm. Personalized **names** are: the Numb, the Distractor, the Runner or the Scroller. The **aim** is to learn to tolerate emotions and to learn other, healthy ways of regulating emotions. Commonly used **methods and techniques** include empathic confrontation, chairwork, challenging beliefs (*I cannot tolerate my emotions*) and practicing emotion regulation.

Suspicious Overcontroller

Almost all schemas may underlie this mode, and your client avoids them. They **feel** hyperalert and possibly suspicious. They **think**: *I have to be careful, people have bad intentions.* What they **do** is test, verify, check and not trust you with things. Personalized **names** are: the Detective, the Scan Mode, the Camera. The **aim** is to learn to let go of controlling behaviour and strengthen trust in others. Commonly used **methods and techniques** are empathic confrontation, chairwork, challenging interpretations of mistrust and injustice, and practicing trust.

Perfectionistic Overcontroller

This mode is the result of an inversion of the Failure, Emotional Deprivation or Insufficient Self-Control/Self-Discipline schemas. Your client **feels** pressure, a tense sense of responsibility and an underlying fear of failure. They **think**: *It has to be perfect. I have to have everything in order.* What they **do** is control, overwork, obsessively organize, worry or maintain control in other ways. Personalized **names** are: the Perfectionist, the Organizer, the Compulsive. The **aim** is to learn to let go of control and to learn to tolerate imperfection. Commonly used **methods and techniques** are empathic confrontation, chairwork, challenging perfectionist rules and practicing allowing mistakes.

Attention and Approval Seeker

This mode is the result of an inversion of the Emotional Deprivation, Defectiveness/Shame, Social Isolation/Alienation or Emotional Inhibition schemas. Your client **feels** insecure and craves attention and recognition. They **think**: *I have to stand out to be seen.* What they **do** is dramatize, exaggerate emotions or eroticize. Personalized **names** are: the Confirmation Seeker, Drama Bug, Attention Buddy. The **aim** is to strengthen self-esteem and self-confidence. Commonly used **methods and techniques** are empathic confrontation, chairwork, challenging cognitions related to self-image and practicing adequate self-expression.

Self-Aggrandizer

This mode is the result of inversion of a schema; this can be almost any schema. Your client **feels** inflated self-esteem and irritability when limits are set. They **think**: *I am more important than the rest.* What they **do** is brag, dominate, make demands and belittle others. Personalized **names** are: the Know-It-All, the Lord of the Manor, Miss Universe, the Arrogant One. The **aim** is to improve the underlying self-image. Commonly used **methods and techniques** are empathic confrontation, chairwork, limit setting, challenging cognitions related to self-image and rules, practicing perspective-taking and treating others with respect.

Bully and Attack

This mode is the result of inversion of the Abandonment, Subjugation, Unfairness or Mistrust/Abuse schemas. Your client **feels** anger, tension and underlying fear of humiliation. They **think**: *I must attack before I will get hurt.* What they **do** is bully, intimidate, and display verbal and physical aggression. Personalized **names** are: the Fighter, the Bully, the Attacker. The **aim** is to stop the threatening or intimidating behaviour and teach your client to deal with underlying triggers in an appropriate manner. Commonly used **methods and techniques** include limit setting, empathic confrontation, chairwork, challenging cognitions that justify the attack in your client's eyes (the other person provoked me) and practicing alternative behaviour.

Conning and Manipulation

This mode is the result of an inversion of the Abandonment or Unfairness schemas. Your client **feels** opportunism and an underlying fear of losing control. They **think**: *I have to play it smart to get what I want.* What they **do** is lie, manipulate, deceive, withhold information to avoid rejection or punishment, or to gain an advantage. Personalized **names** are: the Joker, Twister, Sly. The

aim is to teach your client to take responsibility. Commonly used **methods and techniques** include setting limits within a safe relationship, empathic confrontation, chairwork, challenging cognitions that elicit deceitful or manipulative behaviour from your client, and practicing taking responsibility.

Predator

This mode is the result of an inversion of the Unfairness schema. Your client **feels** coldness and vengeful feelings, and is calculatingly calm. They **think**: *I must eliminate this risk. I must not show weakness.* What they **do** is strategically inflict damage, exploit and oppress. Personalized **names** are: the Iron Hand, the Hunter. The **aim** is to stop the associated behaviour and ensure safety. Commonly used **methods and techniques** include setting strict limits, empathic confrontation, examining threat perceptions, risk assessment, and learning and practicing alternative ways of dealing with triggers for this mode.

Functional modes

Healthy Adult

In this mode, there are positive schemas (see section, Positive schemas). Your client **feels** a certain degree of calm, stability, confidence and (self) compassion. For example, they **think**: *I can handle this. My needs are important, but I also take others into account.* What they **do** is take care of themselves, solve problems, help others without losing themselves and set boundaries for themselves where necessary. Personalized **names** are: the Captain, Wise … [client's name], Strong … [client's name]. The **aim** is to strengthen this mode. Commonly used **methods and techniques** are future-oriented imagery, chairwork with the three steps of the Healthy Adult, integrating realistic beliefs and behavioural experiments.

Happy Child (also belongs to the category of 'child modes')

In this mode, there are positive schemas (see section, Positive schemas). Your client feels spontaneous, safe, playful, connected and relaxed. They **think**: *I am allowed to play. I am OK the way I am.* What they **do** is enjoy themselves, be creative, engage in social interactions and be spontaneous. Personalized **names** are: Dancing … [client's name], Radiant … [client's name], Happy. The **aim** is to stimulate the Happy Child. Commonly used **methods and techniques** are imagery focused on safe, fulfilling experiences; modelling spontaneity and play; and trying out activities that bring joy and energy.

PART II: Assessment Phase

Determining that schema therapy is indicated

Schema therapy is indicated in cases of personality disorder or recurrent or persistent syndrome disorder for which previous guideline treatment has been ineffective. Comorbid problems or mild intellectual disability are not contraindications for schema therapy. There is some evidence that schema therapy can be effective with autistic people and people with personality problems (Vuijk et al., 2024). However, it should be emphasized that more research is needed and specific treatment models need to be developed. In cases of comorbid substance use disorder, it may be necessary to address the substance-related problem first. At the same time, schema therapy can help clients gain insight into the underlying functions of their substance use and manage emotions and cravings in a more adaptive way, thereby increasing their motivation to change and the likelihood of successful addiction treatment.

Rationale for schema therapy

Explain to your client what schema therapy entails, so they know what to expect. See Appendix 1: Rationale for schema therapy for an initial introduction of schema therapy. During the assessment phase, while exploring emotional needs, schemas and modes, you can continue to incorporate elements of the rationale so that your client gains a better understanding of their patterns and how schema therapy can help.

Goal of the assessment phase

The goal of the assessment phase is to investigate how your client's presenting problems are related to unmet emotional needs in childhood and to the schemas and modes that were developed as a result. You incorporate this into an individual case conceptualization, which is therefore an explanatory model for the current presenting problems. The case conceptualization is the end product of the assessment phase and forms the basis for the treatment plan.

Setting up the assessment phase

In the assessment phase, you can use various methods and techniques to explore emotional needs and identify the most relevant schemas and modes of your client. Make sure you use not only cognitive methods (by thinking and talking about it), but also experiential methods (by feeling and experiencing it).

Methods and techniques you can use in the assessment phase include:

- discussing current presenting problems
- discussing themes from previous therapies
- life history (with attention to family-of-origin rules and trauma)
- downward arrow technique
- therapeutic relationship
- heterogeneous anamnesis
- tests and questionnaires
- childhood photographs
- diagnostic chairwork
- diagnostic imagery.

With so many different methods and techniques available, it is wise to plan the content of the assessment phase in advance to make sure you use a wide range of cognitive and experiential methods. Experiential techniques, such as diagnostic imagery, not only provide a wealth of information, but also convey an important message to your client: therapy is not just about talking, but often involves experiential exercises.

In the following chapters, you will find methods and techniques that are of great value in the assessment phase.

Chapter 3: Diagnostic Imagery

Objective

To experientially explore which emotional needs were not met in the past and which schemas arose from this, leading to the current presenting problems of your client. In this assessment phase, the aim of the imagery is only to explore and not yet to rescript.

Guidelines

Step 1: Rationale
Step 2: Safe place imagery
Step 3: Imagery of a recent schema-activating event
Step 4: Affect bridge
Step 5: Exploring the childhood experience
Step 6: Safe place imagery
Step 7: Reflection

Explanation of the guidelines

Step 1: Rationale

Introduce diagnostic imagery early in the assessment phase so that it is clear to your client that experiential exercises are part of treatment. Briefly explain the procedure of the exercise and how long it will take, and offer safety and reassurance by indicating that your client is in control and can stop at any time if they wish.

Step 2: Safe place imagery

Ask your client to visualize a place where they feel safe and at ease. This can be a place they have been to or would like to go to, or a place that only exists in their imagination. Ask them about sensory details in the present tense (*What do you see / hear / smell / feel?*) to evoke the positive experience as strongly as possible. Then ask what they feel and where they feel that in their body.

Step 3: Imagery of a recent schema-activating event

Ask your client to let the pleasant image fade and to visualize the recent schema-activating event. Again, ask for sensory details in the present tense: *What do you see / hear / smell now?* Explore the cognitive, emotional and physiological responses in this situation.

Step 4: Affect bridge

Ask your client to focus on these responses. Have they experienced this before? If they recognize those responses as familiar, guide them to let the image of the recent event fade and observe which images from their childhood come to mind.

Step 5: Exploring the childhood experience

Guide your client to experience the childhood image through the eyes of their 'younger self' in the image by asking for sensory details in the present tense: *Who do you see, what is happening, what do you feel?* Ask about their emotional needs in that situation, in a way that is appropriate for the age of their 'younger self'.

Step 6: Safe place imagery

Ask your client to visualize their safe place again. Help them to focus on the pleasant, relaxed feeling this place evokes. Conclude the exercise by asking your client to let this image fade away and open their eyes.

Step 7: Reflection

Give your client a moment to come back to the present and discuss the exercise. Discuss the link between the childhood memory and the schema-activating situation in the present. Explain that this 'old pain' is what causes them to experience such intense feelings and/or exhibit strong behavioural responses. Discuss explicitly the emotional need that does not seem to be fulfilled.

Example

Therapist: I'm curious to know what made you so angry yesterday that you saw red, as you just said. I'd like to do an exercise to explore where that comes from, because not everyone who is looked at on the street will get so angry, right?

Tim: Most of my friends would, but not everyone, no…

Therapist: OK, then we'll do an imagery exercise where I'll ask you to visualize the moment when that boy looked at you like that, and then we'll go back in time to see if we can understand where your anger comes from.

(*Tim nods.*)

Therapist: Close your eyes and feel your feet touching the ground, your body touching the chair … Now, can you picture a place where you feel good and at ease, simply because it's a nice place to be?

Tim: Last summer I was in the Ardennes; there was a clearing in the forest, and I felt very calm there.

Therapist: Tell me a little more about that clearing, as if you were there. What do you see when you look around you now?

(*Tim describes what he sees, the therapist also asks about sounds, smells and sensations [e.g., sun on the skin].*)

Therapist: What do you feel, now that you're sitting on the moss in this clearing, hearing the birds singing and feeling the sun on your skin?

Tim: I feel calm, relaxed, happy.

Therapist: That's wonderful, enjoy that for a moment … And now let the image fade away. Instead, visualize that boy who looked at you on the street.

Tim: Ugh, yes, I can see him right away, with his challenging gaze.

Therapist: Focus on that. What do you see in that look?

Tim: He looks cheeky, arrogant. As if he's *'the man'* and I'm his little dog. I don't like that…

Therapist: As if you're a little dog? How does that make you feel?

Tim: Angry. It feels like he's above me, as if I'm nothing. I need to pay close attention at all times.

Therapist: What do you feel in your body?

Tim: Tension in my hands, arms. And on my chest, but actually in my whole body.

Therapist: Just concentrate on that tension in your body, on your chest and in your hands and arms. And on that feeling that he's standing above you, that you're nothing. Is this a familiar feeling?

[Tim nods]

Therapist: Let the image of that boy fade, while you hold on to this feeling. Can you go back to a childhood memory in which you had roughly the same feeling? Just wait and see what images come to mind

Tim: ...Yes, I see myself in the village square, with all these older children around me.

Therapist: How old are you here?

Tim: I think seven or eight.

Therapist: Be that seven- or eight-year-old boy. You're in the square, and those older children are standing around you. What happens?

Tim: They're bullying me, calling me names. They say I'm not allowed to play in the square. They say I smell and that my clothes are stupid. A few boys keep making movements as if they're going to hit me.

Therapist: (*Soft voice:*) What do you need right now?

Tim: For them to stop ... For me to be allowed to play with them...

Therapist: I completely understand, of course you want that. You can let go of this memory now. Let it fade, and then go back to your nice place in the forest, that clearing.

(The therapist assists Tim in recalling the image of his safe place and stepping into it by repeating the sensory details he described earlier. After observing that Tim has regained a sense of relaxation, he ends the exercise and asks him to open his eyes. He then asks Tim how he experienced the exercise and explains that, based on this and other childhood experiences, Tim has come to believe that others will do him harm [lack of safe attachment to others, Mistrust/Abuse schema], that he may not belong [Social Isolation/Alienation] and that he is inferior to others [Defectiveness/Shame]. These beliefs and associated feelings may be triggered by situations in the present, for example, when someone looks at him in the street, leading to intense anger and coping responses of acting out or acting big [Bully and Attack, Self-Aggrandizer modes].)

What if your client:

- ...does not want to close their eyes?

  Explain that closing their eyes will lead to a better focus on the exercise. If they keep refusing, let them focus on a fixed point on the floor.

- ...cannot visualize a safe place or chooses an unsuitable place?

  Sometimes clients choose an image in which they display coping behaviour (e.g., a park where they regularly smoke cannabis) or one that activates a negative feeling (a client who visualizes their own home, while being admitted to an inpatient clinic and feeling homesick). You can help your client create a safe place in imagery by building it up step by step (inside or outside, colours, smells, etc.).

- ...speaks in the past tense or as an observer (in the third person)?

  Summarize in the present tense. For example: 'OK, you *are* in the square, what *do* you *see* around you *now*? As long as schemas are sufficiently activated, you can let your client talk in the past tense or as an observer during the exercise and discuss this afterwards.

- ...cannot bring up a memory using the affect bridge?

  Remember that there are several ways to identify meaningful images from the past, such as a preliminary discussion of the exercise with questions such as: *Which images are the most vivid?, When did your symptoms start / worsen?, Which memories evoke the strongest feelings of...?, Which experiences prove emotionally that...?* You can also use images from the childhood photos you looked at together.

- ...describes multiple memories after the affect bridge?

  All memories are probably meaningful. Choose the earliest memory or the memory that evokes the strongest feelings.

Variations

If schemas are already activated and your client talks emotionally about a recent event, you can skip Steps 2 and 3. Ask your client to close their eyes and reflect on the emotions and cognitions evoked by the recent schema-activating event (use the downward arrow technique if necessary, see Chapter 5: Downward Arrow Technique) before starting the affect bridge in Step 4.

Preferably, throughout the exercise, speak in the present tense and in the first person from your client's perspective (*I am* in the square). If this is too overwhelming for your client, you can choose to guide them through the exercise with a little more distance by letting them watch the younger version of themselves as an observer, or by allowing them to speak in the past tense.

In a group setting, the presence of other group members can cause so much tension that it is very difficult for clients to visualize a safe or happy place. In group therapy, you can therefore do a guided exercise, in which the therapist describes an image that is likely to evoke positive feelings in everyone, such as visiting a toy shop where you can walk around and choose whatever you want, or an ice cream parlour where you can choose your favourite flavour (see Farrell and Shaw, 2012). After this happy place exercise, diagnostic imagery can be divided into sections, with the group members sharing their experiences with each other and the therapists after each step (recent unpleasant event, affect bridge, image from the past).

Chapter 4: Creating a Timeline

Objective

To map out important events in your client's life so that you can form hypotheses about the extent to which emotional needs have been met and about the schemas and modes that have been formed as a result.

Guidelines

Step 1: Draw a line from birth to the present
Step 2: Place positive and negative events on this line
Step 3: Ask about (unmet) emotional needs for each period or event
Step 4: Link the events or periods to the emergence of schemas and modes
Step 5: Reflect and integrate (make connections with presenting problems)

Explanation of the guidelines

Step 1: Draw a line from birth to the present

Draw the line on a large white sheet of paper or whiteboard. Divide the line roughly into developmental stages (early childhood, primary school, secondary school, young adulthood and adulthood).

Step 2: Place positive and negative events on this line

Ask your client about important events in their life for each period. If your client only mentions negative events, explicitly ask about positive events, and vice versa. Ensure that traumatic events and important life events, such as school experiences, experiences of loss, moving house and victories or successes in your client's life, are discussed. Ask about relationships with parents, peers and other important people during each period. How did your client experience these relationships? Ask them to describe this in order to form hypotheses about (unfulfilled) emotional needs. When discussing early childhood, it is also useful to consider temperament (*What were you like as a young child?*). If your client knows little about this, you can ask them to check with their parents or, in consultation with your client, invite a parent to attend a session. You can use symbols or colours to indicate important events.

Step 3: Ask about (unmet) emotional needs for each period or event

When discussing events or periods, ask your client how they felt, what they needed at that point in their life and to what extent the people around them met those needs. Link this to the core emotional needs within schema therapy: safe attachment to others, self-expression, autonomy, spontaneity and play, realistic limits, fairness and self-coherence (see Chapter 2: Overview of Concepts for a description of the core emotional needs).

Step 4: Link the events or periods to the emergence of schemas and modes

Based on the information you receive about emotional needs, form hypotheses about the schemas your client has developed and the events that led to the formation of those schemas. Include both positive and negative schemas. Ask questions such as: *What did you start to believe about yourself or others at that time?, How did that make you feel?* Also, explore how your client dealt with those messages, so that you can gather information about coping styles and the emergence of relevant modes.

Step 5: Reflect and integrate (make connections with presenting problems)

After creating the timeline, first ask your client how they feel about mapping out their life in this way. What emotions and thoughts does this evoke? Discuss together which events your client considers to be the most relevant or life-defining, and mark these events (e.g., using a colour, symbol or other indication). Next, ask your client what connections they see between past events and their current problems. Present your own hypotheses to them and explain that they may be overreacting to situations in the here and now because old pain is being triggered at those moments.

Example

Therapist: Today, I'd like to gain a better understanding of the course of your life in order to better understand the problems that brought you here. Everyone experiences things in life, both positive and negative, that contribute to how you develop and that sometimes even determine your life. I've just drawn your timeline here, from birth to now, and I'd like to fill it with events that have been important to you. Are there any events that immediately come to mind?

Tim: Yes, I think my parents' divorce was important. I was only five and there was a lot of arguing at the time.

Therapist: That does seem like an important event. (*Marks a point on the timeline that coincides with the age of five and notes 'parental divorce'.*) How did you experience that period?

Tim: Well, it was very unpleasant. I mainly remember the arguments. And that from one day to the next, I suddenly went to live somewhere else with my mother and little brother, with a strange man who was suddenly my stepfather.

Therapist: That must have been very intense for a five-year-old boy. How did you feel at the time?

Tim: I was confused and also a bit scared, because my father would sometimes suddenly show up at the door and then there would be shouting.

Therapist: What did you need at that moment?

Tim: Just for there to be no shouting and for my parents to sort things out between themselves.

Therapist: Yes, I understand, you needed security and predictability. And that your parents would sort things out and you could stay together as a family?

Tim: Yes, that would have been best, of course. Because I missed my father too; he could do fun things with us, and suddenly that was gone too.

Therapist: I can imagine that this period also influenced how you came to see yourself and others. For example, that others can suddenly disappear from your life, or that others might pay little attention to you because they're so preoccupied with their own problems. Do you recognize any of this, or did you start to believe something different about yourself or others during that period?

Tim: Yes, I think both. Everything was swallowed up by the arguments and the hassle; they weren't really concerned with me. And, yes, I realized that someone can suddenly leave. I haven't had any contact with my father for a long time.

Therapist: How did you deal with that at the time?

Tim: I don't know. I just carried on; I think I switched off my feelings or something. I find it difficult to recall; I don't remember much about the past.

Therapist: Ah, that's something we recognize from the here and now, isn't it? That you still tend not to pay too much attention to what you feel. I can well imagine that these experiences were so intense for you as a child that you learned to switch off your feelings as a way to cope and 'survive'. Were there any other events that contributed to this lack of emotions?

What if your client:

- ...has few memories of their childhood?

  Just start by asking questions about the different periods in their life and the different themes. Usually, this will bring back enough memories. If necessary, ask your client to bring photos from their childhood to stimulate memories.

- ...seems distrustful?

  Explain again why you want to create the timeline and reassure your client. Start by discussing positive events.

- ...says that a (traumatic) event has taken place, but does not want to talk about it?

  Explain that it is important for you to know about the event in order to tailor the treatment to your client as effectively as possible, but leave the decision of whether to discuss it up to your client. This is only the assessment phase, so the therapeutic relationship may need to develop further first. Ask your client about the age at which the event took place and mark this on the timeline so that you can return to it later.

Variations

When working with children and adolescents, materials can be used instead of drawing, for example, by laying a rope on the floor to represent the timeline. During the discussion of the various events, you can move along this rope. Symbols can be placed along the rope to mark the events (e.g., stones for negative events and flowers for positive events, or an object of your choice for each event).

Chapter 5: Downward Arrow Technique

Objective

To identify schemas that give rise to automatic thoughts.

Guidelines

Step 1: Select a problem situation

Step 2: Ask about thoughts, feelings and associated meanings

Step 3: Keep asking questions until there is no further depth

Step 4: Show empathy and label the schema

Step 5: Connect this schema to unmet emotional needs in the past and the current presenting problems

Explanation of the guidelines

Step 1: Select a problem situation

When a client brings up a problem situation in a therapy session, it is often one to which they overreacted (e.g., being overwhelmed by sadness, fear or anger; excessive worrying; shutting down). This indicates that a schema has been triggered, although it may not always be apparent from the client's narrative which schema that is.

Step 2: Ask about thoughts, feelings and associated meanings

Asking further questions about the thoughts or feelings can provide access to the underlying schemas. Ask questions such as: *Suppose this is true, what would that mean for you?, What would be so bad about that?, What makes you most angry / sad / anxious?, If that is true, what does it say about you as a person?*

Step 3: Keep asking questions until there is no further depth

Continue to ask probing questions, each time building on the client's answer to your previous question. If you keep repeating this, you will arrive at the deeper level of the schema. The schema activation that then takes place often leads to immediate emotional reactions.

Step 4: Show empathy and label the schema

Tell your client that you fully understand why they hold this belief and how strongly it affects them, especially in light of past experiences that have given rise to this schema. Try to label the schema (or give a quote) in terms that resonate with their own experience.

Step 5: Connect this schema to unmet emotional needs in the past and the current presenting problems

If you do not know much about this yet, ask your client if they recognize this belief from other situations or from their childhood. Name the unmet emotional needs in their history and make connections with the formed schemas and the strong emotional reactions in current problem situations.

Example

Mary: I completely shut down at work again yesterday; I just wanted to walk out of the office and go home.

Therapist: What was going through your mind at that moment?

Mary: I thought: I can't do it, it's too much.

Therapist: And suppose that's true, that you can't do it or that it's too much? What would that mean for you?

Mary: (*Shrugs.*) That I'm failing.

Therapist: And suppose you do fail, what would be so bad about that?

Mary: That others would see that too and think I can't do it.

Therapist: And if others see that and think that, what would that mean for you?

Mary: That's terrible, because then they won't accept me.

Therapist: And suppose they won't accept you, does that say something about you as a person?

Mary: (*Begins to cry.*) Yes ... That I'm an outsider. I've always been different from the rest! I can't take it anymore!

Therapist: Oh ... I can see how this affects you. This is a painful issue for you, isn't it? And I understand from what you're saying that this would be a repeat of previous experiences in your life?

Mary: Yes, I just never really belonged. I already felt that way at school: I liked different things and found different things interesting than my classmates, and that's why I never felt connected. I often just did what they did or tried to talk with them; that helped a little, but of course it didn't really work.

Therapist: So, what you missed most as a child was that feeling of belonging, the connection that every child needs so badly. And because that wasn't there, it left a wound, a wound of sadness, loneliness, the feeling of being different, of not belonging (*schema Social Isolation/Alienation*). Is that right?

(*Mary nods.*)

Therapist: And you learned to adapt as much as possible, to go along with the rest, to avoid being confronted with that feeling of not belonging as much as possible.

Mary: Yes, I think so.

Therapist: Let's go back to the situation at work, that feeling that you wanted to run out of the office. How does that relate to this?

Mary: Um ... I think that at work, I feel like I'm always walking on eggshells. And I'm always trying to do my tasks the way my colleagues do them. And it makes me so tired...

Therapist: It's good that you mention that. So, it's not really about the belief that you can't do something or that you will fail, but that you don't belong if you don't do your tasks the way your colleagues do. And that's an important need; everyone wants to be accepted by others. And to try and fulfil that need, you keep adapting, like you're walking on eggshells.

What if your client:

- ...after repeatedly being asked about the meaning, still can't get to the bottom of it, but you also don't feel that you've really identified the relevant schema?

  Try to vary your questions. In addition to asking what it means to your client or what is so bad about ..., you can also ask what it says about other people or about them as a person. Repeat the downward arrow technique at different moments and in different situations, so that you get more and more information about the relevant schemas.

- ...does not seem to be affected, even though you think you have identified the underlying, most relevant schema?

  It may happen that your question activates the schema and your client switches to a certain coping mode, for example, the Detached Protector. You will then see no emotion. You can point this out and, if necessary, switch to one of the techniques for working with coping modes (see PART V Treatment Phase: Working with Coping Modes).

Variations

If desired, the process can be visualized by writing down the thoughts and drawing ladders or arrows between them.

Chapter 6: Diagnostic Chairwork

Objective

To gather information about your client's modes and mode dynamics.

Guidelines

Step 1: Notice the mode
Step 2: Label the mode
Step 3: Rationale
Step 4: Have your client sit in another chair
Step 5: Interviewing the mode
Step 6: Add an extra chair or chairs for any other modes
Step 7: Reflection from the original chair or standing
Step 8: Homework

Explanation of the guidelines

Step 1: Notice the mode

Chairwork is not only an important tool for gathering information about the modes, it is also a message to your client that they will be doing such exercises in therapy. Identify the active mode in the session or in your client's story – is it a child mode, a coping mode or an inner critic mode?

Step 2: Label the mode

Describe to your client what (emotional, cognitive and behavioural) state you observe: What does your client say, in what tone and with what facial expressions? Support this description with gestures: When talking about this state, point to a place next to your client, almost as if you were talking about a third person. This supports the process of becoming aware of the modes.

Step 3: Rationale

Explain that this technique helps to gain insight into the modes and their relationship to the presenting problems. Explain to your client that they remain in control and can therefore stop the technique whenever they want.

Step 4: Have your client sit in another chair

Place an extra chair in the designated spot for the modes. Be directive in guiding the exercise, as this will provide clarity for a technique that may initially feel strange and uncomfortable for your client. For example, say: *'In this chair, I want you to completely identify with that side. I will also address you as such.'*

Step 5: Interviewing the mode

From this point on, address your client as if they are the mode, using 'you' rather than 'that side'. Depending on the mode, you ask different questions. You ask a child mode about emotional experiences: *What do you feel?, Where do you feel that in your body?, What makes you so sad/afraid/angry?* You ask a coping mode about its protective function: *How would they (pointing to the client's original chair or the chair of the Vulnerable Child) feel if you weren't there?, How do you help them?* You ask an inner critic mode what it is critical of: *What don't you like about them or about what they have done (pointing to the original or emotional chair)?*

Step 6: Add an extra chair or chairs for any other modes

Depending on how the interview progresses, you may want to add an extra chair. For example, the coping mode says that they work so hard because otherwise they would feel very bad about themselves (indicating an inner critic mode). You can then add an extra chair for that inner critic mode and interview it.

Step 7: Reflection from the original chair or standing

Regularly ask your client to join you in taking a step back and looking at the mode(s) you have just interviewed. After a short interview, you can invite them to stand next to you and review the modes from that standing position. This gives you the opportunity to reflect the dynamics of the modes by, for example, placing the chair of the protective coping mode in front of the chair of the Vulnerable Child, symbolizing how that coping mode shields the child mode.

Step 8: Homework

Summarizing and reflecting in between the steps of this technique is a first step in consolidating awareness of the modes. As a homework assignment, you can ask your client to record situations in which their modes are activated in a mode diary.

Example

Therapist: How have you been feeling this past week?

Sandra: Bad … I'm fed up with myself. I'm just a burden to my family.

Therapist: Listening to you, it sounds as though you're in a state right now (*points to the space next to Sandra*) where you're looking at yourself, but not with kind eyes; rather, with anger and criticism.

Sandra: Yes, that's right, but it's the truth: it's stupid that I can't just do it.

Therapist: So, once again, I hear that perception (*gestures to the same place next to Sandra*) that criticizes you, that is angry at what you do and don't do. Shall we do an exercise that will help us better understand why that inner critic is there? I'll put an extra chair here (*places an extra chair in the spot of the inner critic mode*) and then I'll ask you to sit in that chair and tell me what you're angry and critical about. In that chair, you *are* that inner critic. I'll then ask you to get up from that chair, and then we can look at this inner critic together. Distancing from it will help us gain some more insight. Shall we just give it a try? You can always stop if it doesn't feel right for you.

Sandra: OK, let's give it a try.

Therapist: Good, now please come and sit in that chair. (*Sandra sits in the chair of the inner critic mode.*) OK, in this chair, I want you to really get into that criticism; as if you are that inner critic. And then I will also address you as such. Well, if I understand correctly, you (*gestures to Sandra in chair of inner critic mode*) have all kinds of things to say about her (*gestures to Sandra's original chair*)? What don't you like about her?

Sandra: Well, she just makes a mess of things, makes all kinds of mistakes, doesn't do anything anymore!

Therapist: OK, OK, stop for a moment. Sandra, could you please get up and stand next to me for a moment, so we can look at what's happening together. But when you stand up from that chair, you can leave that inner critic behind, as if it were glued to the seat with superglue.

(*The therapist stands up, and Sandra comes and stands next to him.*)

Therapist: Right, let's take a step back and look at what happened. I heard a lot of criticism in that chair (*gestures towards the chair of the inner critic mode*): 'You're not doing anything anymore, you're making mistakes.' And not only did the words sound angry, but the tone of voice was angry too, almost condescending.

(*Sandra nods.*)

Therapist: How long has she been so critical? Is this something that has happened in recent years, or has it been going on for longer?

Sandra: No, it's been like that my whole life.

Therapist: And where do those words come from? Children aren't born with that kind of language.

Sandra: Well, I think they're a bit like the things my father used to say to me, that I was always making mistakes and that I was difficult, even as a child.

Therapist: So, when we listen to her (*gestures towards the chair of the inner critic mode*), we're actually listening to your father's voice? (*Sandra nods.*) Then I wonder what that must have been like for you as a child; how did she feel with all that criticism? (*Therapist gestures towards the original chair.*)

Sandra: Sad, alone…

Therapist: I understand, no wonder, with so much criticism. How did she cope with all that criticism and that sad feeling?

Sandra: …I don't know, I think by withdrawing, shutting herself off.

Therapist: Right, that makes sense, as if she withdrew behind a wall. (*Therapist takes another chair and places it between the chair of the inner critic mode and Sandra's original chair, and stands next to Sandra again.*) Something like this?

Sandra: Yes, I think I quickly stopped talking and withdrew.

Therapist: So basically, she (*gestures again to the chair between the inner critic mode and the Vulnerable Child*) protects you from that sadness and loneliness by distancing herself from others, by withdrawing?

Sandra: Yes, and when I look at it that way, I think others mainly see her (*points to the chair in the middle, representing a coping mode*), because that's what they always say, that I'm so quiet and so on.

Therapist: Well, it feels like we're both gaining more insight into what's going on inside you, how that works with those different sides of you. I'd like to ask you to pay attention over the next week to see if you can recognize those different sides. Is that alright with you?

Sandra: Yes, I can do that.

Therapist: Maybe it would help you to take a photo of these chairs, just as a reminder?

(*Sandra picks up her mobile phone and takes a photo of the chairs.*)

What if your client:

- ...thinks it's a stupid exercise and doesn't want to participate?
  This is probably a coping mode that has been activated. Don't dismiss the technique too quickly, because it is one of the most effective elements of the therapy. You can tell the coping mode that you understand that it's a bit of a strange exercise, but that you want to do everything you can to help your client, even things that seem a bit strange at first. You can suggest trying it once before drawing any conclusions.

Variations

You can ask your client to sit in the chair of the Vulnerable Child mode while you, as the therapist, have a conversation with the coping mode. Did your client feel seen in the chair of the Vulnerable Child or did the coping mode stand in the way of that? In this way, the client can experience the adverse effect of the coping mode.

By moving the chairs around, you can illustrate what the therapy goals could be: you want to negotiate with the coping mode (move the chair of the coping mode slightly to the side) and fight the inner critic mode (remove the chair of the inner critic mode).

Chapter 7: Dialogue with a Coping Mode

Objective

To learn to recognize a coping mode and explore its origin and function.

Guidelines

Step 1: Name the coping mode and have the client draw it
Step 2: Interview the coping mode with the drawing in front of your client's face
Step 3: Test different positions
Step 4: Reflection
Step 5: Generalizing through homework

Explanation of the guidelines

Step 1: Name the coping mode and have the client draw it

Drawing the mode helps to render it more ego-dystonic, as it places your client in a more reflective stance. Make sure that drawing the coping mode does not take too much time (it is not about your client's drawing skills!).

Step 2: Interview the coping mode with the drawing in front of your client's face

Ask questions such as: *How do you help [client's name]?, What exactly do you do?, How long have you been doing that?, Why is that important?, What would happen if you wouldn't do that?* Explicitly validate the origin and function of this mode.

Step 3: Test different positions

Because it takes energy for your client to hold the drawing in front of their face during the interview, you will often see the drawing drop down a little during the interview. Here you can use the metaphor that constantly 'putting on' the coping mode can be exhausting. Clients typically recognize this, especially with regard to a Detached Protector. You can then make contact with your client over the edge of the sheet of paper and remark that you are pleased to be able to see your client now and that eye contact is possible. By letting your client play around with moving the drawing in front of their face (to the side, a little further away, closer), they can experience which position of the coping mode feels most comfortable for them.

Step 4: Reflection

Now that there is more eye contact and you can look at the paper sheet with the drawing of the coping mode together with your client, you can reflect on what they have just experienced and on the origin and function of the coping mode. Your client has probably also realized that it is not always pleasant when their coping mode is active, but also stands in the way of your connection.

Step 5: Generalizing through homework

As a homework assignment, you can ask your client to keep a mode diary to record the situations in which their coping mode is activated and what their feelings, thoughts and behaviour are at that moment.

Example

Therapist: I notice that you start every session by saying that you're doing well. I also notice that when I ask about difficult moment during the week, you shrug your shoulders and respond with brief answers.

(Mary shrugs.)

Therapist: Yes, exactly that. As if you don't want to talk about what's going on inside you. Is that right?

Mary: I just don't know. I don't have much to say, that's just how I am.

Therapist: You told me that you're more relaxed in other situations, for example, when you meet up with your best friend. I therefore think that this quieter attitude in the sessions means that there's a side to you that tries to help you out in new or difficult situations. Shall we explore that?

Mary: OK.

Therapist: Here's a piece of paper and a pencil. Would you mind drawing this side of you, the one that doesn't say much, shrugs its shoulders and says that everything's fine? Just a few pencil strokes, a sketch.

(*Mary draws a robot.*)

Therapist: Aha, a robot. I'd like to talk to that robot. Would you mind holding your drawing of the robot in front of your face? Then you can become the Robot, so that I can have a brief conversation with that side of you.

(*Mary holds the drawing in front of her face with both hands.*)

Therapist: Hello Robot, you make Mary a bit quieter. How does that help her?

Mary: Um, well, then she can't say anything strange.

Therapist: What could happen if she said something strange?

Mary: Then others would think I was strange, and not like me.

Therapist: I see, so you protect Mary from rejection. How would she feel if you weren't there to do that?

Mary: I would feel really bad.

Therapist: Aha, by being quiet, you're trying to help Mary to not feel so bad. Is that also what happens in therapy? That you prefer her not to speak, because you're worried that I might think she's strange?

Mary: Yes, I think so. (*Mary lowers her arms slightly.*) My arms are getting a bit tired from this.

Therapist: I can imagine. Isn't that exactly what happens in real life? It takes a lot of energy to constantly let the Robot shield you. You often feel tired, don't you?

Mary: Yes, that's right. Could that be the reason?

Therapist: It could be. If the Robot keeps getting in the way, you can never be yourself. And then you might find it harder to relax or enjoy pleasant interactions or enjoyable things. What strikes me is that now the Robot is lowering a little, I can see more of you. I like that; it feels like we have more contact when I can look at you, for example. How does that feel for you?

Mary: Hm, I'm not sure. Not unpleasant, I think ... But it does feel a bit 'exposed'.

Therapist: I understand, you're so used to the Robot shielding you. Would you like to move the Robot around a bit, hold it in different positions to see what feels right for you? Try a position where we can see each other, but where it still feels right for you. (*Mary moves the drawing back and forth, further away and closer. The therapist keeps asking how that feels.*)

Mary: (*Mary holds the drawing halfway in front of her face.*) I think this is the most comfortable.

Therapist: Great! I'm glad I can see part of you and that we can interact more. How does that feel for you?

Mary: It's pleasant, but also a little tense.

Therapist: Yes, I understand. Because that Robot is there for a reason. It's trying to help you in this new situation, in which you don't yet know exactly what I can do for you and what you can expect from me. But in order to get to know each other, it's useful to be able to interact.

Mary: Yes, that's right.

Therapist: Today, we've gained a little more insight into the Robot and why it's active in our sessions. But you said that there are other situations in which the Robot 'pops up'. Would you mind filling out this registration form over the next week, so that we can learn more about the Robot and the situations in which it gets activated?

What if your client:

- ...refuses to draw the mode?

  Try to find out why your client refuses to do so, as this is itself important information that could contribute to the case conceptualization. If necessary, do the drawing yourself by asking your client how they see the coping mode, or use a set of mode cards and ask the client to hold the card of the coping mode in front of their face.

- ...draws excessive details, which takes too much time?

  Explain the purpose of the assignment and ask your client to make a quick sketch. If your client enjoys drawing, ask them to continue working on the drawing for the next session as homework.

- ...seems to have tireless arms and won't put the drawing down?

  Ask your client if holding the drawing up takes energy. If the answer is 'yes', you can still use the metaphor. If the answer is 'no', skip this and ask your client to move the drawing in front of their face.

- ...remains convinced that the coping mode is only beneficial to them, without realizing that it can also be limiting?

  Perhaps that is how your client feels at this moment, or in this situation. That shows how strong this 'survival strategy' is. The homework assignment may reveal examples where it is clearer that the coping mode may also have limitations. Or use one of the other techniques from this book to examine the coping mode (assessment phase) and work on it (beginning of treatment).

Variations

This technique may be used as an alternative to chairwork. With children, it can be fun to literally build a wall out of boxes between you and your client, from which one or more boxes can be removed gradually to make contact.

In group therapy, you can perform this exercise with several clients, asking them to join the group with their coping mode in front of their face. You can also ask the clients to engage in conversation with each other from their coping mode, so that they can give each other feedback on how this affects the other person and the group as a whole.

Chapter 8: Interpreting and Providing Feedback on Questionnaire Scores

Objective

To discuss the scores on the questionnaires in order to select the most relevant schemas and modes of your client, taking into account other information from the assessment phase.

Guidelines

Step 1: Select the schemas and modes with the highest scores
Step 2: Note down corresponding items with a score of 5 or 6
Step 3: Select other schemas and modes and note down their 5 and 6 item scores
Step 4: Ask your client what they experienced while completing the questionnaire
Step 5: Explain the questionnaire structure
Step 6: Discuss the preselected schemas and modes
Step 7: Determine which schemas and modes will be included in the case conceptualization

Explanation of the guidelines

Preliminary remark: The questionnaires are only one source of information when it comes to selecting your client's most relevant schemas and modes. Therefore, do not blindly include schemas and modes with high scores on these self-report questionnaires in your case conceptualization (see Chapter 9: Case Conceptualization), but ensure you proceed in a hypothesis-testing manner.

Step 1: Select the schemas and modes with the highest scores

In practice, the two most commonly used questionnaires are the Young Schema Questionnaire (YSQ) and the Schema Mode Inventory (SMI).

Although a new version is under investigation, the YSQ-S3 (Young and Brown, 2005) is currently the most recent questionnaire for measuring schemas in adults. The questionnaire measures all 18 schemas originally developed by Jeffrey Young with 90 items (for an overview, see Chapter 2: Overview of Concepts).

The current SMI (Young et al., 2007) has 118 items and measures 14 modes. Discuss the modes with the highest scores.

Step 2: Note down corresponding items with a score of 5 or 6

For both the SMI and the YSQ, it is recommended that, prior to discussing with your client, you check which items from the previously selected schemas or modes were scored with a 5 or 6. These are likely to be items that most accurately represent the schema or mode of your client. Note them down so that you can discuss them with your client later.

Step 3: Select other schemas and modes and note down their 5 and 6 item scores

Higher scores generally indicate that a schema or mode is present. Conversely, lower scores do not always mean that a schema or mode is not present. For example, if your client was in the Detached Protector mode while completing the questionnaire, this may have lowered the scores. Therefore, use other sources of information from the assessment phase to determine which (lower-scoring) schemas and modes you want to discuss with your client as hypotheses, and check whether these schemas and modes have items with 5 and 6 scores.

Step 4: Ask your client what they experienced while completing the questionnaire

The answer to this question may provide information about the presence of schemas. Examples: *I don't have the concentration to complete such a long list* (hypotheses: Insufficient Self-Control/Self-Discipline schema; Undisciplined Child mode); *It took me hours; I doubted everything and overthought everything* (hypotheses: Failure schema; Perfectionistic Overcontroller mode).

Step 5: Explain the questionnaire structure

Explain that the questionnaires consist of different groups of questions about how your client sees themselves, others or the world (YSQ) or about different sides of your client (SMI), and that your client seems to recognize themselves in a number of groups.

Step 6: Discuss the preselected schemas and modes

Start with the highest-scoring schemas or modes, and mention the high-scoring items (5 or 6 scores). Ask your client what they recognized in themselves from these items, and connect this to the insights you have gathered from other sources in the assessment phase.

Step 7: Determine which schemas and modes will be included in the case conceptualization

To determine this, consult all the information you gathered during the assessment phase. Sometimes, based on the discussion in the previous step, it becomes clear that a schema or mode that your client scored highly on in the questionnaire is not applicable or relevant to the case conceptualization after all. For example, your client scores high on the Insufficient Self-Control/Self-Discipline schema, but the discussion reveals that your client mainly feels that they are unable to persevere with tasks because they set such high standards for themselves (Unrelenting Standards/Hypercriticalness schema). So, before you include schemas or modes in the case conceptualization, ask yourself if the presenting problems are likely to change when you start working on these schemas/modes.

Example

Therapist: We've now had a few sessions in which we've discussed all kinds of things and done exercises. You've also completed questionnaires about your different sides and how you see yourself and others. Today, I'd like to discuss the questionnaires with you and also take into account the other information we've already gathered together. How did you experience completing the questionnaires?

Mary: Well, it was difficult. I kept having doubts. I would have found it easier if you'd sat next to me or if you could have given me some explanation.

Therapist: Right. In the questionnaire about how you see yourself, others and the world, there is a group of questions about these kinds of doubts. I saw that your scores were higher on those kinds of questions. For example, here, on the item *My judgement cannot be counted on in everyday situations* (Dependence schema). What do you recognize in this?

Mary: Well, I find it difficult making decisions. It can be about even the smallest things. For example, not only when filling out the questionnaires, but also about what clothes to wear. Or yesterday, when I had to call the bicycle repairman, but I got anxious. I didn't know how to go about it, so my partner ended up doing it.

Therapist: Yes, I recognize that from our previous conversations. It's actually Little Mary, isn't it, who feels she can't do things on her own? That vulnerable side of you that we talked about in previous sessions?

Mary: Yes, that's something I've had my whole life.

Therapist: Yes, it indeed reminds me of Little Mary: as a child, you didn't get much space to do things your own way. Your mother was very concerned and tended to take care of everything for you. I think that that sense of dependency on others is very old and has become deeply ingrained.

Mary: Yes, I think so too.

Therapist: And what you just said about calling the bicycle repairman, that you got anxious. What exactly were you afraid of?

Mary: Gosh, so many things. That I wouldn't be able to express myself, that I wouldn't understand him, that I'd say something stupid. He's such a nice man, but I don't know, I just don't dare to interact with others, especially if I like them. I always start stammering, and afterwards I feel terribly embarrassed.

Therapist: I hear something here that belongs to another group of questions on the questionnaire, namely the expectation that you'll do or say something embarrassing, that you'll fall short as a person. In the questionnaire, this concerned statements such as *No man/woman I desire could love me once he or she saw my defects or flaws* and *I am unworthy of the love, attention and respect of others* (Defectiveness/Shame schema).

Mary: Yes, I often feel that I'm less valuable than others.

Therapist: Yes. I can understand that when I think about your history, especially the bullying you went through.

Mary: Yes, and I couldn't talk to anyone about it. No one understood me at the time. My parents were always too busy with their work to listen to me, of course.

Therapist: What you're saying makes me think that you may have come to believe that no one is really there for you or supports you, and that you don't receive the warmth, attention and love you need (Emotional Deprivation schema). Your questionnaire scores were not particularly high on this schema, but I do recognize this theme from previous sessions. How does that sound to you?

... [etc.]

What if your client:

- ...scores very high on all schemas and/or (dysfunctional) modes?

  There may be complex issues at play (especially when it comes to the schema questionnaire), or your client may have completed the questionnaire at a time when a certain (coping or inner critic) mode was active. Discuss this with your client to generate hypotheses about the explanation for the high scores. Base your choice of the most relevant schemas and modes on the other sources of information from the assessment phase.

- ...scores very low on all schemas and/or (dysfunctional) modes?

  There may be no problem, but that would be surprising given that schema therapy is indicated. It is more likely that your client completed the questionnaire from a coping mode or benefits in some other way from minimizing their problems. We see this kind of *overnormality* in the forensic sector, for example. Discuss your observations with your client and base your choice of the most relevant schemas and modes on the other sources of information.

Variations

You can help clients complete the questionnaire if necessary, but be aware that your presence may influence the scores. A brief version of the YSQ-S3 is available for adolescents (Santos et al., 2018). At the time of writing, no validated questionnaires have been released for children under the age of fourteen. In Germany, a schema questionnaire has been developed for primary school-aged children, the Düsseldorf Illustrated Schema Questionnaire (DISC; Loose et al., 2018). In the Netherlands, a version of the SMI for adolescents (SMI-A; Roelofs et al., 2016) was published.

In addition, there is a development with regard to positive schemas. By including positive schemas in the case conceptualization, they can be used as sources of strength and support towards (behavioural) change and recovery. The Young Positive Schema Questionnaire (YPSQ; Louis et al., 2018) measures fourteen positive schemas with fifty-six items (see Chapter 2: Overview of Concepts).

Chapter 9: Case Conceptualization

Objective

To explain your client's presenting problems by linking them to modes, underlying schemas and unmet emotional needs. This will clarify which emotional needs must be met during treatment and which schemas and modes must be worked on in order to reduce your client's presenting problems. The case conceptualization therefore serves as the basis for your treatment plan (see Chapter 11: Setting Goals and Creating a Treatment Plan).

Sections

The other chapters of the book describe steps that can be used as guidelines for implementing techniques. For case conceptualization, we outline its various sections and highlight points of attention for each.

A case conceptualization form must contain at least the following sections:

- brief description of your client;
- current presenting problems;
- temperament and biological factors;
- upbringing
- other relevant life events/memories;
- family-of-origin rules;
- deficiencies in the fulfilment of emotional needs;
- relevant schemas;
- schema-activating situations;
- coping responses;
- modes;
- therapeutic relationship and interaction patterns between client and therapist.

A case conceptualization form is usually very extensive, which means that completing all sections is often not feasible in daily practice. However, always create a case conceptualization model in which the information from a case conceptualization form is clearly summarized (see Appendix 5: Case conceptualization model – Tim).

Based on the intake sessions, you can already fill in various parts of the case conceptualization form, either completely or partially. Any information you do not yet have can be gathered during the sessions with your client. During these sessions, you can also test your hypotheses about their schemas and modes. To gather the information you are looking for, you can use the methods and techniques described in this book (PART II Assessment Phase).

Explanation per section

Brief description of your client

Briefly describe the background information about your client. Consider age, gender, education and/or occupation. How does your client function in terms of work, leisure, family relationships, romantic relationships and friendships? What is your client's self-care or lifestyle like?

Current presenting problems

List the problems your client is experiencing, as well as the (intrapsychic and interpersonal) patterns they are struggling with. How long have these problems and patterns existed? Has your client received help for them before?

Temperament and biological factors

List the temperament and biological factors that may influence the presenting problems. Try to obtain information about what your client was like in early childhood (e.g., through hetero-anamnestic interviews) in order to rule out the influence of environmental factors as much as possible. For clients who grew up in complex circumstances, it is difficult to describe pure temperament factors. You can also include your own impressions here: Does your client seem to be more of an extrovert or an introvert by nature? Does your client seem to be temperamental, or do they give the impression of being naturally calm? In any case, mention all biological factors that may have played a role in the development of the problem or that may complicate the therapeutic relationship (e.g., physical disorders, characteristics of autism, attention and/or concentration problems).

Upbringing

How does your client describe the character and parenting style of their parents and/or other caregivers, and how do they experience their relationship with them? What were the important messages they received during their childhood? In this part of the form, you can already make some connections between these background factors and the deficits in the fulfilment of basic emotional needs, and the resulting schemas and modes, for example: 'Father was often absent, and when he was at home, he paid little attention to the client (lack of safe attachment to others, Emotional deprivation schema).'

Other relevant life events/memories

Describe (traumatic) events that are thought to have contributed to the formation of schemas.

Family-of-origin rules

What rules did your client learn during their upbringing and within the context in which they grew up? Look for assumptions that are often conditional (*If I tell someone something about myself, they will take advantage of it*) or rigid (*I must always be there for others / I must never disappoint others*). In this section, also consider the typical sayings and expressions that were used in the family of origin.

Deficiencies in the fulfilment of emotional needs

For each emotional need, assess the extent to which it was met during childhood. If many emotional needs were not met, it is advisable to describe the 'top two or three'. This will provide focus and clarity: How will you shape your limited reparenting attitude with respect to this particular client? If relevant, it is advisable to always include safe attachment to others in such a selection, as this is the most primary emotional need.

Relevant schemas

Select a maximum of five schemas to include in the case conceptualization. If you select more, there is a risk that you will lose track and will not be able to properly specify your limited reparenting attitude or treatment plan. Although it is useful to mention the scores on the schema questionnaire (self-report) here, it is important not to let these determine the selection of the most relevant schemas (see Chapter 8: Interpreting and Providing Feedback on Questionnaire Scores).

Schema-activating situations

For each schema, describe which (internal or external) situations in your client's daily life can activate this schema. Ensure that the triggering situations truly function as conditioned stimuli for your client, rather than being inherently so aversive that they account for the intensity of the emotional response. If your client 'overreacts' to certain situations, this is an indication that one or more schemas have been activated.

Coping responses

In schema therapy, coping is conceptualized as responses to activated schemas, rather than responses to external threats (as in the case of freeze, fight or flight). Therefore, for each of the selected schemas, describe what resignation, avoidance or inversion of that schema might look like. What does your client feel, think and do in each of the three coping responses? Although clients typically may have a preferred coping style, they often display multiple coping responses to a schema, depending on the circumstances at the time.

Modes

Select the modes that are most relevant to your client's presenting problems. Do not rely solely on the scores on the mode questionnaire (self-report); use the information gained from other methods and techniques of the assessment phase too. Describe the feelings, thoughts and behaviour of each of these modes and ask your client to give personalized names to their modes. Always include the healthy modes (Healthy Adult and Happy Child), as well as the Vulnerable Child in your mode model. Make clear how the Vulnerable Child is protected by avoidance and/or inversion of the associated schemas by coping modes. The Angry Child mode is typically included in the mode model, or in any case when your client experiences too much (e.g., in borderline personality disorder) or too little anger (e.g., in avoidant personality disorder). The rule of thumb is to select no more than four coping modes and to choose only one inner critic mode, in which you can incorporate different variants (e.g., both Punitive and Demanding). Incorporate the schemas into the mode model to specify the messages of the inner critic mode, e.g., *You are worthless and deserve punishment* (Punitiveness schema) and *You must perform better* (Unrelenting Standards/Hypercriticalness schema).

Ensure that all presenting problems are accounted for by the selected modes and schemas. Which modes show problematic behaviour? Which modes are responsible for self-criticism and intense emotions? Once you understand where the presenting problems originated in the developmental history and which emotional needs of your client have not been sufficiently met, you can draw up a complete and meaningful treatment plan (see Chapter 11: Setting Goals and Creating a Treatment Plan).

Therapeutic relationship and interaction patterns between therapist and client

In order to be prepared for transference and countertransference, it is important to know your own schemas and modes (fill in the relevant questionnaires yourself!) and to consider which of your client's schemas or modes might trigger yours. Describe this in cyclical processes: Which schemas or modes could be activated in you when interacting with this client (and their schemas and modes), What effect could this then have on their schemas and modes? Investigate which of your schemas or modes clash with each other (e.g., in the case of Self-Aggrandizer modes on both sides) and which are complementary to each other (e.g., the therapist's Compliant Surrenderer and your client's Undisciplined Child). This allows you to investigate whether you are (unconsciously) reinforcing certain schemas and modes of your client and to devise a plan to prevent this.

> **Example**
>
> See Appendix 2: Case conceptualization – Sandra and Appendix 4: Case conceptualization – Tim for examples of completed case conceptualization forms.

Variations

There are several variants of the case conceptualization form and model in circulation. Make sure you choose one that contains the core elements described here.

The case conceptualization form is a form that you, as a therapist, fill in, so it does not need to be simplified in terms of language or complexity to be tailored to, for example, the (cognitive) abilities of your client. However, it is important to summarize the case conceptualization for your client in a case conceptualization model or (simplified) mode model, to create a shared understanding of the background of the presenting problems and to provide a common starting point for treatment.

Chapter 10: Creating a Mode Model

Objective

To represent the modes and their mutual dynamics in a clear model, so that it can be easily referred to during therapy.

Guidelines

Step 1: Choose a mode model

Step 2: Select the most relevant modes and schemas based on your case conceptualization/assessment information

Step 3: Choose which mode (category) to start with

Step 4: Place a mode in the mode model

Step 5: Connect mode with schemas and unmet emotional needs

Step 6: Repeat Steps 4 and 5 and discuss the dynamics between the modes

Optional Step 7: Ask your client which modes they want to change in therapy

Explanation of the guidelines

Step 1: Choose a mode model

Creating a mode model together with your client is an essential part of schema therapy. You can draw the mode model or represent it with figurines, mode cards or other materials. One format is not necessarily better than another. Choose a format that suits you (and your client). It is also important to choose a format in which the modes are positioned logically in relation to each other, so that you can immediately discuss the dynamics between the modes (see Step 6). The advantage of working with figurines, mode cards or other materials is that you can move the position of the modes in relation to each other. This allows you to show desired changes during therapy (see optional Step 7) and easily adjust the mode model.

Step 2: Select the most relevant modes and schemas based on your case conceptualization/assessment information

Select the most relevant modes and schemas based on all the information you have gathered using methods and techniques in the assessment phase (i.e., not just based on scores in self-report questionnaires). Do not make the mode model too complex: for example, choose one or two coping modes under which you can group all the variants you have noticed. Later in the treatment, you can always differentiate further if necessary.

Although you may wait until the end of the assessment phase to have all the information needed, you may also decide to start building an initial concept of the mode model earlier. You can then use it as a means of gathering information or explaining patterns you observe to your client. Problem situations that your client brings up or that arise in the therapeutic relationship can, for example, be represented by figurines that represent their different modes in that situation.

Step 3: Choose which mode (category) to start with

There is no fixed order that you must follow when creating the mode model. The choice of which mode (category) to start with can depend on various factors, such as your client's mode that is active at the time of the session. For example, if it is a coping mode, discuss this first and validate its function by placing it as a coping mode in front of the Vulnerable Child.

Your client may also tell you about a recent schema-activating situation. In that case, you can place the modes that were active in that situation in the mode model and compare or expand them with the information you have gathered so far in the assessment phase.

Step 4: Place a mode in the mode model

Tell your client which mode you want to discuss (for example, '*that side of you that doesn't say much and withdraws*') and place it in the mode model. Discuss what feelings and thoughts your client experiences in this mode and what behaviour they exhibit. If necessary, write this down in keywords in the mode model and together come up with a suitable name for this mode. Match your client's language and perception of the world, but take a guiding role if the name your client comes up with could hinder the goal of the therapy (e.g., 'the Weakling' for the Vulnerable Child). Also, your client's own name may appear in child modes (Little/Sad/Anxious/Angry Sandra) and healthy modes (Big/Balanced Sandra) that you want your client to identify with, but not in inner critic modes, because you want to guide your client to adopt a more ego-dystonic perspective on these modes.

Step 5: Connect modes with schemas and unmet emotional needs

In the case of child modes and inner critic modes, your client feels, thinks and acts as if the schema is 'true' (resignation). Discuss what expectations they have about themselves, others and the world, and note these in the mode model as statements from the child and inner critic modes. Briefly summarize how your client developed these schemas from deficiencies in the fulfilment of emotional needs in childhood. When placing the coping modes, discuss how they used to have an important (survival) function and are often still experienced as helpful in the short term in the present. Do not forget to discuss and reinforce the adaptive modes (Healthy Adult and Happy Child), and give them a personalized name. Connect these modes to your client's positive schemas.

Step 6: Repeat Steps 4 and 5 and discuss the dynamics between the modes

Repeat these steps until all relevant modes are included in the mode model. Always include the Vulnerable Child, Healthy Adult and Happy Child in the mode model, as well as the Angry Child (in any case, when too much or too little anger is experienced by the client). As a rule of thumb, you can choose five other modes that are most relevant to the problem (see also Chapter 9: Case Conceptualization).

The mode model gains meaning by discussing the dynamics between the modes: an inner critic mode puts pressure on the Vulnerable Child, who in turn is protected by coping modes, but there is also a Healthy Adult, who can (learn to) deal with schema activation in an adequate manner.

Optional Step 7: Ask your client which modes they want to change in therapy

Once the mode model has been constructed, ask which modes bother your client the most or which modes they would like to work on in therapy. To help your client with this, you can explain the general objectives of the therapy: validating the needs of the child modes, combatting and reducing the inner critic modes, moving beyond the coping modes and strengthening the Healthy Adult. Based on this, your client's therapy goals may be formulated (see Chapter 11: Setting Goals and Creating a Treatment Plan).

Example

Therapist: You just told me about your boyfriend getting angry with you yesterday and how you panicked. (*Picks up a figurine representing the Vulnerable Child and places it on the table.*) Look, I have this figurine for that part of you that can feel so overwhelmed. What exactly are the emotions associated with that?

Sandra: Fear, panic, but also sadness. Loneliness.

Therapist: And what goes through your mind at those moments? For example, yesterday, when your boyfriend was angry with you?

Sandra: Well, all I could think was, 'He's right, I've ruined it.' It's so stupid of me not to have said I'd be late.

Therapist: Here I hear that side of you that we previously called the Punisher (*adds a little figurine for this Punitive Critic*), which thinks your boyfriend was right to be angry. Do you remember when we said that this is similar to the messages your father used to give you, that you ruin everything and that you're worthless? (*Writes 'you're worthless' on a sticky note next to the figurine of the Punitive Critic.*) I understand that this makes you sad and also a little panicky, at the thought that you have ruined everything and are worthless. (*Points to the Vulnerable Child figurine.*) Just like Little Sandra used to feel so anxious and sad when your father was raging. When your boyfriend gets angry now, feelings from Little Sandra come to the surface again. (*Writes down feelings and statements such as: 'I ruin everything' [Failure schema] and 'I'm worthless' [Defectiveness/Shame schema] next to the Vulnerable Child figurine.*) How did you deal with these feelings yesterday?

Sandra: Well, basically, I made sure to make it up to my boyfriend: I prepared his favourite meal, and we went to see that film that I really hate, but that's OK, because he really wanted to see it.

Therapist: That sounds like a side of you that completely adapts to what someone else wants, even if it's something you really don't like yourself.

Sandra: Well, I did have something to make up for, I was ashamed of what I did.

Therapist: I think I hear that Punitive Critic again. (*Points to that figurine.*) It says you have something to make up for because you messed up, and that makes you feel ashamed and panicky. (*Points to Vulnerable Child figurine.*) Could it be that you then do everything you can to make your boyfriend happy again, so you don't have to feel that shame or fear anymore?

Sandra: Yes, I think that's right.

(*The therapist and Sandra call this coping mode the Pleaser and continue working until all modes are included in the mode model.*)

Therapist: How do you feel about seeing all your different sides and important beliefs laid out like this?

Sandra: Well, it's good, because it's true, but it's also quite confronting. I hadn't realized that the Punisher had so much influence.

Therapist: Yes, I think it's important that we combat that Punisher, so that it doesn't get under your skin so much and Little Sandra gets a little more space to feel what she feels and needs. (*Moves the Punitive Critic figurine away from Little Sandra.*) How would that feel for you? What would change?

What if your client:

- ...does not recognize or acknowledge a certain mode or pattern, while you are convinced that this mode or pattern is present and relevant to the problem?

  Try to explain why you think this is the case by giving examples. The Vulnerable Child, the Happy Child and the Healthy Adult are always included in the model, and this is often also the case for the Angry Child mode (whether there is too much or too little of it). For the other modes and associated schemas, leave them out of the mode model for the time being if your client really cannot identify with them. Discuss them again with your client as soon as you think they are being activated.

Variations

For primary school-aged children and clients with mild intellectual disabilities, it is recommended to keep the mode model as simple as possible. Choose only one mode from each mode category and use materials that are appealing to them. For example, you can have your client dress up as their modes and take photos of them to create personalized mode cards.

In group therapy, group members share their mode models and sometimes hang them on the wall during sessions. This makes it easy to refer to a mode when it appears to be active in the session.

Chapter 11: Setting Goals and Creating a Treatment Plan

Objective

To prepare a treatment plan to guide the content of the sessions and help you respond flexibly to your client's active modes and schemas.

Guidelines

Step 1: Consult the general schema therapy goals
Step 2: Set individual treatment goals
Step 3: Specify the limited reparenting attitude
Step 4: Decide which methods and techniques to use
Step 5: Determine the duration of the treatment

Explanation of the guidelines

Step 1: Consult the general schema therapy goals

In schema therapy, the following goals are pursued:

- validating the emotional needs of the child modes;
- negotiating with coping modes;
- combatting inner critic modes;
- strengthening the Healthy Adult.

Step 2: Set individual treatment goals

Ensure that the individual treatment goals are aligned with your client's presenting problems and request for help. Usually, you can summarize your client's most important desired changes in two or three individual therapy goals. Below are a number of intermediate steps for setting individual goals:

- **Positive:** Formulate the goals as positively as possible instead of (only) mentioning what needs to change. What does your client want to do/think/feel more, so that their presenting problems are reduced? For example: 'I want my mood to improve and I want to undertake social activities more often' instead of 'I want to feel less depressed'.
- **Concrete:** Try to make the goals as concrete and measurable as possible, so that they provide direction and you can monitor progress. If necessary, add a visual analogue scale, frequency or other measure of desired behaviour.
- **Linked to schema therapy goals:** Make the connection with one or more general schema therapy goals. According to your case conceptualization, which modes (and underlying schemas and emotional needs) do you need to work on to achieve this treatment goal?

Example

I want to learn to take notice of and prioritize my feelings (Vulnerable Child and Healthy Adult) instead of constantly adapting myself (driven by my inner critic mode and Compliant Surrenderer), so that my mood improves (currently a 2 on a scale of 0–10, I want to get to a 6) and I undertake more social activities (currently once a month, I want to get to at least once a week).

Step 3: Specify the limited reparenting attitude

Based on your case conceptualization, you have identified the top two or three unmet emotional needs. In your treatment plan, you specify how you will implement your limited reparenting attitude so that your client's most important emotional needs are met (and so that you provide an antidote to your client's schemas). In line with the goal 'I want to learn to take notice of and prioritize my feelings', limited reparenting could focus on promoting connectedness and self-expression by helping your client to explore and validate their emotions and underlying emotional needs, to put these into words, and to support and comfort them when they experience overwhelming emotions.

Step 4: Decide which methods and techniques to use

Now that you have described which modes you will work with to achieve the therapy goals, decide which methods and techniques you can use to do so. Some techniques are characteristic of schema therapy, such as imagery rescripting and chairwork. You can supplement these with other interventions. The aim is to give direction to the treatment and to be able to fall back on it during preparation of sessions.

- **Choose experiential, cognitive and behavioural techniques:** Ensure that you use experiential, cognitive and behavioural techniques so that you are working on changing the modes through different channels (feeling, thinking and doing). Changing schemas and modes not only requires corrective emotional experiences, but also the resulting cognitive restructuring, which then contributes to actual behavioural change.
- **Take phasing into account:** The different phases in therapy require an adjustment of your limited reparenting attitude (from caring and guiding to a more coaching stance, until you are on the sidelines and encouraging your client to independently meet their own emotional needs) and in the techniques (from modelling to increasingly challenging the Healthy Adult). You can work with subgoals, which you can evaluate at the end of each phase. An example:
  - **Initial phase:** I can recognize my inner critic and Compliant Surrenderer modes, and I know where they come from and how they influence me. I notice that reflecting on my feelings during the sessions leads to pleasant experiences.
  - **Middle phase:** I can contradict my inner critic mode, and I usually manage to put my Compliant Surrenderer aside so that I can make room for what I feel and need, at least during therapy sessions and in some situations outside of it. I usually manage to do things that I find important or enjoyable, which means I undertake more social activities and my mood improves.
  - **Final phase:** I can recognize my inner critic mode and ignore it; I know it will remain with me, but I don't have to listen to it. I can deliberately activate my Compliant Surrenderer when I think it will help me given the situation, but I can also 'switch it off' again. Every day, I consciously connect with my feelings and needs, which helps me to understand better how I want to live my life. I can also apply this to my daily life, although that can sometimes be difficult. With these changes, I am able to undertake a social activity at least once a week and my mood is more stable and positive.

Step 5: Determine the duration of the treatment

The choice of the duration of therapy can be based on research and on the relevant emotional needs of your client. Studies have shown that schema therapy can be effective in the treatment of borderline personality disorder over a period of two or three years (Giesen-Bloo et al., 2006; Nadort et al., 2009). The treatment of cluster C personality disorders has proven effective with fifty sessions (Bamelis et al., 2014). However, based on the relevant emotional needs, you can also deviate from these guidelines, for example, if your client with an avoidant personality disorder has also had a severe lack of safe attachment to others and you estimate that fifty sessions will therefore not be sufficient. The guideline is to agree on a timeline with your client, working towards a clearly defined end of therapy. So, give your client an idea of how long the therapy will last, and divide it into initial, middle and final phases of therapy. Make sure that there is enough time left in the final phase to work towards completing the treatment.

Example

See Appendix 6: Treatment plan – Tim for a detailed description of the treatment plan mentioned below.

Goals:

- I want to understand where my anger comes from (the Super Angry and Little Tim) and learn to express it in a healthy way (Calm Tim), so that I no longer get into trouble with the police because of my aggression (the Attacker).
- I want to improve my relationship with my mother by:
  - sharing more of what is going on inside me (Little Tim and Calm Tim) instead of shutting her out ('I don't care' side) or putting myself above her (the Great One);
  - negotiating rules with her in a respectful way (Calm Tim) instead of getting very angry (Super Angry Tim) or rebelling against them ('Screw it' side).

Limited reparenting attitude: Primarily fulfilling safe attachment to others and realistic limits and self-control (being predictable, reliable and available; limit setting without being punitive).

Duration and session frequency: One to one and a half years, motivate for two sessions per week at the start, evaluate every two months.

Involvement of loved ones: Involve mother in sessions and plan separate sessions with mother.

Methods and techniques:

- **Initial phase:**
  - **Experiential:** Empathic confrontation Angry Protector, chairwork with coping modes and Punitive Critic mode versus Vulnerable Child, letting the Angry Child rage and express creatively, imagery rescripting for Angry and Vulnerable Child.
  - **Cognitive:** Consciously reflecting on new experiences in therapy, mode sequences, safety plan, Socratic dialogue and motivational interviewing, pointing out the Healthy Adolescent mode to Tim whenever it's activated.
  - **Behavioural:** Practicing sharing emotions and experiences in the session, limit setting to impulsive behaviour and practicing postponing needs.
- **Middle phase:** (Think of motivating/giving direction/limit setting with respect to drug use.)
  - **Experiential:** Allowing more self-negotiation with coping modes and combatting the Punitive Critic with chairwork, imagery rescripting (rescript together or encourage Tim to rescript himself; rescripting may also be focused on the need for realistic limits and self-control).
  - **Cognitive:** Consolidate corrective emotional experiences, use mode sequences with more attention to underlying needs, historical test, continuum technique, courtroom technique.
  - **Behavioural:** Practicing healthy responses to each other with mother and Tim, practicing calming oneself down when angry.
- **Final phase:**
  - **Experiential:** chairwork in which the therapist plays coping or inner critic modes, future-oriented imagery, expressing emotions around the termination of therapy.
  - **Cognitive:** consolidation of corrective emotional experiences and influence of healthy choices on feelings and thoughts, independently adjusting dysfunctional cognitions, discussing cognitions around the termination of therapy.
  - **Behavioural:** encourage Tim and his mother to independently discuss conflicts and present their solution in the sessions.

What if your client:

- ...does not (yet) want to work on a particular goal, while you think it is relevant or necessary?

  A dysfunctional (coping) mode is probably activated, causing your client to not want to change in that area. Try, if you can, to agree to a goal that has to do with working on that mode. For example, your client does not want to process traumatic experiences because they are afraid of being overwhelmed by emotions and becoming suicidal, but they agree on the following goal: 'I want to learn to allow my emotions more (Vulnerable Child) instead of suppressing them (Detached Protector), so that I can learn to deal with them in a healthy way (Healthy Adult instead of suicidal tendencies of Detached Self-Soother)'. Agree that you will reassess whether you can include trauma work in the treatment plan during the initial phase or at the next evaluation.

- ...is not benefiting sufficiently from the treatment, meaning that the treatment goals are not being achieved?

  Continue to monitor progress throughout the therapy. If you notice that the goals of the current treatment phase are not being achieved, discuss this. By evaluating progress at regular intervals, you can identify obstacles as quickly as possible. Do not be too quick to decide to adjust the timeline: the time pressure of the treatment plan can prove to be an important tool for clients to overcome blockages.

Variations

Some clients (e.g., young people, forensic clients) may not have voluntarily sought help, and therefore they may say that they have no therapy goals. In that case, suggest doing a few sessions to get to know each other and find out if there is anything you can help your client with, regardless of the desire for change that others have for them. The motivation for this assessment phase may still be extrinsic *(at least then my parents will stop nagging me / then the judge will be satisfied)*. After the assessment phase, you can often formulate a therapy goal based on the mode model (Which mode would you like to have reduced?).

In group therapy, the duration and goals of treatment will be determined in advance, as will the programme. However, within that structure, there is still plenty of room for individual treatment plans, which can be drawn up in parallel individual sessions and shared with the group.

PART III: Treatment Phase – Working with Child Modes

Child modes

In a child mode, your client is in a state of mind that is coloured by unfulfilled emotional needs and associated emotions, thoughts and behaviour from their childhood. In this state, your client feels the same emotions they experienced as a child and is inclined to think like a child, and react primarily to these emotions and thoughts. In child modes, your client may be overwhelmed by emotional experiences, because these are not only triggered by a current situation, but also intensified by the schemas that are activated (in child modes, the client resigns themselves to the activated schemas). However, the degree of (emotional) intensity depends on various factors, such as your client's temperament and type of presenting problems. For example, the Vulnerable Child mode in borderline personality disorder will appear much more emotional and intense than the Vulnerable Child mode in obsessive–compulsive personality disorder. These child modes must therefore always be observed in your client's individual context.

How do you recognize the child modes?

The case conceptualization developed during the assessment phase can serve as an important tool for recognizing child modes in session. This conceptualization will already include initial recognition cues. During sessions, child modes can be further identified and differentiated from other mode categories by drawing on four sources of information:

- ***What* does the client say?:** Child modes are characterized by primary emotional, cognitive and behavioural responses. So, in a child mode, your client shares more about their feelings and experiences than in a coping mode. To differentiate from inner critic modes, be aware of harsh or judgemental experiences towards themselves ('I am such a failure'). In a child mode, your client will talk about how they feel ('I feel like a failure').
- ***How* does the client say this?:** The emotional experiences in child modes sound more 'primitive' and 'raw' compared to coping modes. The tone of voice in inner critic modes can also sound raw and, for example, angry, but the anger is mainly directed at themselves.
- **What is your primary *emotional response* as a therapist?:** Because child modes are primary emotional or behavioural expressions of activated schemas, you will feel more connected to your client and possibly have more empathy and compassion for them compared to the countertransference you may experience when they are in a coping mode or inner critic mode.
- **Pay attention to *contrasts* in the presentation:** Modes reflect changes in transient states. It can therefore be helpful to be alert to contrasts in your client's state. At the start of the session, you may think that they are in a child mode, but after fifteen minutes, they suddenly become much more emotional and, looking back, you recognize the initial presentation as a coping mode.

What is the goal in working with child modes?

The goal in working with child modes is to provide healing, corrective emotional experiences by validating the emotional needs that have not been met in the past. This section describes methods and techniques that can help you do this. However, the most important tool for validating unmet emotional needs is the therapeutic relationship of limited reparenting. A guiding question in limited reparenting is, '*What would I do or say if this were my foster child?*'

Because your clients may have different emotional needs, you need to tailor your limited reparenting stance to each client. For example, the unmet need for realistic limits requires a different form of limited reparenting than a lack of safe attachment to others. Let your client's case conceptualization (including a top two-to-three list of unmet emotional needs) guide you in determining your limited reparenting stance.

Initial Phase

The child modes are often still strong in the initial phase of therapy: clients are overwhelmed by emotions, experiences and behavioural tendencies without seeming to have any control over them. When your client is in a child mode during this phase of treatment, it is useful to perceive them as a primary school-aged child, as this corresponds to their emotional age in that moment. Seeing childhood photos of your client can help you mentally picture that child within your adult client.

One of the main goals in the initial phase of therapy is to help your client become more aware of their unmet emotional needs, schemas and modes. The 'paper knowledge' from the assessment phase must now be recognized in everyday practice. A second goal is to bring about corrective emotional experiences that can serve as a basis for your client's Healthy Adult mode.

In this initial phase, you take the lead in sessions: you provide psychoeducation about needs, schemas and modes, and you help to verbalize emotions. You are also the one who offers corrective emotional experiences as a role model for the caregiver that should have stepped in when they were a child.

On the following pages, you will find techniques and methods for dealing with your client's child modes in the initial phase of treatment.

Chapter 12: Providing Care to the Vulnerable Child (Limited Reparenting)

Objective

To provide a corrective emotional experience, once schemas are activated, by validating core emotional needs. This experience needs to be consolidated so that it contributes to the growth and strengthening of the Healthy Adult.

Guidelines

Step 1: Connecting with the Vulnerable Child – Schema activation
Step 2: Compassion for emotional responses
Step 3: Validating relevant emotional needs
Step 4: Consolidating corrective emotional experience

Explanation of the guidelines

Step 1: Connecting with the Vulnerable Child – Schema activation

The Vulnerable Child mode is characterized by primary emotional responses to triggers in the here and now, but these are also emotions that were experienced in similar situations in the past. Because this old pain also plays a role, the emotional reactions of the Vulnerable Child are often disproportionately strong in relation to what is happening in the here and now.

The Vulnerable Child may be immediately visible, but you may also need to do some preliminary work to get your client into this mode. Especially in the initial phase of treatment, the aim is to get your client into Vulnerable Child mode in every session, because changes in that mode correlate with a more positive therapy outcome (Yakin et al., 2020). Keep in mind that the Vulnerable Child may manifest differently depending on your client's personality and presenting problems. The classic image of a Vulnerable Child in borderline personality disorder, where your client is overwhelmed by intense emotions, is very different from the image in your client with obsessive–compulsive personality disorder. In the latter case, the Vulnerable Child may be characterized by a subtle vulnerability (and absence of hard work), without your client showing tears or other intense emotions.

If your client is not yet in Vulnerable Child mode, more schema activation is needed. Other chapters describe techniques that can help with this, such as imagery or chairwork. Apart from these techniques, you can also simply ask your client to focus their attention on schema-activating triggers, such as an argument with their partner, comments from their boss and other triggers. Having them describe these trigger situations in detail can help activate the schemas.

Step 2: Compassion for emotional responses

Acknowledge your client's emotional responses when schemas are activated. Make it clear that these are partly normal emotional responses that anyone could have: '*Of course you feel (sad/anxious/angry), that's a very normal feeling in such circumstances. Anyone could feel that way in that situation.*' However, you also want to explicitly indicate that old pain has been activated: '*With what you have experienced in the past, this is yet another time that you feel (sad/anxious/angry). With so much old pain involved, I can understand that you are now somewhat overwhelmed by all these feelings.*' Take your time with this acknowledgement: compassion for the pain felt has a calming effect, allowing your client to better hear and understand the validation of emotional needs.

Step 3: Validating relevant emotional needs

The way you validate emotional needs depends on the specific unmet emotional need that is connected to the felt pain. The need for connection is to be validated differently to the need for self-expression or realistic limits. Validating emotional needs always has two elements: on the one hand, it is a corrective emotional experience, and on the other hand, it is a form of cognitive restructuring, in which old schemas are adjusted and new, positive schemas are built. You offer care through your limited reparenting stance, the tone of your voice and the way you connect with your client, using words to underline the validation of the emotional needs. In Chapter 2 Overview of Concepts, you will find an overview of the possible words you can use when validating the various emotional needs.

Step 4: Consolidating corrective emotional experience

Validating the relevant emotional needs is a corrective emotional experience that you want your client to remember. Consolidating such experiences requires attention and repetition. Focus your client's attention on that experience by asking questions such as: *Is this a better or worse feeling than just now?, Where in your body do you feel this better feeling?, Is it a warm or cool feeling?* Further consolidation takes place by repeating the experience, for example, by listening back to the recording of the session or an audio flashcard (see Chapter 45: (Audio) Flashcard). In addition, you can use a *transitional object* to help your client remember that experience after the therapy session.

Example

From the case conceptualization, we know that Sandra's relevant emotional needs are safe attachment to others and self-expression. Sandra enters this session appearing emotional following an argument with her boyfriend Mark, yet she seems to be holding back her emotions.

Therapist: I know how difficult arguments can be. Can you tell me what happened?

Sandra: I don't know. We were at a party, and it was fun until he got very drunk again.

Therapist: OK, and what happened then?

Sandra: He said all sorts of stupid things and became aggressive … shouting and swearing at me…

Therapist: Oh, Sandra, that's intense … What went through your mind when he did that?

Sandra: All I could think was: Why do you have to ruin it? I didn't do anything.

Therapist: So, you were taken aback that he just started shouting and swearing out of nowhere?

Sandra: Yes … And then he was immediately like, 'You're stupid…'
(*Sandra starts crying.*)

Therapist: (*In a soft voice.*) That sounds really awful, Sandra. That must have been very unpleasant for you. Of course, you feel sad and maybe anxious too. I think anyone would feel that way in such a situation … And what happened next? I really want to understand what you went through.

Sandra: …I tried to talk to him a few times to tell him to stop, and then he shouted in my face and I … I just packed my things and went home alone.

Therapist: How awful, Sandra … It reminds me of when you were a small child – you had to deal with situations like then then, too… With your father shouting at you, getting angry and walking away. Of course you'll be upset now, by that situation with Mark ... Because for you it's the umpteenth time you've had to deal with anger and shouting ... Is that about right?

(*Sandra nods, sad, but a little calmer.*)

Therapist: And what happened next?

Sandra: I just went home ... I was very sad, and I felt very alone ... I didn't know what to do.

Therapist: What was going through your mind, feeling so alone and sad at home?

Sandra: I just wanted it to stop ... so ... I did it again.

Therapist: Do you mean cutting yourself?

Sandra: ...Yes...

Therapist: ...I understand your pain, and at the same time, I feel terrible knowing that you felt so bad, so desperate, that you couldn't do anything else but hurt yourself at that moment...

Sandra: I just didn't know what else to do.

Therapist: I'm glad you're telling me about this, Sandra. I know it's difficult for you to share this, so I'm very happy that you're doing it anyway. I'm even proud of you for telling me what happened. Now I know what you've been through. When you hear me talking like this, do you feel that I understand you, that I understand a little bit of what you've been through?

(*Sandra nods.*)

Therapist: And how does that make you feel, hearing that I'm glad you're sharing this with me and that I seem to understand how you felt? Does that make you feel worse or better?

Sandra: A bit better...

Therapist: I'm glad you feel that way. And where in your body do you notice that you feel a little better when you hear that I seem to understand you?

(*Sandra gestures towards her chest and stomach.*)

Therapist: In your chest and stomach? Can you put your hand there? And if you keep in touch with that place and you hear me saying that I'm glad you're sharing things with me, that I think it's great that you're talking about those moments that are so difficult for you ... That I seem to understand that in those moments you can be so desperate that you feel you have no choice but to hurt yourself. And that I understand you and want to understand you ... does that feel good?

(*Sandra nods.*)

Therapist: And is that a light or a heavy feeling?

Sandra: Light...

Therapist: Is that a feeling of being alone or of being together, connected?

Sandra: Connected, I feel more connected...

Therapist: Let's make a recording so that you can hear those words when I'm not there, so that we can stay connected even then. So that you can feel that you are not alone and that it is safe to share things, even the painful, difficult things ... I want you to learn to carry that feeling of warmth, safety and connection with you ... so that you can feel more often that you are connected to someone, like you are now.

What if your client:

- ...is overwhelmed by emotions and can hardly calm down?

  Continue to speak in a soft but audible voice, repeating your client's name. In the stormy sea of emotions, your voice and care can be a lifeline for your client.

- ...does not seem to feel much?

  This may be a sign that a coping mode is active. Ask your client to focus their attention on the schema-activating triggers and the emotions that you know they often feel. By continuing to focus attention on the Vulnerable Child, you can sometimes bypass the coping mode and help your client connect with their emotional experiences. Take into account the context of your client's personality and presenting problems: you may not see many emotions, but this may already be a very emotional situation for your client. In that case, you do not need to stir up those emotions even more, but you can offer care as described above.

Variations

In a group, the other group members can contribute to providing care for your client in Vulnerable Child mode. In this way, the group members practice skills that they also need to learn to use for themselves: recognizing feelings and needs, self-compassion and validating emotional needs. You can do the same in a couples' session: ask the partner to express recognition and compassion.

When working with children and adolescents, you may need to be more active in helping them put their feelings into words.

Chapter 13: Offering Guidance (Limited Reparenting)

Objective

To change behaviour patterns with the help of the therapeutic relationship of limited reparenting.

Guidelines

Step 1: Recognizing and identifying behavioural patterns
Step 2: Compassion with underlying schemas
Step 3: Discussing positive schemas
Step 4: Explaining healthy behaviour patterns

Explanation of the guidelines

Step 1: Recognizing and identifying behavioural patterns

When schemas are activated, your client, especially in the initial phase, is inclined to fall back into old coping styles of resignation, avoidance or inversion. The aim of the initial phase is to make your client aware of their emotional needs, schemas, coping styles and modes and to offer corrective emotional experiences. The emphasis in this phase is not yet on behavioural change; this becomes increasingly important in the middle and final phases of treatment. However, it may be necessary to adjust behavioural patterns when they can lead to unsafe and schema-confirming experiences. Explore the situation that activates such behavioural patterns.

Step 2: Compassion with underlying schemas

Begin by acknowledging the unmet emotional needs and schemas that underlie the behavioural patterns to be adjusted. Expressing explicit recognition and compassion has a soothing, calming effect, allowing your client to better hear and accept the suggestions you want to give. For a detailed description of this step, see Chapter 12: Providing Care to the Vulnerable Child (Limited Reparenting).

Step 3: Discussing positive schemas

After you have said that you recognize and understand the activated schemas, you actively work on forming new, positive schemas. In this initial phase of treatment, your client's Healthy Adult is still limited in its presence. When forming healthy, more positive schemas, you will need to take the lead and offer more guidance. This may mean that you need to be firm in your statements in order to counterbalance the negative schemas: *You are valuable. You are not a failure; you have many abilities. Your opinion matters; I think it is important to know how you feel and I want you to tell me about your feelings and needs.*

Step 4: Explaining healthy behaviour patterns

Explain that you want your client to stop displaying the old behaviour in order to break the behavioural pattern. Also explain what you want your client to do instead in order to learn to validate their emotional needs in a healthy way. In this initial phase, you will also need to be firm, more so than you may be used to in other forms of therapy. Just as when guiding young children, in this initial phase you will need to use phrases such as: *I don't want you to… [old behaviour pattern]* or *I want you to… [new behaviour pattern].* Like a lighthouse, you will not make cautious suggestions, but give clear, guiding messages: *Don't go here, go there.*

Example

Sandra: Yes, so a few days ago we had another argument … I just couldn't take it anymore. I left, and I ended up going to a bar to have a drink, and well … that's when I ran into that man.

Therapist: Tell me, how did that go?

Sandra: Well, I mean, nothing happened or anything, and I don't want anything to happen. But he was nice, and we had a really nice conversation, maybe an hour or two, and when I got home later, I suddenly realized: I don't want those arguments with Mark and his aggression anymore; I'm just done with it.

Therapist: I hear that on that evening you realized more clearly how you actually feel and how you actually miss things in your relationship with Mark, is that right?

Sandra: Yes. I can just have a nice conversation with a man.

Therapist: Someone who is kind and interested.

Sandra: Yes, exactly!

Therapist: And you deserve that, interest and kindness.

Sandra: And I don't really have that with Mark, maybe I never did … So … I've decided to stop seeing Mark.

Therapist: That's a big decision. And it sounds like you've been feeling really overwhelmed by everything that's happened in the past week, is that right?

Sandra: Yes, but I mean, those arguments, they just keep going on and on, but that evening I realized that things could be different.

Therapist: Yes, it was a kind of relief perhaps? That it doesn't always have to be like that, those arguments and struggles.

Sandra: Yes, exactly…

Therapist: That's a very important realization, and I notice that you're much more in touch with what you're feeling than you used to be. And now that you're in touch with your emotions, you're also starting to notice what you need. Over the last few sessions, I've seen that you seem to be noticing more and more what you feel and also what you need. And I think that's really great, it's a very nice change. Those old messages from your father, that your feelings don't matter, aren't true. Your feelings are very important, very much worth listening to and discussing. So well done for starting to listen to your needs better and also starting to take better care of yourself. After all, that's exactly what we want.

Sandra: Yes, that's right.

Therapist: And what I hear you saying is that in an argument with Mark, you actually feel unsafe and lonely again – exactly the feelings you've had so often in your life. And while you're starting to feel that you actually need something else, you meet this man and notice how nice it can be to have a safe connection with someone who is genuinely interested in you. I can imagine that this is nice – perhaps overwhelmingly so. Maybe even a little confusing…?

Sandra: Yes, it is a bit, I'm not so sure of anything anymore. But what I do know is that I don't want those arguments anymore, so I'm going to break up with Mark!

Therapist: I'm really very happy that you're trying to listen to your needs, and I want you to continue doing so. At the same time, you're in a difficult situation: the reality is that you're still in a relationship with Mark and that you've built something together – you live together. Although I want you to listen to your needs, I don't want you to make a hasty decision based on your feelings without thinking it through calmly first. So, I'm very glad you're talking to me about it, and I'd like to invite you to think about it calmly together. Because ultimately, I want you to make choices that really suit you, that you can stand behind, not only now, but also later. Do you understand what I mean?

Sandra: Yes, I understand that, but I can't stay in a relationship where I'm not happy, can I?

Therapist: No, indeed, I don't want you to be in a relationship where you feel unhappy. But I also don't want you to end the relationship right away, without first trying to talk about it. I'd actually like you to try to talk to Mark and tell him how you feel and what you're missing in the relationship. I understand that this is very difficult and stressful for you. This is understandable, as feelings were never discussed in your home, so what I'm suggesting may seem very uncomfortable, frightening and perhaps even foolish to you. Nevertheless, I'd like to assist you in attempting to do so. Ultimately, I want you to learn how to deal with the confusing feelings you encounter in life in a healthy way. And this is one of those moments where I actually want us to try that together, so that you can learn to deal with your feelings in a different way, rather than immediately making a decision and throwing yourself into something, or walking away from something, as you tend to do now. What do you think? Shall we try together to see how you could do that?

Sandra: Yes ... That's fine...

What if your client:

- ...is not open to your suggestions and still sticks to old patterns?

  You have no control over your client. Hopefully, your investment in the therapy relationship has led to your opinion mattering to your client. But activated schemas can evoke such strong emotional experiences that your client keeps falling back into old habits. Keep this in mind, and do not confuse offering guidance with limit setting. When you say, '*I don't want you to rush into a new relationship*', you are explaining in a personal way how your client can learn to deal with their needs in a healthy way. Limit setting means that your client's behaviour must stop and that there will be consequences if your client does not comply. That is not the case here.

Variations

In addition to trying to influence your client's behaviour patterns in a personal way, involving others can also be helpful. For example, ask cognitive questions such as: *What would you advise your best friend / daughter / partner to do if they were in a similar situation?*

In a group setting, you can ask other group members to think about different ways in which your client could deal with the situation.

Chapter 14: Limit Setting for the Undisciplined/ Impulsive Child

Objective

To fulfil the core emotional need for realistic limits within the framework of your limited reparenting stance by limit setting in a personal, calm and consistent manner.

Guidelines

Step 1: Preparation
Step 2: Announcement
Step 3: Describe the undesirable behaviour and its effect
Step 4: Set limits in a personal way
Step 5: Name the desired behaviour
Step 6: Reflection

Explanation of the guidelines

Step 1: Preparation

Many therapists find it difficult to set limits to undesirable behaviour. One possible explanation for this is that they tend to be sympathetic to the behaviour because of their client's problems. This may make it more difficult for these therapists to problematize the behaviour. Another explanation may be that they are afraid of jeopardizing the therapeutic relationship when they set limits to undesirable behaviour. However, limit setting is an important part of limited reparenting: it is a form of care, in the sense that it provides clarity and predictability about what is and is not allowed within the therapeutic context. When limits are set in a respectful, personal and consistent manner, it can be a corrective emotional experience for your client, who may not have had sufficient healthy limits set for them in their past.

In preparation for limit setting, try to identify your client's undesirable behaviour in as detailed a manner as possible: What exactly is the client saying/doing? How are they saying/doing it? Consider what emotional, cognitive and behavioural responses you notice in yourself when confronted with this undesirable behaviour. If you know that you find it difficult to set limits, think about what you need in order to do so, for example, discussing it with a colleague before and/or after the session, or concentrating on your own Healthy Adult mode before the session.

Step 2: Announcement

Next, prepare your client by announcing that you want to discuss something, for example: '*I want to discuss something with you that is important for our collaboration.*' This ensures that your client does not feel overwhelmed, but at the same time pays sufficient attention to this important topic.

Step 3: Describe the undesirable behaviour and its effect

Describe the undesirable behaviour as precisely as possible and ask your client if they recognize it. Give examples of moments when this behaviour occurred. Use self-disclosure to explain to your client what effect this has on your emotions, cognitions and behaviour, and how this, in turn, can affect the therapy or the therapeutic relationship.

Step 4: Set limits in a personal way

Set limits clearly and in a personal way: '*I don't like it when you [undesirable behaviour] and I need you to stop…*', '*I think it's important that you do more / less…*' One way to explain why you are setting limits is to make it reciprocal: '*Just as I want you to feel comfortable during our session, I need to be able to feel that way too. When you do / say …, it makes me feel uncomfortable.*' Do not hide behind rules set by the institution or society in general: the client may challenge or ignore such general rules. However, you and your limits will be less easy to ignore, and if that does happen, you can attach consequences to it.

Step 5: Name the desired behaviour

Clearly describe the behaviour you would like to see from your client. Try to make this as specific as possible, so not: *I need you to treat me with respect*, but *I need you to wait until I have finished speaking rather than talking over me during our sessions*. Make the desired behaviour observable and specific, phrase it positively and link it to a context (Where/when do you want this behaviour to be displayed?). Explain to your client what effect it will have on you as a therapist when your client displays the desired behaviour.

Step 6: Reflection

Give your client the opportunity to respond to your limit and tell you how it affects them, but not to question the limit itself. If this threatens to happen, repeat the limit setting. If possible, explain which modes play a role in your client's behaviour. Try to come up with ways together to prevent the undesirable behaviour from recurring and to encourage the desired behaviour. Also make agreements about what to do if the undesirable behaviour recurs, for example, that you will then point it out to your client or, if necessary, explain what the consequences will be. If necessary, you can announce and implement consequences of increasing severity. Ensure that the consequences are appropriate to the undesirable behaviour (e.g., having to submit homework before the session in the event of repeated disregard for homework assignments) and increase the likelihood that your client will exhibit the desired behaviour.

In this step, also consider any corrective emotional experience your client may have just had: How did your client feel about you setting limits in a respectful and personal manner, and what does that mean for your relationship? Compliment your client for being open to this.

Example

Therapist: I've noticed something that I'd like to discuss with you, because I think it's important for our collaboration.

Sandra: Oh?

Therapist: Yes, it's about the homework assignments. We've been working together for a while now, and I've noticed that when I ask you to think about something or write something down, you usually don't do it, or only do it partially. You say that something came up, that you forgot, or that you had other priorities.

Sandra: Oh, yes. Sometimes I do think about it, but then I don't write it down.

Therapist: And I notice that you then no longer remember the situation exactly as it was, and that it takes quite some time for you to recall things. I also notice that it gives me the impression that you may not be taking me or the therapy very seriously. When that happens, I find myself thinking: never mind, and I feel less inclined to give you assignments, even though I believe they're really important.

Sandra: Oh, but I do take the therapy seriously. I just don't always feel like doing those assignments, or I'm busy.

Therapist: Still, I think it's important that you do the homework assignments. I give them to you for a reason. I believe that you need to continue working on your process between sessions, to ensure that you can apply the things you learn in the sessions to your daily life. Only then will you really benefit from the therapy. There is a side of you that tends to set other priorities and perhaps also a more avoidant side, which is afraid that you won't do well. But you'll never know unless you try. So, I expect you to try the assignments and not avoid them anymore.

Sandra: Yes, I understand that.

Therapist: Let's take a moment to look at what you can do to ensure that you prioritize completing the assignments, and whether I can help you with that in any way. But first, I'd like to compliment you on the way we've been able to discuss this. I know you find it difficult when someone tells you what to do, or when you feel that someone is criticizing you. How did that feel for you?

Sandra: Yes, at first, I found myself thinking for a moment: 'What am I doing wrong now?' But I did appreciate you explaining why you want me to do those assignments; I understand that. It's for my own good, but I just can't always manage it.

Therapist: Yes, I understand, let's look at it that way. But I'm very pleased to hear that you appreciate my explanation and that you were able to let go of that feeling that you did something wrong. Of course, it's not my intention to make you feel that way. I'm discussing this with you so that we can continue to work together on your problems and not be distracted by other things.

What if your client:

- ...does not recognize the undesirable behaviour?

  This is unlikely if you describe the behaviour in very concrete and factual terms. Also, give examples of recent situations in which the behaviour occurred. If necessary, you can use chairwork to make your client more aware of the undesirable behaviour. See also the explanation under the heading 'Variations'.

- ...feels that they do not need to change their behaviour?

  Reiterate the effect of their behaviour on you as a therapist and that it can also have adverse effects on them or your working relationship. Stick to your limits and, if necessary, announce appropriate consequences if they do not change their behaviour.

- ...says they will change their behaviour, but in fact continues to exhibit the undesirable behaviour?

  Continue to point out and address the undesirable behaviour each time it occurs. Enforce the consequences you announced earlier and emphasize that you expect your client to exhibit the desired behaviour in the future. Announce more severe consequences to make it clear how important it is for your client to stop their undesirable behaviour.

Variations

If necessary, you can use a chair or another representative of the mode exhibiting the undesirable behaviour to make your client more aware of (the effect of) their undesirable behaviour. In the case of chairwork, you can sit in the chair of the client (or the mode of the client) and act out the undesirable behaviour. You can let your client sit in your chair to experience the effect this behaviour can have on another person. Then switch chairs again and continue with the steps in the guideline.

Chapter 15: Validating the Angry Child

Objective

To learn that anger is a normal emotion and may be expressed.

Guidelines

Step 1: Give space to vent angry feelings

Step 2: Empathize

Step 3: Reflection and cognitive restructuring

Step 4: Behaviour modification

Explanation of the guidelines

Step 1: Give space to vent angry feelings

First and foremost, give space to your client's anger. Remain calm and present, so that they feel that you can tolerate their anger. Even if the anger is directed at you, refrain from commenting or explaining at first. Instead, ask neutral questions, such as: *What else makes you angry?, Is there anything else you're angry about?, Has anyone else done anything to make you angry?* This gives your client the opportunity to express themselves fully. It's a somewhat crude comparison, but letting off steam is like squeezing a pimple: it can only heal properly once all the gunk is out. Of course, you need to set limits when their expression of anger is destructive to themselves or others: '*You're allowed to be as angry as you are, but I don't want you to damage anything. So please, tell me what's making you so angry.*'

Step 2: Empathize

After giving space to vent angry feelings, often your client's anger subsides somewhat and underlying vulnerability comes to the surface. You can now let go of your more neutral stance and show empathy for the underlying emotional pain. Empathize with the realistic aspects of your client's anger: '*Gosh, I would find that unfair too*', and make the connection between their anger and the unmet emotional needs and activated schemas: '*Of course, this touches a sore spot for you, the feeling that people don't take you seriously and don't really care about what you think. It's a feeling you know all too well, and it makes you feel so angry and powerless.*'

Step 3: Reflection and cognitive restructuring

See if your client can already distance themselves somewhat from the activated schema and the associated thought. This will not always be feasible in the initial phase of therapy, in which you will need to actively guide your client to evaluate the cause of the anger (schema-activating situation) as realistically as possible. See also Chapter 51: Cognitive Behavioural Therapy Techniques. Also, ask your client how they felt about you giving space to vent their anger: What effect did that have on their feelings, thoughts and behaviour?

Step 4: Behaviour modification

In the initial phase, you help your client recognize the behaviour they exhibit as a result of their anger. In later phases, you also discuss how they could express their anger earlier and in a healthier way in the future, rather than letting it build up. When appropriate, use self-disclosure to share how the client's anger affects you, helping your client understand its effect on others. Did they notice that you were able to listen to them better when they were not exhibiting destructive behaviour? Give your client homework to gain insight into their anger and schema-activating situations (initial phase) or to practice new ways of dealing with anger (middle and final phases).

Example

Sandra: (*Speaking in an agitated tone.*) That's not normal, is it? That he just sends me a text like that and I have to come running again, when he didn't respond to my messages the days before. Complete radio silence! And then he thinks he can just snap his fingers and I'll be there for him again. That's not how it works.

Therapist: So, you're angry about the text message he sent you. Are there any other things you're angry about?

Sandra: Well, that's just how it always is with those men. They're not worth a penny. They make you think you're special to them and all that. But meanwhile, they can't even respond to a message. He said he was with a friend, but surely you can always find a moment to reply, right? But no, apparently that's too much to ask. Well, I've had enough of men, they just frustrate me.

Therapist: Are there any other things that make you angry or frustrated?

Sandra: Well, plenty! For example, yesterday I called my friend to make plans, but she couldn't because of the children. I think her children are adorable, but they're always whining when we're trying to chat. And when I want to plan a night out so she can get away from home and we can have fun like we used to, she suddenly has a thousand and one reasons why it might not be a good idea. I think that's so stupid!

Therapist: So, there are several things bothering you at the moment. Has anyone else, or perhaps myself, done anything else to make you angry?

Sandra: Well, to be honest, I didn't like it last week either that it took you a whole day to call me back. For all I knew, something could have happened, or I could have been in crisis! And you just waited a whole day to call me back. It wasn't even your day off, so I don't understand why it had to take so long.

Therapist: It's good that you're pointing this out. What bothered you most about me not calling you back?

Sandra: Well, you always say that I can speak my mind to you, and then I do, and you're not there. You don't even respond!

Therapist: And what made you so angry about that?

Sandra: That you just don't see me! I've been worrying about it all week. And then all those other things happened on top of that, so I'm a bit fed up with it all. (*Here, Sandra's tone of voice softens, and there is more emotion in her voice, sadness.*)

Therapist: I can understand that. I hear that I disappointed you by not calling you back sooner, that you felt a bit abandoned. That also seems to be the theme in what you're telling me about Mark and your friend. That you feel they don't really pay attention to you, and that you just have to conform to their schedule or situation.

Sandra: Yes, that's true. Story of my life… (*Tears are visible and Sandra falls silent.*)

Therapist: I can see your sadness when you say that … So, it's not just pain about what's happening now, but also old pain, right? What does it remind you of?

Sandra: It used to be like that at home too. I had to conform to everyone else, no one listened to me.

Therapist: That must have made you feel very powerless and frustrated. No wonder these situations with me, Mark and your friend evoke so much anger and frustration in you.

Sandra: Yes, that must have something to do with it, indeed.

Therapist: How do you feel about me letting you talk about this and express your anger? How are you feeling about your anger now?

Sandra: I'm feeling less angry now, actually. I appreciate that you didn't interrupt me and that I could just get it all out.

Therapist: Very good, it's important to vent from time to time. I'm very sorry that my late phone call affected you so much. Let's talk about that for a moment and about what you can expect from me in that regard.

What if your client:

- ...is angry, but doesn't express this (easily)?

  See Chapter 17: Stimulating the Angry Child about stimulating the expression of anger.

- ...is very angry with you, even though it is unjustified?

  Remember that their anger is not only a reaction to the situation with you, but also that it is 'old' pain and anger that is triggered by this situation. Stay calm and just follow the steps. Only in Step 3 should you explain your own behaviour that triggered your client's anger.

- ...is so angry that they exhibit destructive behaviour in Angry or Enraged Child mode?

  Set gentle but clear limits to the destructive behaviour and continue to encourage your client to express their anger in a way that allows you to give it your full attention.

Variations

In some cases, it can help to allow your client to vent their anger physically, for example, by smashing blocks of clay, throwing a ball against the wall, hitting the edge of a table with a rolled-up newspaper or using a punching bag.

In the description and example mentioned, it was the need for self-expression that needed to be validated. For some clients, for example in the forensic sector, the need for realistic limits is also relevant. Instead of just giving space to vent their angry feelings, limit setting should also be incorporated in Step 1 (you want your client to express their anger at a reasonable volume and to discuss the sources of their anger rather than resorting to shouting of threatening violence).

Chapter 16: Creating a Safety Plan

Objective

To train healthy ways of regulating emotions. Your client learns to deal with schema-activating situations in a healthy way rather than resorting to risky and/or dysfunctional behaviour.

Guidelines

Step 1: Select a format for the safety plan
Step 2: Identify the (risky) behaviour
Step 3: Operationalize the behaviour
Step 4: Create mode sequences
Step 5: Describe healthy coping strategies your client may adopt
Step 6: Describe how others can help support them

Explanation of the guidelines

Step 1: Select a format for the safety plan

The safety plan is a practical tool for recognizing early warning signs of destabilization or crisis and responding appropriately to prevent risky behaviour. It gives your client self-insight, control and security. There are various formats in use. Ensure that attention is paid to specifying the behaviour, and to actions that your client can take themselves and that others in their environment can take to support your client.

There are usually three phases in a safety plan:

- **Green phase:** in which mainly the Healthy Adult and the Happy Child modes are active;
- **Orange phase:** in which schemas are activated and dysfunctional modes are at work, without your client being completely overwhelmed by negative emotions or exhibiting highly risky behaviour;
- **Red phase:** in which your client experiences very intense emotions and exhibits risky behaviour due to schema activation.

Safety plans are used in various forms of therapy; in schema therapy, the modes are added to the safety plan.

Step 2: Identify the (risky) behaviour

First, define the (risky) behaviour that the safety plan focuses on. What exactly do you wish to prevent? Sometimes you can combine several risky behaviours in one safety plan. For example: certain situations trigger feelings of loneliness and social isolation in your client, causing them to withdraw (orange phase), after which they feel even more lonely and isolated and try to avoid this feeling through self-harming behaviour (risky behaviour 1) or drug use (risky behaviour 2) (red phase).

However, if different modes precede certain behaviours (e.g., aggression and self-harm), it is better to create two different safety plans. Of course, it is important to keep it feasible and therefore refrain from using many different safety plans for one client. Therefore, only select the riskiest behaviours. It is possible, however, to draw up a 'mode user manual' with your client in addition to the safety plan, where you describe, for each mode in the mode model, in which situations it becomes active, what it looks like, what your client can do and what others can do (see 'Variations' at the end of this chapter). By focusing the 'user manual' on modes, you can incorporate different forms of risky behaviour into that one manual.

Step 3: Operationalize the behaviour

In collaboration with your client, specify what the risky behaviour looks like. What are the observable signs of the behaviour? Which modes of your client exhibit this behaviour?

Step 4: Create mode sequences

To gain clarity on how the chosen risky behaviour develops, it is important to work with your client to create mode sequences based on situations in which your client exhibited the behaviour. Which situations can trigger this behaviour? And which modes often follow each other before they exhibit the risky behaviour? See Chapter 44: Mode Sequence on creating a mode sequence.

Based on the mode sequences, examine the pattern that often leads to the risky behaviour. Which modes become active in the orange phase? In addition to the mode that exhibits the risky behaviour, is there another mode that becomes active in the red phase? Enter these modes in the safety plan and specify the behaviours of those modes in the different phases: How does your client notice that this mode is active, and what may other people observe then? Do not forget to specify this for the Healthy Adult and Happy Child modes in the green phase as well.

Step 5: Describe healthy coping strategies your client may adopt

Now that it is clear which modes are active in the different phases of the safety plan and what behaviours they exhibit, describe what your client can do in each of the phases to deal adequately with the activated schemas and modes. What has your client already tried that works? If your client does not yet have an answer to this, give them homework to try out healthy coping strategies and add effective strategies to the safety plan as the therapy progresses. Consider asking for help, pursuing a hobby, writing exercises, relaxation exercises, going outside, being creative, exercising, self-compassion and positive self-talk, distracting yourself and postponing/slowing down, among other things. Don't forget that you can also include the use of the therapeutic relationship in this plan: contacting the therapist and reading or listening to (audio) flashcards.

Step 6: Describe how others can help support them

Discuss with your client what significant others can do to help them return to the green phase. Explore with your client what is most effective, and keep in mind that what your client *desires most* at that moment (or rather, what a certain dysfunctional mode of your client desires most at that moment) is not always the same as what your client *needs*! For example, if your client says, 'When I withdraw, others should just leave me alone', it may be that their coping modes *desire* that, but that (the vulnerable side of) your client actually *needs* connection with the other person. Discuss with your client and their loved ones what approach is most effective: Should the other person simply encourage your client to make contact, or is it more beneficial for your client if the other person also exerts some gentle pressure at these times? Based on their experience with certain modes or behaviours of your client, significant others can often make important contributions to the safety plan and can also learn how to support your client in preventing risky behaviour.

What if your client:

- ...displays many different types of risky behaviour, each of which involves a different configuration of modes?

  Usually, it is possible to cluster behaviours based on similarities in their pattern of modes. If not, prioritize the behaviours your client wants to work on first and create a safety plan for those. Alternatively, choose to create a modes user manual with your client (see 'Variations' at the end of this chapter). Keep in mind that a safety plan does not attempt to offer a perfect solution, but that its use is a form of emotion regulation training, so that the Healthy Adult mode can learn to deal with schema-activating events.

Variations

Adjust the language, complexity and layout for children, adolescents or clients with mild intellectual disabilities. When working systemically (family therapy/couples therapy), you can include mode clashes or mode collisions with loved ones in the column, *What can others do?* Briefly describe the mode of the significant other that can be activated in response to your client's behaviour in that phase and what they can do to respond to your client from their own Healthy Adult mode.

If a safety plan does not seem necessary, or if there are many different risky behaviours, you can choose to create a modes user manual with your client. Together with your client, describe the following elements for each mode in a table:

- Triggers (What situations can activate this mode?)
- Modes (What does your client think, feel and do in that mode?)
- Healthy coping strategies (How would your client like to deal with this situation/mode in their Healthy Adult mode?)
- Support from others (What can others do to help when this mode is activated?)

Example

Which mode is active?	What do I and/or others notice (behaviour, thoughts, feelings, bodily sensations)?	What can I do?	What can others do?
	I feel good I am connected to my feelings and needs I'm thinking: 'I can handle this' My body feels relaxed I am enjoying myself and am feeling happy	Enjoy! Prepare for difficult situations in the future, ask for help if necessary	Compliment me Have fun with me ☺
	I feel lonely, sad My inner critic is saying: 'It's all your fault', 'You're worthless', 'You can't do anything' My body feels tense, I feel a knot in my stomach I withdraw, become quiet, and avoid contact. I feel empty and zombie-like	Read the flashcard I developed with my therapist Take the dog for a walk Write counterstatements to my Punitive Critic mode and visualize sending it away and locking it in a cupboard	Ask if I'm putting myself down and gently challenge it Spend some time playing a game with me, without pressuring me to talk about it Check whether I want to talk about something, and reassure me that you're there if I do
	I become panicked, feel overwhelmed by sadness, and believe there is no way out My Punitive Critic side tells me, 'See, nothing will ever come of you'. I engage in self-harm (scratching or cutting) to avoid feeling, and at times because my Punitive Critic side tells me I deserve it	Listen to the flashcard my therapist recorded for me Knead clay and focus on it until I calm down Listen to the safe-place exercise Ring Aunt Karin and use the code word	Acknowledge that you see I'm having a hard time and reassure me that you're there for me Stay with me, unless I clearly indicate that I don't want you to Remind me of my safety plan or flashcard

Middle Phase

The emotional growth that began in the initial phase indicates that the child modes in the middle phase can be compared to children in puberty. This implies that, as your client develops with regard to their emotional age, the objectives of the therapy change. The objective now is for the client's Healthy Adult to become more visible and to learn to validate their own basic emotional needs. Your role as a therapist also changes in this phase, from being directive and guiding to coaching and working side by side.

With this change in attitude, the methods and techniques from the initial phase can also be used in the middle phase. When providing care or guidance, you can, for example, ask the client what they think you would say now, to allow them to independently retrieve the healthier messages you provided earlier from their memory. In this phase, further practice is also given to the safety plan, which is constantly being adapted on the basis of new insights and experiences. In the following chapters, you will find other techniques that are appropriate for working with the child modes in the middle phase.

Chapter 17: Stimulating the Angry Child

Objective

To teach your client to recognize anger, to see it as a normal emotion that has benefits, and to express it in a playful way.

Guidelines

Step 1: Rationale
Step 2: Adjusting assumptions about anger (cognitive restructuring)
Step 3: Practice expressing anger (behaviour modification)
Step 4: Consolidation

Explanation of the guidelines

Step 1: Rationale

In the case conceptualization, you included the Angry Child, even though anger was not visible at the time. In the initial phase, you demonstrated healthy forms of anger in challenging the punitive and demanding messages of the inner critic modes and standing up for your client's needs. In the middle phase, you now explicitly discuss that you want to help your client to better express their anger. When your client denies experiencing anger, you can explain that anger is in human DNA: you don't have to teach a baby to scream when it is not fed quickly enough, it does so naturally. The fact that your client no longer experiences anger does not mean that it is not there, but that they have not learned to connect with it.

Step 2: Adjusting assumptions about anger (cognitive restructuring)

Before you can encourage your client to practice expressing anger, it will often be necessary to adjust negative assumptions about anger. It may help to list all the positive aspects of anger on a whiteboard, such as:

- Anger helps you set boundaries.
- Anger helps you recognize and express your needs.
- Anger gives you energy.
- Anger allows you to show who you are, which can strengthen relationships.
- Anger is fun (e.g., comedians who get angry about all sorts of things).

Step 3: Practice expressing anger (behaviour modification)

Use playful methods to learn how to express anger, such as a 'rant game' (see 'Example' later in this chapter). This way, your client learns to associate anger with a playful light-heartedness instead of the fear and heaviness that has been associated with it since childhood.

Step 4: Consolidation

Pay attention not only to the anger experienced, but also to its positive aspects. For example, ask: *Now that you are angry, do you feel more tired or more energetic?* Or make your client aware of the observable changes when expressing anger (*'I see you having some fun now that we are practicing expressing anger'*).

In addition to focusing on these positive experiences during the exercise, you can give homework to further consolidate them. This could include noting down all the moments during the week when your client feels anger, in combination with noting down the level of energy felt. In this way, your client can repeatedly learn that expressing anger has positive consequences for themselves (regardless of the reaction of others).

Example

Therapist: I think it's really impressive what you've achieved in therapy so far; you've already become better at recognizing your Pleaser, you feel what you need more often and you're listening to that more and more. And you're also managing to push back against your inner critic more often.

(*Mary nods and smiles.*)

Therapist: However, I do think you could get a little better at feeling anger and expressing it.

Mary: Well, I'm just not angry that often, so I don't know if I can really change that…

Therapist: I understand that you still find it difficult to feel your anger and recognize it as such. But as we said at the beginning of therapy, anger is an emotion that every human being has. It's in our DNA – you don't have to teach a baby to get angry, it will naturally start screaming furiously if it isn't fed quickly enough. So, I think you do have anger, but that it's difficult for you to connect to it, and even more difficult to express it. I'd like to suggest that we work on that today.

Mary: Well, I don't know if I want to … It doesn't seem right to me to get angry more often, does it?

Therapist: I think I'm hearing that inner critic again with all those negative thoughts about anger. But last time we explored together whether those thoughts are accurate, right? What was it again that was good about anger?

Mary: Well, you said that anger helps to set boundaries and express needs.

Therapist: Exactly! So, there are all kinds of reasons why anger is actually quite good. And with everything you've been through in the past, you haven't learned that anger can even be a little bit fun.

(*Mary looks at the therapist in disbelief.*)

Therapist: I can see from the way you're looking at me that you don't believe a word of it. But I think we can practice with that anger in a way that can also be fun. Shall we give it a try?

(*Mary nods.*)

Therapist: Then I suggest we play a 'rant game' together. We'll take turns saying something we don't like about life. It can be anything. The important thing is that we get it all out and rant about things we don't like. Let me start … Well, when the alarm went off this morning, I really didn't like that! I had this feeling of 'ugh!

(*Mary chuckles.*) Do you recognize that? (*Mary nods.*) And what's something you don't like?

Mary: Well, when I came here, it suddenly started pouring with rain, even though they'd said it would stay dry. I really didn't like that, no.

Therapist: And what did you think when it started raining?

Mary: I don't know ... Something like, 'Yuck'.

Therapist: Say that again, but twenty per cent louder?

Mary: (*In a slightly louder voice.*) Yuck!

Therapist: Very good! And I know that feeling too, that feeling of 'Yuck'. When I was travelling by train last week, they suddenly announced that the train would terminate at the next station. Well, I was pretty grumpy then too, and I had that feeling of 'Yuck!' Do you recognize that?

Mary: Well, no, I don't travel by train very often, but when I drive, I sometimes get grumpy too. Recently, there was a guy on the motorway who suddenly cut me off.

Therapist: And what did you think then?

Mary: Well, to be honest, I thought, 'What a jerk!' Maybe some other things too, but I'm not going to say them now.

Therapist: But say that again. Say 'What a jerk', but a little louder, as if you really mean it, as if you're back in the car and it's happening again.

Mary: ...What a jerk! (*Chuckles a little.*)

Therapist: I see you smiling a little. How do you feel right now?

Mary: Well, it's a bit strange, but it's also nice to be able to just say it.

Therapist: I get that feeling too, and let's focus on your body. Do you still feel tired and heavy, as you often do, or do you have a little more energy?

Mary: ...Well, I do feel more energetic, yes.

Therapist: And where do you feel that in your body?

Mary: (*Points to her chest and shoulders.*) Here, as if it's all a bit lighter.

Therapist: Very good! What I like is that you now realize for yourself that what we talked about is true – anger gives you a little more energy and can even be fun.

Mary: (*Smiling.*) Yes, that's true, in a way.

Therapist: We'll continue the ranting game in a moment, but I want to say that you can also do this at home this coming week – just take a moment every day to allow yourself to rant about the things that have irritated you. And don't just say it to yourself, say it out loud – like when you think of that 'jerk' in traffic. I think it's very good to practice being angry and expressing anger more often. And you see, it's not as unpleasant as it seemed at first.

(Mary nods.)

What if your client:

- ...denies feeling anger?

  In addition to the approach described above, you can also have your client do general exercises to become aware of emotions. For example, give them homework such as *Which music / film / series makes you happy / sad / angry?* Try using different wording so that the negative associations with the word 'angry' are not activated too much. Consider descriptions such as 'not feeling very happy', 'finding something irritating' or 'finding something annoying'.

Variations

In addition to the ranting exercise, there are other exercises to stimulate anger: tearing up paper, skipping or popping an inflated balloon, hitting the edge of a table with a rolled-up newspaper, bouncing a ball on the floor as hard as possible, sticking cocktail sticks into an apple while saying what you are angry about, kneading and smashing balls of clay, and thinking up funny swear words and saying them out loud (increasing the volume each time), among other things.

Chapter 18: Stimulating the Happy Child

Objective

To teach your client to recognize happy, spontaneous impulses within themselves, to see happiness as a normal emotion and to express these impulses.

Guidelines

Step 1: Rationale
Step 2: Adjusting assumptions about having fun (cognitive restructuring)
Step 3: Practice having fun (behaviour modification)
Step 4: Consolidation

Explanation of the guidelines

The steps for stimulating the Happy Child are the same as those for stimulating the Angry Child (see Chapter 17: Stimulating the Angry Child). When your client has not learned to recognize happy and spontaneous impulses as normal, good and natural, they will have trouble expressing joy, spontaneity and play.

Step 1: Rationale

In the case conceptualization, you included the Happy Child, even though spontaneity and playfulness were not visible at the time. In the initial phase, you were visibly playful and spontaneous as a role model. In the middle phase, you explicitly discuss that one of the goals of therapy is for your client to learn to recognize and express that spontaneity and playfulness.

Step 2: Adjusting assumptions about having fun (cognitive restructuring)

Negative assumptions about spontaneity and play (e.g., 'Relaxation is a waste of time, you have to work') must first be challenged cognitively. Consider helpful cognitions such as:

- Play is normal in the animal kingdom; in nature documentaries, you often see animals playing.
- Play increases your competence and stimulates your creativity.
- Play and spontaneity give you energy.
- Playing together creates bonds and connectedness.
- Play and spontaneity are fun.

Step 3: Practice having fun (behaviour modification)

Use playful forms to generate joy and learn to express it: watch videos on the Internet (e.g., of kittens playing), tell your favourite jokes, dance, sing along to music, burp the alphabet and play with animals, among other things. Pay attention to sometimes minimal primary emotional responses that indicate pleasure or enjoyment of the activity, and make your client aware of those responses.

Step 4: Consolidation

Further consolidate these positive experiences with play and spontaneity by assigning homework. Explain that your client may feel some resistance at first, but that this is necessary training to get used to the positive aspects of play and spontaneity.

Chapter 19: Chairwork with the Undisciplined/Impulsive Child

Objective

To help your client become aware of their undisciplined or impulsive behaviour and its effects on the therapeutic relationship and on others. Your client can then learn to set limits to their own undisciplined or impulsive behaviour.

Guidelines

Step 1: Identify the undisciplined/impulsive behaviour
Step 2: Switch seats and mirror behaviour
Step 3: Ask about the effect
Step 4: Have the client sit on an extra chair
Step 5: Coach the client in setting limits to the undisciplined/impulsive behaviour
Step 6: Reflection

Explanation of the guidelines

Step 1: Identify the undisciplined/impulsive behaviour

Observe and identify the undisciplined/impulsive behaviour and/or experience (lack of motivation, being reactive and distracted). If necessary, determine which modes are active and suggest switching seats for a moment. Explain that you want to re-enact the behaviour in your client's chair, while they can observe the behaviour from your perspective in your chair. Explain that this can help to gain more insight into what is happening.

Step 2: Switch seats and mirror behaviour

As you sit in your client's chair, mirror their posture, tone of voice and facial expressions. Repeat the statements your client made earlier that are consistent with their undisciplined or impulsive behaviour.

Step 3: Ask about the effect

Ask your client what they think and feel now that they are looking at this behaviour from your perspective. Is it pleasant to be confronted with this behaviour? What is unpleasant about it? Is your client inclined to continue staying open and listening to what you're saying or not? What else do they notice? Indicate that you also notice a similar reaction in yourself when your client exhibits this behaviour. You now both recognize the effect that the mode has on others.

Step 4: Have the client sit on an extra chair

Add an extra chair and ask your client to sit on it, while indicating that the Undisciplined or Impulsive Child mode remains on the original chair. Sit back down in your own chair. Pointing to the empty chair, ask your client what they think of this behaviour from their Healthy Adult perspective. Indicate that this side needs some guidance from your client so that they can achieve their goals and ensure that they get what they need. If necessary, explain that getting what you need is not always the same as getting what you (impulsively) want.

Step 5: Coach the client in setting limits to the undisciplined/impulsive behaviour

Coach your client in addressing their Undisciplined or Impulsive Child mode. Let them start by expressing compassion for that side of themselves; it is a part that also belongs to your client and that sometimes benefits them. Then coach them to express what they think of the behaviour, why it does not help them (at least in the long term) and what they really need. Help them to set limits to this side in their own way. If necessary, demonstrate this or discuss what your client can say to do so. Let them talk directly to the undisciplined or impulsive side on the chair as much as possible. When your client starts making statements that fit this side, you can have your client sit back down in that chair or, with gestures, link those statements back to the chair of the Undisciplined or Impulsive Child mode.

Step 6: Reflection

Ask your client how they felt about doing this exercise. What did they experience when setting limits to their undisciplined or impulsive behaviour? Let them reflect on the positive, powerful feelings that may have been released. Then discuss what they can do in their daily life to deal with these impulses.

Example

Tim: (*In a flat, uninterested tone.*) I didn't do the assignment. I didn't get around to it.

Therapist: Oh, that's too bad, I wanted to discuss the assignment with you now.

Tim: I didn't really think about it anymore. And something else always came up.

Therapist: Hm. 'I didn't get around to it', 'I didn't think about it anymore', 'Something else always came up' … These statements remind me of your 'Screw it' side. (*Points to the mode model in the case conceptualization.*)

Tim: Well, maybe.

Therapist: I think it would be good to take a moment to consider that side of you and what effect it has on the therapy. Would you like to sit here in my chair for a moment? Then I'll sit in your chair. (*Therapist and client switch chairs.*) You can take my role from my chair; you're the therapist. And I'm you, or rather, I'm your 'Screw it' side. Just pay attention to how it sounds, how it feels and what else it evokes in you when that 'Screw it' side is at work. (*The therapist mirrors Tim's posture, facial expression and tone of voice prior to the chair swap and repeats what Tim said earlier about the assignment.*)

Therapist: How does that feel for you, in the role of therapist? When you hear and see me talking like this, does it seem like I'm taking the therapy seriously?

Tim: Um. Well, no, I don't think you're very interested in the whole therapy thing. Apparently, you find other things more important.

Therapist: Yes, I recognize that from my role as a therapist. I get that impression when I talk to your 'Screw it' side. Even though I know that you do think the therapy is important and that you have goals you would like to achieve. (*The therapist pulls up a chair and places it next to the therapist's chair.*) Would you like to sit on this chair? Then I'll go back to my own chair and let your 'Screw it' side sit on its own chair. (*Tim and the therapist move chairs, and the therapist places the Undisciplined Child mode card on the empty chair.*)

Therapist: In this chair, I'd like to ask you to look at that 'Screw it' side from your Healthy side. How do you feel about it going its own way and making other people think that you don't care about things?

Tim: I do think therapy is important, otherwise I would have stopped long ago! And I always come to the sessions; I just often don't do the assignments in between.

Therapist: Yes, that's right. I also know that you think therapy is important, but at the same time he (*Points to the 'Screw it' side.*) doesn't want to spend any time on it between sessions…

Tim: Well, I don't know. It's not that I don't want to, but there are often other things I want to do as well.

Therapist: Yes, I understand. And your 'Screw it' side definitely has its qualities, too. It ensures that you do fun things, that you spontaneously go along with things and that you're independent. But it also needs some guidance from you, so that you can work on the things that are important to you in the long term. If you want to achieve your therapy goals, it's important to keep working on them between sessions.

Tim: Yes, OK. But when all kinds of fun things come along, I just want to do them. That's not strange, is it?

Therapist: Hey, who am I talking to? Is it you, Tim, or is he (*Pointing to the 'Screw it' side.*) at it again? What do you think? Would you like to sit in that chair again? (*Tim moves to the empty chair and says he wants to do fun things when they come along, because they make life enjoyable. The therapist then asks Tim to sit back down on his Healthy side on the other chair and respond to this.*)

Tim: Well, I can still do fun things and schedule the assignment for another time. And I can put it in my phone so I don't forget.

Therapist: Well, I think those are very good ideas you have there. Would you like to tell your 'Screw it' side what you think of his statements and suggest your ideas to him?

Tim: (*Addressing the chair with the mode card on it.*) Well, um, 'Screw it' side, I don't think your statements are very helpful to me. I like doing fun things, but I also want to do more of what's important.

Therapist: Fantastic! How does it feel to say this to your 'Screw it' side?

What if your client:

- ...does not recognize that this is the behaviour of his Undisciplined or Impulsive Child mode?

  Continue to Step 2 anyway; your client may understand what you mean better if you mirror their behaviour and they are confronted with it. If this is not the case, explore with your client which side they think it is. During the case conceptualization and initial phases, you will likely have discussed the undisciplined side on several occasions and probably discussed various examples that resemble the current behaviour. In any case, try to reach agreement on the dysfunctional nature of the behaviour itself. How does the behaviour relate to your client's goals? If necessary, move on to setting (step-by-step) limits to the behaviour (see also Chapter 14: Limit Setting for the Undisciplined/Impulsive Child or Chapter 41: Step-by-Step Limit Setting).

- ...has great difficulty setting limits to their undisciplined or impulsive side?

  Demonstrate the limit setting (modelling), discuss together what your client could say to their undisciplined or impulsive side, or provide guidance by asking your client questions about what they think of the behaviour and what they really need. It is not a problem if your client finds this difficult; at this stage, your client is still discovering their healthy side. Following the steps of compassion, realistic thinking and then changing behaviour is still new and does not happen automatically.

Variations

In the final phase of therapy, you can increase the difficulty level of Step 5 of the exercise by responding from the chair of your client's undisciplined or impulsive side to the limits set by your client's healthy side. Try to do this in their own words as much as possible, so that it remains as close as possible to your client's experience and the need to set limits is as realistic as possible. To support the chairwork, you can use materials to represent your client's undisciplined or impulsive side on the chair (such as the mode card in the example, but this can also be a figurine or another symbol). The steps of this technique can also be applied when dealing with the transgressive or dysfunctional behaviour of a coping mode, but in that case, the limit setting should focus more on the (avoidant or inverted) function of this behaviour.

Chapter 20: Chairwork – Practicing Empathy for the Vulnerable Child

Objective

To learn to to have compassion for the emotions evoked by schema activation, and to recognize and validate the relevant emotional needs.

Guidelines

Step 1: Rationale
Step 2: Have your client sit in the Healthy Adult chair
Step 3: Place an additional chair for the Vulnerable Child
Step 4: Coach empathy for the Vulnerable Child
Step 5: Reflection

Explanation of the guidelines

Step 1: Rationale

In the initial phase, you have consistently shown compassion for the emotions evoked by schema activation and have identified and validated the emotional needs of the Vulnerable Child. Explain that your client will now learn to do this themselves. The chairwork is a tool to help you avoid merging too quickly with the experiences of the Vulnerable Child from the perspective of the Healthy Adult.

Step 2: Have your client sit in the Healthy Adult chair

Use an extra chair for the Healthy Adult. In the beginning, this can also be your therapist's chair; this allows you to make use of the associations of that chair with the compassion you demonstrated in the initial phase. First, ask your client to sit in this chair and make contact with their Healthy Adult (see Chapter 47: Visualizing the Healthy Adult).

Step 3: Place an additional chair for the Vulnerable Child

Place an additional chair for the Vulnerable Child mode with a photo of your client as a child or another symbol on it.

Step 4: Coach empathy for the Vulnerable Child

Encourage your client to express understanding for the emotional responses evoked by the current context and for the old pain that is involved: *'Of course you feel sad / alone / anxious / vulnerable. That is a very normal emotional response in such a situation, especially since this is yet another time you are feeling this pain.'* Ask your client how it feels to repeat these words, and focus attention primarily on the positive emotional responses.

Step 5: Reflection

Your client may feel uncomfortable showing this compassion. Explain that it takes time and practice to get used to a healthy form of self-care (comfort, nurturing, compassion, understanding) that your client has not learned.

Final Phase

In the final phase, the child modes can be seen as young adults. This changes the objectives once again. Now the emphasis is more on behavioural change: breaking old behavioural patterns. After all the healthy experiences you have offered as a therapist in the initial phase, and coaching the client to learn to validate their emotional needs in the safety of therapy in the middle phase, the goal in the final phase is for the client to learn to apply what they have learned independently. Your role as a therapist thus changes to that of a coach standing on the sidelines. Just like in football, that coach is not allowed to cross the white line; the game must be played by the players. As a coach, you can only give some instructions in the hope that the players will pick them up and follow them. You ask the client more questions, using open-ended questions. When a client does not know the answer immediately, you give them some space to figure it out for themselves. In this phase of therapy, the therapeutic stance increasingly resembles that of a cognitive behavioural therapist.

In the following chapters, you will find guidelines for two techniques to supplement the final phase of working with the child modes.

Chapter 21: Chairwork – Warm Letter to the Vulnerable Child

Objective

To practice showing self-compassion in contact with one's own feelings and needs.

Guidelines

Step 1: Rationale
Step 2: Client writes a letter to the Vulnerable Child
Step 3: Place a chair for the Vulnerable Child
Step 4: Client reads the letter out loud to the Vulnerable Child
Step 5: Reflection

Explanation of the guidelines

Step 1: Rationale

Explain that in this final phase, your client will take independent care of the feelings and needs of their Vulnerable Child mode in a warm letter. Your client can write down which emotional needs they have missed, which emotions this has understandably evoked and that they promise to take care of their Vulnerable Child mode.

Step 2: Client writes a letter to the Vulnerable Child

Your client writes this letter as preparatory homework. Do not guide this assignment too much in order to allow room for autonomy.

Step 3: Place a chair for the Vulnerable Child

Place a chair for the Vulnerable Child with a photo of your client as a child, some other symbol or a mirror (a powerful tool to help your client practice self-care) on it.

Step 4: Client reads the letter out loud to the Vulnerable Child

Example

Dear Sandra,

I notice that you are still often sad and doubt yourself. Sometimes, you worry that there is something fundamentally wrong with you. I understand very well that you have these thoughts. You heard so often in the past that you were not good enough, that you couldn't do things. Those were hurtful words, and they should never have been said. There is nothing broken or wrong with you. Of course, you sometimes make mistakes or do things that others may not like. Everyone does that; no one is perfect. Yes, you can sometimes be very assertive, and when you are angry, you can be quite forceful. But that says nothing about your value as a person. It does not make you any less valuable or stupid, and certainly not bad.

I want to ask you to stop listening to those old, nasty voices from the past. You are a warm, valuable and special person. I am proud of who you are.

I care about you.

Step 5: Reflection

Ask about the positive aspects of this explicit self-care. Ask your client to read this letter several times at home. You could also ask them to think of a symbol to remind them of their intention to continue caring for their inner child (for example, a piece of jewellery, screensaver or printed mug).

Chapter 22: Empathic Confrontation with the Vulnerable Child

Objective

To make your client aware of their resignation to schema activation and its consequences, and then to encourage them to adopt healthier forms of emotion regulation.

Guidelines

Step 1: Preparation
Step 2: Identify the behaviour
Step 3: Empathy
Step 4: Confrontation
Step 5: Consolidation

Explanation of the guidelines

Step 1: Preparation

Empathic confrontation is usually focused on (the consequences of) avoidance or inversion of the feelings evoked by schema activation (see Chapter 37: Empathic Confrontation with a Coping Mode). However, you can also confront your client with the negative consequences of their resignation to the activated schemas. In preparation, you try to distinguish that resignation from the schema activation itself. After all, the goal is not to confront your client with the fact that schemas are being activated, something over which your client has no control, but rather with their tendency to resign themselves to strong emotions. This is possible in this final phase because your client is now aware of schema activation and has learned how to deal with the evoked emotions in a different, more healthy way.

Step 2: Identify the behaviour

Describe the emotions you see and the context in which they were evoked. Indicate that your client is resigning themselves to those emotions by, for example, focusing all their attention on them.

Step 3: Empathy

Be understanding and acknowledge the emotions that have been triggered by the current context and the old pain that plays a role in it. Name the Vulnerable Child mode that you recognize in these emotional reactions. Use this compassion to bring your client back into their window of tolerance, so that they can think and talk about the Vulnerable Child mode instead of being fused with it.

Step 4: Confrontation

Your client just seemed to merge with that Vulnerable Child mode, to blend with its emotions. Explain that as a result, you feel as though you are responsible for your client's emotional regulation and that this raises concerns: '*As much as I want to help you with that, I am also a little concerned that you will not be able to cope on your own. The sadness is there, you cannot control that, but you can decide for yourself how to deal with it so that you are not overwhelmed by it.*'

Step 5: Consolidation

Compliment your client on being able to talk about their Vulnerable Child mode while returning in Healthy Adult mode. Ask your client how this feels and focus on the positive aspects of this healthy emotion regulation, such as the connection they feel with the other person or the feeling of competence.

Example

Although the therapy is in its final phase, Mary still often seems to be overwhelmed by emotions. The therapist has to work hard every time to help regulate the emotions and feels increasingly powerless, as if the therapy is having no effect. In the current session, they talk about situations in which Mary feels lonely. The conversation stalls because she seems to be overwhelmed by emotions.

Therapist: Mary, what's happening now?

Mary: ... (*Tears well up in her eyes and she seems unable to speak.*)

Therapist: I see your sadness, I see your tears, and it seems as if you're somewhat overwhelmed by this sadness. Is that correct?

(*Mary nods.*)

Therapist: It pains me to see you so sad. I don't think that's strange, though, because we're talking about an emotional subject for you: feeling alone. That, in itself, is a sad subject, but I know that for you it touches on an old pain.

Mary: (*Somewhat calmer.*) ...Yes.

Therapist: When I see you becoming so overwhelmed by sadness, it feels as if I have to try to keep you afloat. I certainly want to help you, but if I have to do it alone, I feel that it is becoming difficult. It feels as if I'm solely responsible.

What if your client:

- ...becomes even more emotional as a result of the empathic confrontation?

  Show compassion and be understanding: it is also a difficult and potentially painful message that you are conveying. In addition, be kind to yourself, because it may feel uncomfortable to address your client in this way. However, try to think realistically: of course, you can continue to help your client, but the goal of the treatment is for them to become increasingly capable of regulating their own emotions.

PART IV: Treatment Phase – Working with Inner Critic Modes

Inner critic modes

Inner critic modes have traditionally been referred to as 'parent modes' (Young et al., 2003). Following an international research group (Arntz et al., 2021) and the Dutch Association for Schema Therapy, we have chosen to refer to inner critic modes, thereby foregrounding the characteristic aspect of this mode category, namely self-criticism. When talking about 'parent modes', there is a risk that people will think that these modes always and only originate from internalized messages given by (one of) the parents. This is incorrect: an inner critic mode can have many sources. Think, for example, of bullying peers, a strict grandmother, a demanding sports coach or the messages that the child has drawn from learning experiences unintentionally offered by the environment. In the latter case, think, for example, of the hard work of loving parents that was 'read' by the child as a message that this was also expected of him/her. It is therefore likely that your client's inner critic mode has been shaped by a combination of strict or punitive messages given by different people, either explicitly or implicitly.

Inner critic modes involve resignation to schemas such as Unrelenting Standards/Hypercriticalness and Punitiveness. The category of inner critic modes includes the Demanding Critic and the Punitive Critic, with the Guilt-Inducing Critic being a variant of the latter (see Chapter 2: Overview of Concepts for descriptions of these concepts).

How do you recognize inner critic modes?

In the case conceptualization of your client, you have already described what their inner critic modes look like and whether they concern a Demanding, Punitive and/or Guilt-Inducing Critic. During sessions, you can further recognize the inner critic modes by using four sources of information:

- ***What* does your client say?:** When an inner critic mode is active, you will hear your client express demanding, critical, devaluing, punitive and/or accusatory judgements about themselves. In the Demanding Critic and Guilt-Inducing Critic modes, these messages can be subtle: 'It is very important that I put everything aside right now to meet this deadline.', 'It's only logical that I'm there for my mother now: she's old and really can't do this herself.' These could also be statements from the Healthy Adult, but with the inner critic mode, the expectations and demands your client places on themselves are disproportionate, which is at the expense of their (other) emotional needs.
- ***How* does your client express this?:** Your client speaks in a stern tone in the inner critic modes; they are unyielding. They may be angry with themselves and use a punitive and harsh tone or make sarcastic remarks about their own 'flaws'. In the child modes, your client may also make statements about their self-image, but then it is done with more emotion.
- **What is your primary *emotional response* as a therapist?:** When your client is in an inner critic mode, you probably tend to contradict the demanding or punitive messages. If you do this without first 'defusing' your client from the inner critic mode, you run the risk of getting bogged down in an argument. You may also feel indignant or angry about the injustice done to your client by the inner critic mode.
- **Pay attention to *contrasts* in the presentation:** Sometimes, self-critical messages (e.g., 'I never do anything right') may initially resemble messages from the inner critic mode, but on closer inspection turn out to be lightning rods for, say, an Angry Protector: 'It doesn't matter what I do; I might as well not try anymore, because it's never good enough anyway'. As a therapist, you can sense the distance your client is creating and that they are indirectly blaming their environment.

What is the goal in working with inner critic modes?

The goal in working with an inner critic mode is to teach your client to arm themselves against its messages. This part of the book describes methods and techniques you can use to combat inner critic modes. To do this, your client must first learn to recognize their inner critic modes and see them as separate from themselves (diffusion), so that they can contradict or dismiss their inner critic mode and/or not be overly affected by its messages.

Initial Phase

In the initial phase of therapy, your client is often still fused with their inner critic mode. They feel as if they are one with it and believe the messages of their inner critic mode completely or to a large extent. In the initial phase, it is therefore important to constantly point out to your client when you hear or see their inner critic mode. Make your client aware of the changes in their way of speaking, the tone of their voice or their attitude towards themselves when the inner critic mode is active. Help your client to increasingly see this inner critic mode as an external messenger that they have internalized in the past. You do this by 'removing' the inner critic mode from your client, as it were, by giving that side a place or chair in the room or representing it with a symbol, mode card or figurine that they can address directly while fighting it. In this initial phase, your client may still watch as you present counter-arguments against their inner critic mode and limit or send it away: you take the lead in this and thereby stand up for their core emotional needs and goals.

In the initial phase of treatment, limiting or dismissing the inner critic modes will be a form of 'fighting' against them. By taking a clear, dichotomous stance against the messages of the inner critic modes, you offer clear, unambiguous, healthy messages that your client can internalize. In this initial phase, do not give in to the temptation to nuance those critical messages or ask for understanding of the intentions or background of the inner critic modes; that nuance can take place later in the therapy. In this initial phase, compare your client on an emotional level to a young child, where the most important goal is to validate needs; nuance and realistic thinking will only become important later in development (puberty in children, or in therapy, the middle phase).

On the following pages, you will find guidelines for techniques that you can use in the initial phase to combat your client's inner critic mode.

Chapter 23: Imagery Rescripting – The Therapist Rescripts

Objective

To provide corrective emotional experiences by rescripting visualized (traumatic) memories (schema activation) through validating unmet core emotional needs. These experiences must then be consolidated as building blocks for the Healthy Adult.

Guidelines

Step 1: Rationale
Step 2: Imagining a good place
Step 3: Imagining a schema-activating event in the present
Step 4: Affect bridge
Step 5: Exploration of the visualized memory
Step 6: The therapist rescripts the memory
Step 7: Imagining a good place
Step 8: Debriefing and homework

Explanation of the guidelines

Step 1: Rationale

Explain that the aim of the exercise is to imagine a better outcome to unpleasant events in the past in which emotional needs were violated. When you imagine something vividly, your brain perceives it as 'real', allowing the exercise to offer healing experiences.

Step 2: Imagining a good place

See Chapter 3: Diagnostic Imagery. You can skip this step for reasons of time or because your client's schemas have already been activated by recent events or intrusive memories. In that case, you can ask them to visualize those events (go to Step 3) or memories (go to Step 5) immediately.

Step 3: Imagining a schema-activating event in the present

Ask your client to conjure up an image of the unpleasant event in the present and have them describe it in the present tense, from a first-person perspective. Ask about the most schema-activating aspect and ask them to focus on that. This schema activation is necessary in order to access relevant (traumatic) events in the past.

Step 4: Affect bridge

Ask your client about the emotional, physiological and cognitive elements of the experience (*What are you feeling right now? Where do you feel that in your body? What is going through your mind?*). Then ask whether this is the first time they have had this feeling or whether it is something familiar. In the latter case, ask them to let go of the image and allow images or memories from the past to surface that are in some way related to this experience.

Step 5: Exploration of the visualized memory

Ask your client to describe the situation from a first-person perspective: *What do they see now? Where do they see the other person?* (Ask them to point them out.) *What is the other person saying? How does their voice sound?*

Try to get your client to focus on the most schema-activating elements of the image, such as the angry eyes or punitive words of the antagonist.

Step 6: The therapist rescripts the memory

Once your client's emotional arousal is high in the image, proceed to rescripting. Do not be afraid to let those emotions surface: as long as your client is responding to your questions and interventions, they can still process the corrective information you are offering with the rescripting.

In rescripting, you address the antagonist as if you were literally speaking to that person. For example, look in a different direction when you address the other person (where the client was pointing earlier), and use a different tone of voice. The guideline for rescripting is that you have the upper hand in the interaction with the antagonist, which may mean that you send them away from the scene. Addressing the antagonist is not intended to change them, but to allow your client to hear the arguments that counter the critical messages.

Then directly validate the child's needs in a gentle tone, shorten your sentences and tailor your language to the age of your client in the image. Then ask about the primary emotional responses: *Does it feel good or bad when you validate their emotional need?* Probe further into that corrective emotional experience: *Where do they experience that pleasant feeling in their body? Is it a warm or cold feeling? Is it a feeling of loneliness or more of togetherness?* Such attention-focusing questions help to consolidate the experience.

Step 7: Imagining a good place

After the rescripting, you can return to the good place described earlier. However, you can also ask the child in the image where they would rather be than in this stressful situation. In this way, your client learns healthy ways of regulating emotions: after something stressful, it is important to relax for a while. Ask your client about the sensory information in this good place.

Step 8: Debriefing and homework

Focus your client's attention on the corrective emotional experience in order to consolidate it. As with every session, give homework in the form of an (audio) flashcard or an assignment, for example, writing down the most important arguments against the antagonist and frequently reviewing them at home.

Example

When Sandra came to the session, she felt sad and small because of a nasty comment from her boyfriend Mark, who said that her therapy would not help her. The therapist decides to skip the good place and initiate an imagery rescripting exercise in response to the unpleasant feeling.

Sandra: (*With her eyes closed.*) Mark says he wants to do something this afternoon, and then I say I have to go to therapy. Suddenly he becomes very aggressive: 'Do you have to go to that therapy again? It's pointless!'

Therapist: How do you feel now?

Sandra: Sad, and small…

Therapist: Where do you feel that in your body?

Sandra: (*Points to her stomach.*) A knot in my stomach.

Therapist: What's going through your mind?

Sandra: That I'm trying so hard to fight that feeling and then he says this…

Therapist: Do you recognize this feeling? (*Sandra nods.*) Then concentrate on this feeling, and let the image fade away … Let images from the past come to mind that somehow touch on this feeling…

Sandra: …It makes me think of my father, who said exactly the same thing…

Therapist: Where do you see your father now? (*Sandra points to a spot in front of her.*) … How old are you now?

Sandra: Eleven or so…

Therapist: Describe what is happening now.

Sandra: I ask him if I can take piano lessons and he says, 'No, of course not, you're far too stupid for that! It's pointless, and I'm not going to spend my money on that!'

Therapist: OK, pause the image for a moment. I don't think it's right that he shouts at you like that, you're only eleven years old. That's why I want to join you in the image to help you. Can you place me in the kitchen? Where do you see me?

Sandra: (*Points to a spot to her right.*) Over there, near me.

Therapist: I'm going to say something to your father. (*Therapist turns towards where the father is in the image and says in a firm voice:*) Stop it! Have you gone mad, talking to Sandra like that! (*To Sandra, in a soft voice:*) How does he react?

Sandra: He gets angry and says, 'It's none of your business'.

Therapist: (*To the father, in a firm voice:*) I'm here to take care of Sandra; that was your job, but you aren't doing it. You're only making her anxious and making her feel bad. That is why I'm done with this and I want you to leave. (*To Sandra, in a soft voice:*) Look, he's leaving … How do you feel?

Sandra: Better, calmer…

Therapist: That's good. Because he shouldn't shout at you like that, and it's not true that you're stupid. It's logical that it makes you afraid; he shouldn't do that, and what he says isn't true. It's great that you want to take piano lessons, and it's perfectly normal to ask for that. How do you feel now?

Sandra: Good, calm.

Therapist: Where do you feel that calm feeling? (*Sandra points to her chest.*) Just concentrate on that calm feeling in your chest … Is it a warm feeling or a cold feeling?

Sandra: Warm…

Therapist: A feeling of being more alone, or more together?

Sandra: Together…

Therapist: Enjoy that warm feeling of 'togetherness' in your chest … And where would you rather be right now than here? What would be a nice place for you to be?

Sandra: I'd like to go to the river for a swim.

Therapist: That sounds lovely! Just be there now, enjoying the water. I'll keep an eye on things to make sure it stays safe; you just enjoy yourself.

(The therapist and Sandra talk for a while about how nice this place is, and then the therapist concludes the exercise, after which it is discussed.)

What if your client:

- …cannot imagine the therapist defeating the antagonist?

  Use the many possibilities that imagery offers: bring in helpers, make yourself bigger, or make the antagonist smaller. Ultimately, you can also describe the positive outcome as vividly as possible to help your client visualize that the antagonist is being defeated.

- …feels guilty because of the rescripting?

  The guilt is probably triggered by the antagonist's visible or presumed suffering. That suffering is an implicit, punitive message that your client has done something wrong. First, make that implicit message explicit by saying, for example: '*When you look so tired and sigh like that, your child reads that as a message that it is their fault that you are feeling bad right now.*' Pay attention to the cognitive restructuring of these guilt-inducing assumptions, for example: '*I feel sorry for you that you feel so tired, but that is not your child's fault or responsibility. You cannot expect your child to take care of you, because ultimately parents are supposed to take care of children and not the other way around.*'

Variations

When working with adolescents, addressing the parents as antagonists in the visualized image requires extra vigilance. Unlike most adults, adolescents still have to deal with a relationship of authority and dependence with their parents.

Although it is sometimes necessary to address parents firmly in the image, you should do so with respect. If addressing the parents in the image evokes feelings of loyalty and guilt, you can ask your client to recall an image of a warm and caring side of the parent, in addition to the image of the punitive side of the parent. In the image, you address the punitive side of the parent, thereby conveying the message that you are not addressing the parent as a whole.

In a group setting, you can alternate the different steps of the exercise with group discussions, in which everyone shares their experience. This reduces the chance of group members having flashbacks that you are unaware of. Another option is to have the group participate in the rescripting of an image of one of the group members.

Chapter 24: Chairwork with the Demanding Critic

Objective

To learn to recognize the influence of the Demanding Critic, to gain a corrective emotional experience (validating emotional needs) and to cognitively restructure the demanding assumptions.

Guidelines

Step 1: Recognize the Demanding Critic
Step 2: Point out the Demanding Critic
Step 3: Rationale
Step 4: Interview the Demanding Critic in another chair
Step 5: Place the client on the Vulnerable Child chair
Optional Step 6: Charge the Vulnerable Child chair with emotions
Step 7: Challenge the Demanding Critic
Step 8: Validate the needs of the Vulnerable Child
Step 9: Summary, reflection and homework

Explanation of the guidelines

Step 1: Recognize the Demanding Critic

The Demanding Critic criticizes achievements, rather than criticizing the whole person as the Punitive Critic does. Your client feels that they should have worked harder, organized their time/tasks better, etc. They do not sound angry or punitive, but rather frustrated and impatient.

Step 2: Point out the Demanding Critic

Describe the state of mind as a side of your client. Support this description with gestures, almost as if you were describing another person next to your client. After an initial description of the behaviour, talk about the modes in the third person ('he'/'she') in order to create more distance and thus more awareness.

Step 3: Rationale

Briefly explain that the technique not only helps to better understand what your client is experiencing, but also helps them to feel better. If necessary, offer reassurance and control by saying, for example, that the client retains control over the technique and can stop at any time.

Step 4: Interview the Demanding Critic in another chair

Ask your client to sit in the Demanding Critic chair and empathize with that mode. From now on, address your client directly as the Demanding Critic, using the second person form ('you'). Ask what, according to the Demanding Critic, could and should have been done better. Interrupt the interview in good time so that there is enough time left for the rest of the exercise. When you ask your client to get up from the chair, ask them to leave the Demanding Critic behind on that chair.

Step 5: Place the client on the Vulnerable Child chair

Have your client sit in the Vulnerable Child chair and ask about their primary emotional responses to hearing the messages from the Demanding Critic.

Optional Step 6: Charge the Vulnerable Child chair with emotions

If your client has difficulty recognizing emotions evoked by the Demanding Critic, you can help by expressing the possible feelings and needs yourself in the Vulnerable Child chair. In this way, you 'charge' the chair with feelings and needs, as it were:

- Intermediate step 1: Therapist and client switch seats
- Intermediate step 2: Therapist articulates the primary emotional responses:
  - Describe your client as a child as you have seen them in photographs or in imagery exercises.
  - Describe the normal emotional reactions of children in such situations.
  - Describe the emotions in the present tense and as vividly as possible.
  - Describe the underlying emotional needs.
- Intermediate step 3: Switch seats again, and the client repeats their emotions and needs.
- Intermediate step 4: Increase emotional awareness by focusing attention on different components of those emotions.

Step 7: Challenge the Demanding Critic

Both stand up and discuss counter-arguments from a standing position. This stimulates your client's Healthy Adult. The Demanding Critic can be convincing (and therefore difficult to change) because the core of the beliefs sounds logical: 'Trying harder makes you more competent'. Counter-arguments can be found in the realization that there are more emotional needs than just competence. Then, from the Vulnerable Child chair, let your client experience how you use these arguments to counter the Demanding Critic.

Step 8: Validate the needs of the Vulnerable Child

Validate the need for spontaneity and play and other needs that may be relevant. Reflect on the primary emotional responses that validating those core emotional needs evokes, and consolidate by focusing attention on the corrective emotional experiences.

Step 9: Summary, reflection and homework

At the end of the exercise, summarize the main conclusions and experiences. Give homework, such as repeating the arguments against the Demanding Critic. If desired, the exercise can be recorded and listened to again by the client, who can then note down the arguments that convince them on a flashcard.

Example

Therapist: How have you been feeling this past week?

Mary: Well, I don't know, because I've mainly been working. I'd promised to do a number of things, so I had to. I should have planned it differently.

Therapist: Right, I hear you talking mainly about all the 'shoulds'. It sounds as if you're dissatisfied: 'You should have done that differently, you should have finished that'. Is that right?

Mary: Yes.

Therapist: Then I'll get an extra chair and ask you to sit in it and tell me what you think you should have done differently. You were already in that mindset, but by saying it out loud while sitting in that chair, and then looking at it together from a distance, we can better understand what's going on inside you and I can help you further. Would you like to sit in that chair?

(Mary moves.)

Therapist: Now be that Demanding Critic. What do you think Mary (*Pointing to her original chair*) should have done differently?

Mary: You just have to do it; you're paid for it, after all, and others manage it.

Therapist: OK, I'm going to pause you here for a moment. You can now sit on this chair next to me.

(*Mary moves to the chair of the Vulnerable Child side.*)

Therapist: So, she says (*pointing to the chair of the Demanding Critic*), 'You just have to do it, you should have arranged it better', and her voice sounds harsh too. How do you feel when you hear that demanding voice?

Mary: Well, ... it's true, it's all true.

Therapist: I understand that you believe her, but I didn't ask if you believe her, I asked how it *feels* for you when you hear those demands, that pressure?

Mary: ...Well, no different than there, really. I just think, yes, that's right, I have to do all that too.

Therapist: I can see how difficult it is to put into words how you feel about all these demands. I'd like to help you gain some insight into what you're feeling and what you need when there is so much pressure on you. That's why I'd like to suggest that we switch seats for a moment; you come and sit here in my chair, and I'll sit in your chair. I'll try to put into words the feelings you might have about all those demands and criticisms.

(*Therapist and Mary switch seats.*)

Therapist: Sitting here, I've just heard all those 'shoulds'. And now we're talking about last week, but I know that criticism – I've heard it many times before. It brings back memories of how, even as a child, I was told what I had to do better or differently ... Then I feel again that I didn't want to work at all, I just wanted to play ... That doesn't feel good; I feel it here (*Points to chest.*) ... Let's switch chairs again now.

(*Therapist and Mary move.*)

Therapist: Do you remember what I said about how that felt?

Mary: Not nice ... sad ... that you just wanted to play, to be free...

Therapist: Can you repeat that: 'I don't want to work all the time, I just want to be free'?

Mary: I don't want to work all the time, I want to be free...

Therapist: ...How do you feel now when you say that, pleasant or unpleasant?

Mary: Sad…

Therapist: I understand that, of course you feel sad and a little angry when you're criticized for not having done well enough despite all your hard work last week. And especially if you've received that criticism many times before, it's not just this week, but the umpteenth time you've been told that you aren't working hard enough … How do you feel when you hear that I understand you?

Mary: That feels good.

Therapist: So, you're really feeling the effect of that criticism and those demands from over there. (*Points to the Demanding Critic.*) But that doesn't change the fact that you still think what she says is true, is that right?

Mary: Yes, it's true that all those tasks have to be completed…

Therapist: OK, let's take a step back so we can calmly consider whether that all makes sense. Come and stand next to me.

(*Therapist and Mary stand up and stand next to each other, looking at the chairs.*)

Therapist: So, this is what has been going on inside you over the past week: that critical, demanding side of you was constantly sending messages about all the things you hadn't done yet, and that not only made you feel sad, but also a bit angry. And that happens continuously: criticism–sadness–criticism–sadness … What do you think when you look at it that way?

Mary: I find it a bit wretched…

Therapist: What do you think that sadness, that sad child, actually needs? A kick up the backside?

Mary: No, of course not! … just some relaxation…

Therapist: Exactly … What would you like to look back on in twenty years' time, all those demands and criticisms or a little more freedom in your life?

Mary: …The latter…

Therapist: Yes, right … I don't agree with that Demanding Critic either. Would you like to hear why I disagree with her? (*Mary nods.*) Then I'll sit back down in my chair. And maybe you can listen and see how it feels from this chair on the Vulnerable Child side.

(*The therapist sits down in his own chair, turns towards the chair of the Demanding Critic and voices the arguments.*)

What if your client:

- ...stubbornly insists that the Demanding Critic is right?

  Use cognitive techniques to critically examine the assumptions of the Demanding Critic. Combine these cognitive techniques with the chairwork, in which you and the Healthy Adult examine whether the Demanding Critic in another chair is right. Discuss how the unhealthy rules of the Demanding Critic prevent your client from making real progress with certain therapy goals.

Variations

You can also ask your client to observe while standing when you contradict the Demanding Critic. This places more emphasis on cognitive restructuring than on the emotional experience.

You can place symbols (mode cards, figurines or other materials) for the different sides on the chairs.

When working with children and adolescents, it is important to be alert to current messages that your client may still be receiving from parents or other important people on whom your client is still dependent, given their age. In such cases, try to work systemically to stop such feeding from the Demanding Critic where possible. When working with adults, it is also important to pay attention to systemic aspects, such as a demanding partner or demanding working conditions.

Chapter 25: Chairwork with the Punitive Critic

Objective

To learn to recognize the influence of the Punitive Critic, to gain a corrective emotional experience by validating core emotional needs, and to cognitively restructure punitive assumptions.

Guidelines

Step 1: Recognize the Punitive Critic
Step 2: Name the Punitive Critic
Step 3: Rationale
Step 4: Interview the Punitive Critic on another chair
Step 5: Place the client on the Vulnerable Child chair
Step 6: Fight the Punitive Critic
Step 7: Validate the needs of the Vulnerable Child
Step 8: Summary, reflection and homework

Explanation of the guidelines

Step 1: Recognize the Punitive Critic

In the Punitive Critic, your client sounds angry and punitive towards themselves. If your client says punitive things about themselves but sounds sad or desperate, they may be in the Vulnerable Child mode.

Step 2: Name the Punitive Critic

Name the punitive messages while pointing to a spot next to your client, as if you are pointing to the Punisher as an extra person in the room. This way, your client not only becomes aware of this mode, but you also create some distance from it.

Step 3: Rationale

Explain that the technique helps to distance oneself from negative judgements. If necessary, offer reassurance and control by saying, for example, that the client is in control of the technique and can stop at any time.

Step 4: Interview the Punitive Critic on another chair

Place a chair in the spot you just designated. Ask your client to sit in that chair and be the Punitive Critic, and ask questions such as, *What do you have to say about [client's name]?* In this way, invite your client to express their self-criticism, but do not let this go on for too long.

Step 5: Place the client on the Vulnerable Child chair

After you have heard a few punitive messages, ask your client to leave the Punitive Critic behind on the chair and sit down on the chair next to you. Ask how they feel when they hear the punitive messages (repeat them briefly). Clients often respond that they agree with those messages. Explain that you are not asking whether they believe the negative judgements, but how they *feel* about these unpleasant comments: *Is it nice to hear these judgements or not?* Show compassion for the emotions experienced when hearing the punitive messages and indicate that you do not agree with the Punitive Critic.

Step 6: Fight the Punitive Critic

Turn to the (empty!) chair representing the Punitive Critic and present counter-arguments. Many of the counter-arguments can be found in core emotional needs: there is a need for safe attachment to others, self-expression, etc., not for these punitive messages. Also mention your client's positive qualities. The guideline is that you 'win' against the Punisher. If they persist, take firm action against this mode by addressing them while standing and putting their chair outside the door.

Step 7: Validate the needs of the Vulnerable Child

Fighting (or seeing) the Punitive Critic is both a corrective emotional experience for your client and a cognitive restructuring of the punishing messages. Then address your client in the Vulnerable Child chair and validate their emotional needs, for example, by offering safe attachment to others or complimenting them on self-expression. Consolidate this corrective emotional experience by asking your client to be mindful of the primary emotional responses that occur: *Does it feel better or worse when you hear that … [validation of emotional needs]?, Where do you feel that pleasant feeling in your body?, Is it a warm or cold feeling?*

Step 8: Summary, reflection and homework

Further consolidation of the corrective emotional experience occurs through repetition of that experience. Therefore, summarize the most important conclusions from the exercise. Also give homework that allows the experience to be repeated, for example, by recording an audio flashcard that your client can listen to more often or by writing down the arguments against the Punitive Critic that they found most valuable and convincing.

Example

(*Sandra says that she messed up again and hasn't done everything she should.*)

Therapist: It sounds like you're looking at yourself (*the therapist gestures to a spot next to Sandra*), not with kind eyes, but with anger and criticism.

Sandra: Isn't it stupid that I don't even do the things I agreed to do?

Therapist: Now that you're so full of criticism and anger, I want to do an exercise with it. (*The therapist takes a chair and places it where he just pointed.*) You can sit on this chair and really get into that feeling of anger, with all the criticism you have for yourself. Take a seat on that chair.

(*Sandra moves.*)

Therapist: Be that angry, punishing voice here. Say, Punisher, it seems like you have a lot to criticize about Sandra. Tell me what that is.

Sandra: I just mess everything up!

Therapist: So according to you (*gesturing to Sandra in the punisher's chair*), she (*gesturing to her original chair*) is the one who messes everything up?

Sandra: Yes, she's just lazy, she needs to get things done!

Therapist: OK, let's leave it at that for now. You can come and sit in the chair next to me. But when you get up from this chair, you can leave that Punisher behind, stuck to that chair.

(*Sandra sits down in the chair of the Vulnerable Child.*)

Therapist: (*In a softer voice.*) When I listen to that Punisher, it sounds quite dismissive. How do you feel when you hear that criticism?

Sandra: Well, she's right…

Therapist: So, you believe her, but that's not what I asked. I asked how you *feel* when you hear those judgements: Is it nice or not nice to hear that you're lazy?

Sandra: (*In a soft voice.*) Not nice…

Therapist: I understand. I wouldn't feel good about that criticism either. And for you, it's yet another time you've been told off like that. It's logical that you feel sad; that seems like a very normal human reaction to me. I completely disagree with all the criticism she's pouring on you. I want to let you hear why.

Sandra: OK…

Therapist: (*Turning to the empty chair on the Punitive Critic side.*) I want you to stop peddling this nonsense! She's not messing things up at all, and she's certainly not lazy! She works hard in therapy, and her team leader recently said he was pleased with everything she's taking on. (*Therapist turns to Sandra and continues in a soft voice.*) There's really nothing wrong with you. You're not the problem here, she is (*gestures towards the Punitive Critic*). How does the Punisher react when I contradict her like that?

Sandra: Well, to be honest, I don't think she cares. Right now, she's mostly angry at you, like, 'Mind your own business!'

Therapist: Really? But then I'll have a good talk to her. Don't be alarmed, but I'm going to stand over there for a moment, so she can feel that I'm in charge here, not her.

(*Now, the therapist stands up, speaks more fiercely to the Punitive Critic and puts it outside the door, chair and all. He says that the therapy room is a safe place, where there is no room for those punishing messages.*)

Therapist: (*Sits next to Sandra again and asks in a soft voice:*) How do you feel now when you look at the empty place where the Punisher was just a moment ago?

Sandra: Yes, nice … Better…

Therapist: Where do you feel that it's better, in your body, I mean?

Sandra: I think here. (*Points to her chest.*)

Therapist: I'm very glad you can feel that way. I'd like you to feel that way more often, even after this session. That's why I'm going to record some things on your phone that you can listen to again after the session.

What if your client:

- **…is afraid of repercussions from the Punitive Critic when the session is over?**

  First of all, see it as a compliment: you did your best to make it as real an experience as possible, and you succeeded! Emphasize safety: you will always help your client to get rid of the Punisher, you will give them tools that can protect them, and they can trust that the Punisher will become less and less powerful the more you fight it.

Variations

Place mode cards on the chairs so that it is easier for your client to recognize which mode is where.

In group schema therapy, the other group members can stand in front of your client and fight the Punisher together.

When working with adolescents, it is important to be aware of loyalty issues. If punitive messages come from one of the parents or other important figures in the client's life, it is important to determine to what extent your client currently has contact with that person or, given their age, is still dependent on them. It is important to make it very clear that the Punitive Critic consists of internalized messages that you are fighting against together and that a parent or caregiver is not being 'sent away', as it were. Work with the parents or other important loved ones to reduce the punishing messages, if they are still being given to your client in the here and now.

Chairwork for the Guilt-Inducing Critic (a variant of the Punitive Critic) follows largely the same steps. Your client will then emphasize how their actions (may have) led to negative consequences for others: 'Yesterday, during the appointment, I talked about my work problems the whole time, while she is in a bad relationship … She must feel very alone and sad…' There are then two parts where the technique is performed slightly differently, namely *Step 5: Place the client in the Vulnerable Child chair* and *Step 6: Fight the Punitive Critic mode.*

In Step 5, you first make the implicit messages communicated by the Guilt-Inducing side explicit, as if you were subtitling their messages: '*When she paints that picture of your friend sitting at home alone and sad, I think the message you hear is: "She feels bad because of you"*', or perhaps: '"*You are a bad friend." Is that right? How do you feel when you hear that message?*' In Step 6, you pay more attention to the arguments against the guilt-inducing messages. Many clients with a guilt-inducing side have great difficulty understanding why they are not responsible for other people's well-being. One of the arguments against the guilt-inducing side is that it is unfair that it focuses primarily on the (perceived) feelings and needs of others and not on those of your client.

Middle Phase

In the middle phase, your client will hopefully be able to view their inner critic mode with a little more distance: they no longer identify completely with it. They realize more that the messages from the inner critic mode are not (entirely) true or realistic and have seen you stand up for their core emotional needs many times. There is now room to let your client fight against their inner critic mode: encourage your client, for example, to use chairwork and imagery rescripting from their Healthy Adult to contradict the critical messages and stand up for their needs together with you. Although you have already used cognitive techniques in the initial phase, there is even more room for working on cognitions in this middle phase, because your client is no longer completely fused with the inner critic mode. The client is given an increasingly important role in investigating the credibility of the critical messages. Adopt a coaching and encouraging attitude and support your client where necessary.

On the following pages, you will find techniques that you can use in the middle phase to reduce the influence of your client's inner critic mode. These include both new techniques and adaptations or variations of techniques that have already been described in the initial phase.

Chapter 26: Imagery Rescripting – Rescripting Together

Objective

To coach the client's Healthy Adult in standing up for their emotional needs and fighting the beliefs of the inner critic mode.

Guidelines

Step 1: Rationale
Step 2: Visualizing the Healthy Adult
Optional Steps 3: Imagining a schema-activating event in the present and 4: Affect bridge
Step 5: Exploring the memory
Step 6: Therapist and client rescript the memory
Step 7: Imagining a good place
Step 8: Debriefing and homework

Explanation of the guidelines

Step 1: Rationale

Explain that the goal of the middle phase is to teach the client's Healthy Adult to validate emotional needs. In this phase, you coach the Healthy Adult in saying something to the antagonist and the child in the image.

Step 2: Visualizing the Healthy Adult

Ask the client to begin the exercise by visualizing the Healthy Adult (see Chapter 47: Visualizing the Healthy Adult). This first step makes it less difficult for the client to recall the image of the Healthy Adult during the schema-activating memory.

Optional Steps 3: Imagining a schema-activating event in the present and 4: Affect bridge

In the middle phase, it can be assumed that the client has insight into the original events that led to the complaint patterns. You can, of course, still use the affect bridge if necessary.

Note: You can choose to practice with a memory that was already used in the initial phase. This provides an example of rescripting that the client can now do themselves.

Step 5: Exploring the memory

Depending on your specific goal with this exercise, you can ask the client to empathize with the original memory from the child's perspective (if you also want the client to practice defusing from the Vulnerable Child and connecting with the Healthy Adult) or to observe the original memory from a distance (observer perspective, when the emphasis is on practicing rescripting by the Healthy Adult).

Step 6: Therapist and client rescript the memory

Ask the client to visualize you not only as the therapist, but also as the Healthy Adult. Ask the Healthy Adult to help you think of reasons why the antagonist is wrong and what you can say to the antagonist. As the therapist, take the lead and ask the client to repeat your words to the antagonist or to add something themselves. Coaching can also involve asking the client to repeat the counter-arguments a bit louder. This helps the client become more confident in standing up for their emotional needs.

You repeat this coaching when providing care to the child in the image. This also includes suggesting to the client that they hold the child's hand; it is not only about what the client *says* to the younger version of themselves, but also about what they *do* for them.

Step 7: Imagining a good place

Ask the client where they would like to take the child in the image. Take the time to visualize that good place and pay attention to the emotional and physiological responses when visualizing it.

Step 8: Debriefing and homework

In the debriefing, spend time reinforcing the client's competence in standing up for their own needs. Ask the client to repeat the arguments and statements that were particularly meaningful to them and to write these down as homework.

Example

Therapist: Today, I'd like to do another imagery exercise like we did before. The ultimate goal of the therapy is for you, your Healthy Adult side, to be able to meet your emotional needs. That's why I'd like to practice that today, OK?

Sandra: (*Sounds a little hesitant.*) ...OK.

Therapist: You sound a bit hesitant, but don't worry: I'm going to help you with this. Together, we're going to make sure that your Healthy Adult gets stronger. Let's just take a memory we've used before. Do you remember your father not wanting you to take piano lessons? (*Sandra nods.*) I confronted your father about that and comforted the eleven-year-old Sandra in the image. Today, I want us to confront your father together and take care of that girl in the image.

Sandra: OK, yes, that's fine.

Therapist: Take a comfortable position and close your eyes. (*Sandra closes her eyes.*) To begin with, let's bring up an image of that Healthy Adult of yours. What does she look like again?

Sandra: ...Well, it reminds me of that time I stood up for myself to that woman at work who was criticizing me. And I told her I didn't like it. (*Sandra sits up a little straighter, and her voice sounds a little more confident.*)

Therapist: Very good, I can see you sitting up straighter. Describe what that Healthy Adult looks like.

Sandra: Well, she looks confident, she stands up straight, firmly. And her voice sounds calm ... Yes, she radiates calmness.

Therapist: Do you feel that a little bit too, that steadiness and calmness? (*Sandra nods.*) Good, now let that image fade away. We'll come back to it in a moment, but now I want to ask you to recall that memory of your father getting angry when you asked for piano lessons ... What do you see now?

Sandra: I see my father again, in the kitchen, angry.

Therapist: And are you there now, or are you looking at the situation, do you see that eleven-year-old girl standing there too?

Sandra: Well, it's a bit of both, but mainly I see it as if I'm watching it, and that eleven-year-old girl is standing there. (*Points to a spot in front of her.*)

Therapist: Take a good look at what's happening there, and tell me what you see and what you hear.

Sandra: I see my father looking angry, he snarls as he takes a beer out of the fridge. And Little Sandra is standing there, a bit shocked and sad…

Therapist: Then I think this is a good moment to help her, so can you place me and Adult Sandra in the picture, preferably between her father and that girl … Can you see the Adult Sandra and me? (*Sandra nods.*) Good, now try to be Adult Sandra for a moment, so you are there now … and am I standing to your left or right?

Sandra: Here, to my right.

Therapist: What do we actually think of what father says and does? Do we think it's OK how he treats that girl? (*Sandra shakes her head vigorously.*) What could we say to him?

Sandra: (*In a soft voice:*) That it's not right … But he can get really angry …

What if your client:

- …is unable to contradict the antagonist?

  Then take over from your client and fight the antagonist yourself first. You can then ask again if they can repeat your words. Sometimes, that doesn't work, and that's OK; a growth process is not a straight, upward line.

Variations

In group therapy, group members can contribute ideas about what the Healthy Adult might say. The presence of the group members in the image can support the client and make it feasible to address the antagonist.

With adolescents and clients with mild intellectual disabilities, you will need to be more active in presenting the arguments against the antagonist and suggesting what they can say to the child in the image.

Chapter 27: Chairwork with an Inner Critic Mode in the Middle Phase

Objective

To teach your client's Healthy Adult to resist the messages from the inner critic mode.

Guidelines

Step 1: Rationale
Step 2: Place an empty chair as the inner critic mode
Step 3: Preliminary discussion with the Healthy Adult
Step 4: Coach the client in fighting against the inner critic mode
Step 5: Validate the needs of the Vulnerable Child
Step 6: Summary, reflection and homework

Explanation of the guidelines

Step 1: Rationale

Explain that in this middle phase of therapy, your client will learn, with your help, to counter the messages from the inner critic mode. At the beginning of the middle phase, emphasize that you will work together to counter the inner critic mode, while towards the end of the middle phase, you will be standing by 'on the sidelines' to help if necessary.

Step 2: Place an empty chair as the inner critic mode

Place an empty chair opposite your client, in the place where the inner critic mode is always placed in therapy. At this stage, your client may no longer need to express their inner critic mode from that chair, because its messages are now well known. Name some of those critical messages and, if necessary, place a mode card or other symbol of the inner critic mode in that chair.

Step 3: Preliminary discussion with the Healthy Adult

Ask your client to connect with their Healthy Adult (see Chapter 47: Visualizing the Healthy Adult). Your client can do this from their therapy chair, but in the beginning they can also do it from your therapist chair or from a separate chair for the Healthy Adult. You may consider using an extra chair or other symbol for the Vulnerable Child, so that your client can see who they are fighting for.

Step 4: Coach the client in fighting against the inner critic mode

Discuss the arguments your client can use in fighting the inner critic mode. If necessary, remind your client of effective counter-arguments from the initial phase. Ask them to say these arguments out loud to the chair representing the inner critic mode. Coaching may involve adding additional points or asking your client to repeat these counter-arguments with more volume and force. Ask them how it feels to resist the inner critic mode. Focus your questions primarily on the positive aspects of that experience.

Step 5: Validate the needs of the Vulnerable Child

Next, ask your client to explicitly acknowledge and validate the feelings and needs of the Vulnerable Child. For a detailed description, see Chapter 20: Chairwork – Practicing Empathy for the Vulnerable Child.

Step 6: Summary, reflection and homework

Together, summarize the arguments that were most meaningful to your client. In that summary, also mention the positive aspects of the experience. As homework, have your client repeat these arguments and the memory of the experience, for example, by writing down the most important arguments, listening to the recording of this exercise or revisiting the experience in their imagination.

Example

(*Sandra is silent and looks gloomy.*)

Therapist: Sandra, it feels like something is going on. Tell me about it...

Sandra: Well, Mark made another comment when I went to therapy, saying that it wouldn't make any difference and I'd be better off stopping. I understand, I'm not succeeding either. I haven't made any progress; I must be too stupid for this...

Therapist: OK ... Who do you think I hear here? (*Gestures towards the spot in the room where the Punitive Critic's chair has always been.*)

Sandra: Well, OK, it may sound punitive, but it really feels that way.

Therapist: Exactly, that's how it is, isn't it? The Punitive Critic can still be quite dominant. And in this middle phase of therapy, it's important that you learn to defend yourself against the Punitive Critic. I know it's not easy, but practice makes perfect, so I suggest we practice that today. (*Takes an extra chair and places it where the Punitive Critic is always placed.*)

Therapist: Right, there sits the Punisher. We know what he says; I could hear him just now.

Sandra: Yes. That I'm useless ... That I'm stupid, that I'll never learn...

Therapist: OK, let's leave it at that for now. I'll get another chair. (*Places the extra chair on the other side of Sandra, so that Sandra is now sitting between the empty chair and the therapist's chair.*) Sandra, can you sit in this chair? (*Sandra sits down.*)

Therapist: Here, I want you to be the Healthy Adult, Big Sandra. Make contact with her. How do you do that again? (*Sandra sits up straight, and her facial expression becomes calmer.*) I can see it happening; can you feel that calmness? Perhaps with the thought of that time you contradicted that critical woman at the cleaning address?

Sandra: (*Smiling.*) Exactly, that's what I was thinking about.

Therapist: So, that's where the Punitive Critic is (*gestures to the empty chair opposite Sandra*), and with all that criticism, he makes Little Sandra here (*gestures to the empty chair between Sandra and the therapist*) feel very bad. And that Punisher sounds very convincing, but we now know why what he says is not true. What could we say in response when he says you're stupid and that you'll never learn?

Sandra: That's not true. I'm not stupid. We looked into that, with my old school reports, and they were all full of good grades.

Therapist: Exactly! And what do I always say about how you're doing in therapy?

Sandra: That I'm doing well, that I'm making progress...

Therapist: Exactly, now say that to your Punitive Critic.

Sandra: (*Turns to the empty chair.*) It's not true, I'm not stupid, and I proved that with my old school reports. And I'm doing pretty well in therapy too.

Therapist: Very well! Say that again, but twenty per cent louder?

Sandra: (*In a slightly louder voice:*) I'm not stupid! I always got good grades, and a lot of things are going much better now, so what you're saying isn't true at all!

Therapist: Well done, Sandra! How does it feel to tell that side of you what you think?

Sandra: Yes, good!

Therapist: And where do you feel that good feeling?

Sandra: (*Points to her chest.*) Here, as if it's opening up a little, as if I can breathe again.

Therapist: You're doing really well! And what do you want to do with that Punisher now? Do you want it to stay here, or do you want it gone?

Sandra: No, I want it gone...

Therapist: Come on, let's put it outside the door. We'll do it together, you don't have to do it all by yourself; you've already done really well!

(*The therapist and Sandra stand up and, smiling a little, pick up the chair together and place it outside the door. Then they sit down again.*)

Therapist: (*In a softer voice:*) Sandra, you've done really well, but I'd also like it if you could say some kind words out loud to Little Sandra here. What would you like to say to her?

Sandra: (*Turns to Little Sandra's chair.*) It's OK ... I understand that you're sad ... It'll be alright, you're not stupid...

Therapist: Good ... How does it feel to say that?

Sandra: Good, a warm feeling. (*Gestures towards her chest.*)

Therapist: I think you should say that more often, that you're not stupid, that everything will be alright. Would you like to listen to the recording of this part of the session a few times over the next week and write down those messages?

What if your client:

- ...finds it difficult to distance themselves from the inner critic mode and keeps agreeing with it?

  That could be a sign that more coaching and support is needed. Suggest some of the arguments your client could use against the inner critic mode. If this is still difficult in the final phase of the treatment, you could also try an empathic confrontation with that inner critic mode (see Chapter 36: Empathic Confrontation with an Inner Critic Mode).

Variations

By fighting while standing, your client can draw strength from the posture and position by towering above the inner critic mode.

If you have placed an image or symbol for the inner critic mode on a chair, you can have your client tear it up, lock it in a cupboard or destroy it at the end.

Chapter 28: Visualizing and Combatting an Inner Critic Mode

Objective

To detach from the inner critic mode of the past and the messages learned there. Your client learns to distance themselves from the inner critic mode and to combat or ignore it.

Guidelines

Step 1: Prepare the client for the imagery exercise
Step 2: Visualize the inner critic mode
Step 3: Observe and defuse
Step 4: Reflection

Explanation of the guidelines

Step 1: Prepare the client for the imagery exercise

Tell your client that you want to do an imagery exercise, but that you will not be working on any specific memories. Explain that, instead, you will ask your client to use their imagination to give shape, colour and content to their inner critic mode, so that they can then view it with more distance and practice combatting it.

Step 2: Visualize the inner critic mode

Ask your client to close their eyes and concentrate on a recent situation in which they felt very bad about themselves. Ask them to focus on the messages from their inner critic mode in this situation and then to feel what emotions and physical sensations this evoked. Ask your client to let the image of the recent situation fade and to form an image of their inner critic mode that matches the (physical) feeling they have. This can be an abstract image, a person, an animal or a fantasy figure. If your client is unsure what their inner critic mode looks like, you can ask what shape or colour it has, how close it is, etc. Examples of visualizations from clients include a tight corset, a wetsuit, a thundercloud above their head or a monster chasing your client.

Step 3: Observe and defuse

Let your client walk around the visualized image of their inner critic mode in their imagination. What does it look like? What details do they notice? Instruct your client to move the inner critic mode a little further away from them and then a little closer again, if it is a separate object. What does your client experience now? If it is an object that is, as it were, stuck to your client (e.g., a tight suit), let your client play with the distance from an observer's perspective (*'Can you move a little further away from yourself with that tight suit on?'*). Respond to what your client experiences each time. From the middle phase onwards, you can encourage your client to get rid of their inner critic mode. Acknowledge their desire to no longer feel so small/oppressed/agitated, and encourage them to make this happen. For example, the thundercloud can be chased away or blown away, the corset cut open, etc. Ask your client to let their imagination run wild and ask them how it feels to free themselves from their inner critic mode. What powerful emotions does this evoke, and how does it change the previously reported unpleasant (physical) feelings?

Step 4: Reflection

After completion, ask your client how they experienced the exercise and invite them to look back on the change in (physical) feelings. Discuss how your client can further consolidate this experience at home (for example, by listening back to a recording of the session).

Example

Therapist: You just said that you feel exhausted, but you don't have time to rest. You also feel a lot of pressure for the coming weekend; you keep rushing around because you have so much work waiting for you. Which side of yourself do you recognize in that pressure?

Mary: Yes, that Demanding Critic side has me in its grip again.

Therapist: Yes, that's a good way of putting it. It completely takes over at times like this; I can almost feel your anxiety.

Mary: Yes, it feels like I don't have any time to be here and attend the therapy session. In the past, I would have cancelled the session so I could continue working, but I don't do that anymore because I know that it's important to come.

Therapist: Well done! You're doing very well in recognizing what you really need and then making sure you get it. But you're feeling very restless right now. Shall we see if we can do an exercise with that today? I have an imagination exercise in mind, but not one in which we go back to a memory from your childhood. It's an exercise in which you can learn to deal with your inner critic more directly, because we know that it's a part of you that will probably always be there to a greater or lesser extent.

Mary: OK, fine.

Therapist: Close your eyes and take a moment to focus on that restless feeling you have. What exactly are you feeling?

Mary: It's a kind of flow or tingling sensation throughout my whole body. I feel the urge to move, to struggle almost. And at the same time, it feels like I have no room to move; I have to stay in the straitjacket. It makes me feel suffocated, I feel pressure on my chest.

Therapist: While you focus on these feelings, can you try to form an image of your Demanding Critic? Something that could symbolize the side of you that gives you these feelings? See what comes to mind, what shape and colour it has.

Mary: I see that side of me as a tight, black suit. It's all around me like a second skin. It feels stiff.

Therapist: That sounds like it's holding you captive. Can you create some space between you and the suit?

Mary: No, it's really tight. I can feel how it completely clamps me.

Therapist: Well, it really has you in its grip, doesn't it? That does sound like a very oppressive, suffocating feeling. Can you zoom out a bit, as if you were looking at it from a distance? What do you see when you look at yourself in that super-tight, stiff suit?

Mary: I see how it completely envelops me, how I almost disappear in it. I don't want that, I want space.

Therapist: Very good. You've been wearing this suit for too long. You want to get rid of it, you want space to be yourself, to relax. You don't want to constantly have to meet high standards and expectations. What could you do to give yourself a little more space?

Mary: The suit is too stiff to just pull off. But I see a fray at the bottom. I can pull on it to make the suit thinner.

Therapist: What a good idea! Go ahead, pull on that frayed edge. And be aware that you're now getting rid of that pressure, of all those 'musts'. You've had enough! What happens now?

Mary: The suit is getting thinner, more flexible. It's falling apart a bit. I roll it off me.

Therapist: Good! How does that feel?

Mary: Yes, it's strange, but I feel kind of liberated, relieved. Lighter.

Therapist: Very good. Enjoy that. How is the pressure on your chest now?

Mary: It's a lot less.

Therapist: Good. What else would you like to do with the suit to make you feel even better?

Mary: I actually want to set it on fire, so that nothing remains.

Therapist: Very good, go ahead. (*The therapist continues to encourage Mary to do whatever is necessary to feel liberated and relaxed.*) Enjoy that relaxed feeling, the calmness in your chest. Take that calmness with you as we conclude the exercise. You may let the image fade and, when you are ready, open your eyes again … How did you find doing this exercise?

Mary: Well, it was quite strange, actually, but I really felt that pressure lift. It feels clear, relaxed. Very nice!

Therapist: Well, you did a fantastic job! This suit has been clinging to your skin for so long. You have now consciously chosen to let it unravel, to peel it off and burn it! That seems like a very nice and powerful feeling to me.

Mary: Yes, it does feel powerful, strong. And at the same time, I feel how tired I am.

Therapist: Yes, you started today's session by saying how exhausted you are, but that you don't have time for anything, that you have to work all weekend. How can you take this experience with you into the here and now, that experience in which you let go of all those 'musts' and got a very powerful feeling in return?

Mary: Well, I think I need to set priorities. Look at what really needs to be done, because otherwise things will go very wrong, and what I can perhaps leave until after the weekend or what I can pass on to a colleague. Because I'm really very tired. I also need time and space to relax, I realize that now.

What if your client:

- ...can't visualize their inner critic mode?

  Let them focus on their feelings and give them time to form an image. If necessary, give a few examples of what it might look like and then let them fill in the details.

- ...resists your encouragement to get rid of the symbol for the inner critic mode?

  Ask your client about the reason for this resistance. If they give a self-critical answer ('Because I can't do that anyway'/'Because I need it, otherwise I won't do anything at all'), attribute this reason to the visualized symbol (*'I can hear your suit talking now, but that message only makes it squeeze you even tighter! Is that what you want?'*).

- ...doesn't know how to get rid of the symbol of their inner critic mode?

  Let your client consciously connect with their Healthy Adult side (see Chapter 47: Visualizing the Healthy Adult), and ask them again. Remind them that this exercise takes place in their mind, so they are in control. Encourage them to use their imagination. If necessary, make suggestions on how to get rid of the visualized object.

Variations

If necessary, you can have the object express the self-critical messages and add something silly (e.g., a funny voice, a hat) to lighten the mood. The object can also be drawn, modelled in clay or crafted, after which it is viewed from all sides and your client can then get rid of it in various ways (lock it in a cupboard, throw it outside, stamp on it or burn it).

Chapter 29: Historical Role Play

Objective

To generate corrective emotional experiences and change cognitive aspects of a schema by re-enacting a schema-activating memory. Finally, new, healthy behaviour can also be practiced. In this way, work is done on changing schemas and inner critic modes at all three levels (thinking, feeling and doing).

Guidelines

Step 1: Choose a schema-activating memory

Step 2: Round 1

- a: Re-enact the memory
- b: Discuss thoughts/schemas formed

Step 3: Round 2

- a: Replay the memory with a change of perspective
- b: Formulate alternative thoughts
- c: Discuss a healthy way to validate needs

Step 4: Round 3

- a: Replay the memory with desired behaviour
- b: Adjust alternative thoughts if necessary
- c: Discuss the credibility of alternative and original thoughts/schemas

Step 5: Reflection and homework

Explanation of the guidelines

Step 1: Choose a schema-activating memory

Point out statements made by the inner critic mode to the client. Ask the client about the credibility of this message and note it on a visual analogue scale, or express that credibility in another way, for example, as a percentage. Then ask the client for a memory from their childhood that still proves to them emotionally that this statement is true. In principle, all memories are suitable for historical role-playing as long as they can be re-enacted, except for memories of unsafe situations. In those cases, imagery rescripting is recommended.

Explain to your client that you will go through several rounds of role-playing: first, you will help the client understand how that critical message came about, then learn to look at it differently and, finally, reduce the impact of the inner critic mode in your client's daily life.

Step 2: Round 1

a: Re-enact the memory

Once the memory has been selected, stand up and set up the playing area. Do not remain seated in the therapy chairs during the re-enactment to avoid role confusion. Try to bring the situation from the past to life as well as possible. Get clear instructions on how best to re-enact the antagonist. After you have briefly re-enacted the situation (a few minutes at most), check with your client whether it resembled the past experience. If this is not yet the case, you can re-enact the situation again.

b: Discuss thoughts/schemas formed

Sit down again and ask your client what conclusions the child drew about themselves and the other person in the role play. Note the credibility of those thoughts on a visual analogue scale, or express them as a percentage.

Step 3: Round 2

a: Replay the memory with a change of perspective

Explain that you want to explore the situation further by re-enacting the role play, but that you will now play the younger version of the client and the client will play the other person. Ask for details about the other person's situation at that time, so that the client can empathize with the other person's perspective. Go to the playing field and re-enact the same part of the memory from these new roles.

b: Formulate alternative thoughts

After the role play, ask the client if they can remain in the other person's perspective for a moment longer. What did the client think and feel from the other person's perspective? Then sit down again and, together with the client, formulate alternative thoughts about themselves and the other person, for example: 'My mother was having a hard time, which meant she couldn't be there for me. *She* couldn't cope; it wasn't *my* fault/shortcoming.' Check the credibility of these alternative thoughts and note them on a visual analogue scale or express them as a percentage.

c: Discuss a healthy way to validate needs

Ask the client what they actually needed in this situation. In preparation for Round 3, discuss ways in which they could achieve this, for example, by asking for attention more clearly, saying something about the other person's reaction, etc. Make it clear that such behaviour was not something that could have been expected from the younger version of the client, but that they can practice this in the next round with the knowledge and skills they now have as an adult.

Step 4: Round 3

a: Replay the memory with desired behaviour

Your client now plays the younger version of themselves again and you play the other person. In this role play, your client stands up for their needs. Keep the reaction of the other person, whom you are playing, brief or omit it altogether at first; this round is mainly about gaining a corrective emotional experience of standing up for one's emotional needs. Ask your client to become aware of how it feels to stand up for their needs.

b: Adjust alternative thoughts if necessary

Discuss with the client whether you can refine the alternative thoughts, for example: 'I am allowed to be here and I am just as important as others.'

c: Discuss the credibility of alternative and original thoughts/schemas

Ask about the credibility of the original and refined alternative thoughts, and note them again on a visual analogue scale, or express them as a percentage. Do the same again for the original thought that you formulated as a statement from the inner critic mode.

Step 5: Reflection and homework

Ask what the client will take away from the exercise in their daily life. If necessary, give them a flashcard to remind them of the formulated alternative thoughts.

Example

Therapist: Hey, I hear that Punitive Critic of you again, saying that your feelings don't matter. Shall we do an exercise to see how that side has become so active?

Sandra: OK.

Therapist: If you dig into your memories, what event in your childhood gave you this message that your feelings don't matter?

Sandra: There are many. But what comes to mind now is the time I wanted to talk to my mother about my father's aggression. She said I should just let it go. I think I was about fifteen.

Therapist: Fine, let's re-enact that situation to examine exactly what happened then. Let's stand up. Where were you when this happened? (*Therapist and client stand next to each other and begin to set up another part of the room as a play area.*)

Sandra: In the living room. She was sitting at the dining table, and I came up to her. I was sad and wanted to talk to her about it.

Therapist: We'll use this desk as a dining table, and I'll play your mother in this first role play. So, I'm sitting here at the table and you come in? Take a moment to imagine the situation … Picture that situation again, you're that fifteen-year-old girl … Just do as you did back then.

Sandra: (*Walks towards the therapist and says sadly.*) Mum, yesterday Dad was really angry, and he hit me really hard. It's getting out of hand now…

Therapist: (*Responds as mother.*) Oh, you know how he is … It's better to leave it alone, otherwise it will only get worse.

(*The therapist stops the role play and asks Sandra if that's how it went, to which she replies in the affirmative. Back in their chairs, when the therapist asks about her thoughts.*)

Sandra: One, it doesn't matter what I feel or want, and two, my mother doesn't think I'm important. (*She believes the credibility of these thoughts to be 75%.*)

Therapist: We're going to do the role play again, but this time you'll be your mother and I'll be you. Come with me, sit down at the dining table, and put yourself in your mother's shoes. Try to empathize with her … What was her life like back then?

(The therapist and Sandra briefly discuss the circumstances her mother was in at the time, so that Sandra can empathize with her properly, and then they do the role play again.)

Therapist: (*Stops the role play.*) OK Sandra, stay in your mother's role for a moment. How do you, as your mother, view Sandra walking towards you to talk about her father's violence?

Sandra: I'm a little scared, I can't stand up to him. I can't bear her sadness either. I want everything to be fine, I don't want any conflicts.

(Therapist and Sandra sit down again and discuss what this means. They formulate alternative thoughts: 1) What I feel or want is important, even if my mother can't do anything about it, and 2) I wasn't the problem, but my mother had a problem with my father.)

Therapist: Let's think about that situation together. What did you actually need back then? Fifteen-year-old Sandra did really well. But as an adult, what would you want to say in that situation, with everything you know and can do now?

Sandra: I would say that she really needs to listen to me now, otherwise I'll go to the police and report it.

Therapist: That sounds good! Shall we try that out in a third role play? Then you can be yourself again.

(The therapist and Sandra re-enact the situation, with Sandra practicing her new, intended behaviour. She feels powerful as she does this; it gives her a feeling of openness in her chest. The therapist lets her focus on this, and they write the following concluding statement on a flashcard: What I feel and need is important, and I am allowed to stand up for it. The fact that my mother couldn't do that says something about her limitations and not about me. I can and am allowed to do this myself now. The original statement from the inner critic mode has become less credible.)

What if your client:

- **...is unable to take the other person's perspective?**

  You can skip the second role play or choose to use imagery rescripting instead of the historical role play.

- **...does not change their view of the other person's behaviour despite the role reversal?**

You can make suggestions for a different perspective, but do not insist; it may be that the client's assumption about the other person's behaviour is correct. It is not necessary for the exercise to be successful. It is often possible to at least shift the definition of the problem somewhat: 'She always did/does that, but that says more about her than about me.'

Variations

This exercise can also be used to test children's cognitions or coping modes.

For the perspective shift in the second role play, it is necessary for a client to be able to empathize with another person's experiences to some extent. Assess whether your client with mild intellectual disability or autism is capable of doing so. This also applies when working with children and young people. Also bear in mind that the events happened more recently for them and that, as a result, it may be more difficult to distinguish between their younger selves and their current selves in the third role play.

Chapter 30: Cognitive Technique – Continuum Technique

Objective

To transform a negative self-image (with demanding, punitive and guilt-inducing messages) into more nuanced and realistic statements about oneself.

Guidelines

Step 1: Identify the message of the inner critic (self-judgement) mode
Step 2: Rationale
Step 3: Write down self-judgement on a dimension with a positive counterpart
Step 4: Client scores themselves on the dimension
Step 5: Think of characteristics that fit
Step 6: Client scores themselves on the characteristics
Step 7: Reflection
Step 8: Formulate a more nuanced self-assessment

Explanation of the guidelines

Step 1: Identify the message of the inner critic (self-judgement) mode

Notice when the inner critic mode is speaking and draw your client's attention to this. At this stage, you will already be familiar with the message from the inner critic mode. Write the judgement (e.g., 'worthless') on a scale (see Figure 30.1).

Example

Message from my inner critic mode – I am ...

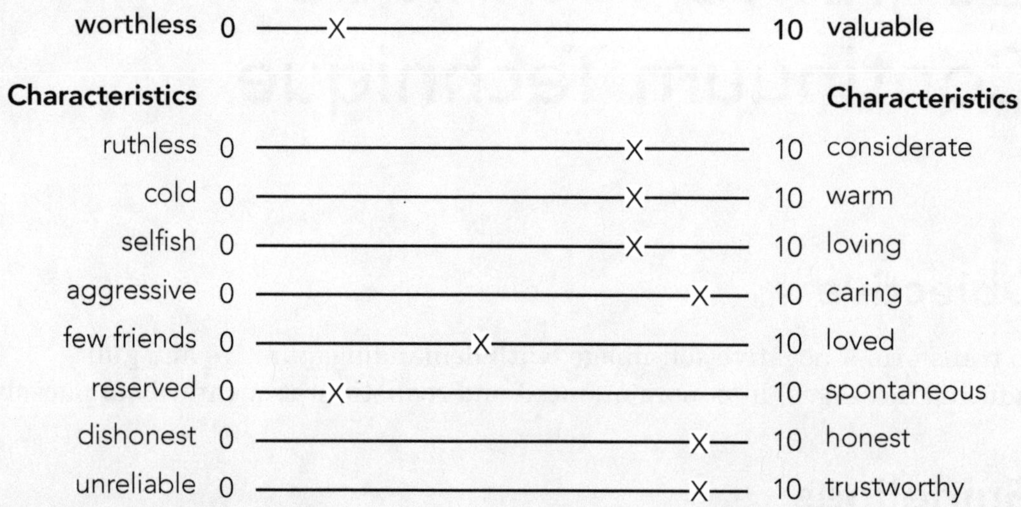

Alternative message:
I am reserved, but not worthless. I have many qualities that make me valuable.

Figure 30.1: A scoring scale for the inner critic mode

Step 2: Rationale

Suggest exploring this message together. This cognitive technique works best if your client is already able to view their self-criticism with some distance, i.e., from the middle phase of treatment onwards. If you use this technique too early and your client is still completely fused with their negative self-image, the exploration will be less effective.

Step 3: Write down self-judgement on a scale with a positive counterpart

Write down the self-judgement on the left side of the first scale and ask your client what the opposite of the self-judgement is (e.g., 'valuable'). Write this on the right side of the scale.

Step 4: Client scores themselves on the scale

Let the scale run between 0–10 (0 = worthless, 10 = valuable), and let your client mark where they stand on this scale according to the inner critic mode.

Step 5: Think of characteristics that fit

Ask your client what characteristics make someone … [negative self-judgement]. Ask them to think of someone they consider to be the most worthless person, for example, and ask them about the characteristics that make that person so worthless. Write down these characteristics on the left-hand side of new scales and, together with your client, think of positive counterparts to these characteristics, which you write down on the right-hand side (see Figure 30.1).

Then ask your client about the characteristics that make someone the opposite of the critical message. For example, who is the most valuable person your client knows, and what characteristics make that person so valuable? Add these to the characteristics on the right-hand side of new scales and, together with your client, think of the negative counterparts to these positive characteristics.

You have now drawn a line between 'worthless' and 'valuable' (or another judgement from the inner critic mode) with several lines underneath it showing characteristics that contribute to the judgement 'worthless' or 'valuable'. After this step, take a moment to reflect: apparently, there are several characteristics that contribute to the judgement of a person; it is therefore more complex than the simple position taken by the inner critic mode.

Step 6: Client scores themselves on the characteristics

Ask your client to score themselves on the lines between the characteristics that contribute to the judgement 'worthless' or 'valuable'. For each characteristic, consider the underlying factors that contribute to the assigned score. This exercise in realistic thinking may be even more valuable than the final outcome of the investigation.

Step 7: Reflection

If you connect the crosses (where your client has placed themselves) on the characteristics and compare them with the cross on the main scale (worthless–valuable), you will probably notice that the scores on the characteristics are not (all) as negative as those on the main scale. Discuss the significance of this with your client ('*Perhaps you are not as worthless as your inner critic says*', or: '*It seems that the fact that you have few friends does not necessarily mean that you are worthless*').

Step 8: Formulate a more nuanced self-assessment

Together with your client, consider how you can transform the original message from the inner critic mode into a more nuanced, positive and realistic statement about themselves. Write this message down and, if necessary, give it to them as a flashcard.

Example

Therapist: OK, so the Punitive Critic calls you worthless. Even though we've fought this side and this message many times before, apparently the Punisher remains credible when he says things like that. Today, I want to explore with you whether what the Punisher says is true.

Sandra: OK.

Therapist: So, he says you're worthless. On a scale from worthless (0) to valuable (10), where does he place you?

(*Sandra puts a cross on the board at '1'.*)

Therapist: OK. He says that, but what do we think about it?
Do we agree?

Sandra: Well, not entirely. Maybe a 2 or 3 is more appropriate? (*Sandra adjusts this on the board.*)

Therapist: Let's explore that. What characteristics make someone a worthless person? Who do you think is the most worthless person you know?

Sandra: Well, I'm thinking of that rapist who was convicted this week, who was all over the news.

Therapist: OK, and where would you place him on this line?

(*Sandra places the rapist at the extreme end of the line, at 0: 'extremely worthless'.*)

Therapist: When you see that rapist standing there at 0, does your 2 or 3 still feel right? Are you almost as worthless as that rapist?

Sandra: ...Well, not as bad as that rapist, I mean, I would never do something that bad.

Therapist: Should we put a new cross, one that better indicates how worthless you are? Apparently, a little further away from that rapist?

Sandra: ...Yes. (*Takes the marker from the therapist and places a cross on 4.*)

Therapist: It's good that we're exploring this, because it's already clear that the Punitive Critic was very wrong to put that cross on 1 and you weren't quite right with 2 or 3 either. Let's continue our exploration. What characteristics does that rapist have that makes him so worthless?

Sandra: Well, he felt no guilt whatsoever, had no empathy for the victim.

Therapist: What do you call someone who doesn't feel guilty?

Sandra: Ruthless.

Therapist: (*Writes on the board.*) And someone who has no empathy?

Sandra: Cold.

(*Therapist writes on the board and asks for more characteristics and writes them down.*)

Therapist: Now let's look at 'ruthless'. What is the opposite of someone who is ruthless?

Sandra: I think … Someone who is considerate of others?

(*The therapist takes notes and also asks about the positive counterparts of the other characteristics.*)

Therapist: (*Takes a step back to look at what is written on the board from a distance.*) Let's take a look at what we've discussed so far. When we started this investigation, you said that the Punitive Critic thinks you're worthless because you can't make choices and you make mistakes, remember? (*Sandra nods.*) What strikes me is that none of those traits come up when we talk about what makes someone worthless.

(*Sandra looks thoughtful.*)

Therapist: Apparently, those are not the characteristics that immediately come up in our research when it comes to what makes someone worthless. I would think that means something…

Sandra: Yes, now that you mention it…

Therapist: Well, let's move on. Do you know anyone who is very valuable?

Sandra: Yes, my cousin. She's really wonderful. Everyone always likes her and thinks she's sweet.

Therapist: And what qualities make her so valuable?

(*The therapist adds these characteristics to the right-hand side of new lines and then asks for the negative counterparts of these characteristics to be noted on the left-hand side.*)

Therapist: OK, so now you see all these qualities here that determine the extent to which someone is valuable or worthless. Looking at the first one, 0 = ruthless and 10 = 'considerate', where would you score yourself?

Sandra: I think a 7.

(The therapist asks Sandra why she scores herself that way and discusses considerations that contribute to the score on the characteristics.)

Therapist: Good, so you initially scored yourself on how valuable you are, and then we looked at which characteristics actually determine how valuable someone is. What strikes you when you look at the crosses?

Sandra: Well, that the crosses on the characteristics are more to the right than the first cross for how valuable I think I am.

Therapist: Yes, indeed! What do you think that means?

Sandra: Well, maybe it's not always entirely true that I'm worthless. But it is true that I don't have as many friends as my cousin, for example.

Therapist: Yes, indeed. But that's not the only aspect that determines whether you are valuable, if we look at it this way. What do you think about that?

Sandra: Yes, that feels good in a way. I also have qualities that make me valuable. But it doesn't always feel that way…

Therapist: Yes, you certainly do! And it's OK that it doesn't always feel that way yet; that's the Punitive Critic that keeps telling you that you're worthless. But we don't have to accept those judgements all the time. And now we have more arguments to fight that side. Shall we write them down and see what positive counter-messages we can formulate?

What if your client:

- ...scores themselves negatively on the characteristics?

  Although you want to stay as close as possible to your client's experience, you can challenge their judgement by asking questions about it. Try to add characteristics that can be assessed objectively and/or ask your client to ask their loved ones to assess them on the various characteristics.

- ...says that one or more characteristics were scored too high during the assessment and that this makes the outcome more positive?

  In that case, you can rescore those characteristics, probably more negatively, and look at the total again. This allows you to discuss that the relative contribution of a single characteristic is limited: how valuable or worthless someone is determined by multiple characteristics and not by one or a few characteristics.

Variations

If necessary, adapt the explanation and terminology to the age or cognitive abilities of your client.

Instead of putting crosses, you can also make a list of valuable and worthless characteristics and ask your client to give themselves a score for each of those characteristics. You then calculate the average score (mirror scores on negative characteristics: a '2' becomes an '8'), which expresses how valuable your client ultimately turns out to be. This is often higher than they initially thought. You can also ask your client to think of and score only positive characteristics, if they are able to do so. The advantage of this is that the emphasis is placed on your client's qualities.

Chapter 31: Cognitive Technique – Courtroom Method

Objective

Practice examining and distancing yourself from negative self-beliefs from a critical perspective, so that your client starts to think about themselves in a more nuanced and realistic way.

Guidelines

Step 1: Rationale
Step 2: Formulating the belief as an indictment
Step 3: Setting up a 'courtroom'
Step 4: Gather evidence for the prosecutor (inner critic mode)
Step 5: Gather evidence for the defence
Step 6: Final judgement by the judge
Step 7: Formulating an alternative belief
Step 8: Reflection and homework

Explanation of the guidelines

Step 1: Rationale

Observe that your client's inner critic mode is active in the session and sending negative messages about your client. Explain that you are going to examine that critical message in detail, as if it were an indictment being assessed for its truthfulness in a court of law.

Step 2: Formulating the belief as an indictment

Write down the critical message as if it were an indictment. This could be a message from a Demanding Critic mode (*'[client's name] must not make mistakes'*), a Punitive Critic (*'…is a worthless person'*) or a Guilt-Inducing Critic (*'Event X is the fault of …'*). Ask your client to rate the (emotional) credibility of this thought on a scale of 0–100%.

Step 3: Setting up a 'courtroom'

Set up a court in the therapy room by placing chairs for the judge, the prosecutor, the defence lawyer and the defendant.

Step 4: Gather evidence for the prosecutor (inner critic mode)

Have your client sit in the prosecutor's chair and, from their inner critic mode, tell you what the charges are and what evidence they have to support them. They address the 'judge'; this can be an empty chair, or you can sit there yourself for a moment. Wherever you are, guide this process by pointing out to the 'prosecutor' that you are in court and that they must therefore provide concrete evidence rather than their opinion. Write the prosecutor's arguments on a whiteboard.

Step 5: Gather evidence for the defence

Ask your client to sit in the defence chair. Together, examine what evidence there is against the charge and what counter-arguments the defence can put forward. Think of relativizing insights, positive qualities and your client's good intentions, successes and positive contacts with others. Also, include the effects of the critical message on your client, the burden it places on them. If necessary, have your client sit in the defendant's chair and tell the judge about this from their Vulnerable Child perspective. Then have your client sit in the defence chair and present the counter-arguments to the judge from their Healthy Adult perspective, and write down these arguments.

Step 6: Final judgement by the judge

Then have your client take the judge's seat and go through the arguments of the prosecutor and the defence together, mentioning the feelings and emotional damage of the defendant. What judgement would your client now pass as judge? Has the charge been proven? Make sure you leave room for nuance: *'Perhaps you sometimes feel worthless because you are not working at the moment, but you are not worthless as a whole.'* Let your client, as judge, deliver the verdict aloud to the (empty chair of the) defendant. If necessary, you can then have your client sit in the defendant's chair to receive the verdict and reflect on how it affects them.

Step 7: Formulating an alternative belief

Have your client translate the judge's statement into an alternative belief in the form of an 'I-message' and write it down. For example: 'I may feel worthless sometimes, but that doesn't mean I am. I have qualities that make me valuable, and my friends show that too.' Have your client rate this belief on the credibility scale and also ask how credible the original belief still feels (0–100%).

Step 8: Reflection and homework

Ask your client how they felt about doing this exercise. What did they take away from it? Give your client the arguments on paper so that they can read them again at home. You could also ask your client to do the exercise as homework in the form of a writing assignment for another critical message.

Example

Therapist: So, your Moaner (*Punitive Critic*) is ready with his judgement again; he's saying that everything you do fails? Shall we really examine that for once? Where are judgements mainly given, and verdicts passed? In a court of law, right?

(*Tim nods hesitantly.*)

Therapist: So, let's use all the knowledge and expertise of a court of law to determine whether the Moaner's judgement is correct. As if we were in court and a judge ultimately had to decide whether the charges against you are correct.

Tim: Eh, OK.

Therapist: So, the accusation is: 'Everything Tim does fails.' I'll put some chairs here so it looks like we're in court. (*Explains who sits where.*) Would you like to sit in the prosecutor's chair first? Tell the judge what you think of Tim (*points to the defendant's chair*) and why.

Tim: (*Addressing the judge's chair:*) Well, Tim just always fails at everything. That's just the way it is, he's useless.

Therapist: Well, prosecutor, we're in court here, so you'll have to come up with arguments and examples.

Tim: OK … Well, for example, at school. He only gets failing grades; this week he got another 3 in maths. He just messes around.

Therapist: Stick to the facts, prosecutor. Failing grades and a 3 in maths, so… (*Writes this down.*) What are some other concrete examples of things that go wrong?

Tim: During my internship, I handed over the wrong tools; that was really stupid. And when I mentioned it at home, my uncle was there and he said that was just like me; he was basically laughing at me.

Therapist: (*Writes down:*) 'Tim handed over the wrong tools' and 'His uncle said that was just like him and laughed'. (*Tim gives a few more examples, which the therapist writes down.*) Tim, would you like to take the chair for the defence now, as if you were defending yourself in the chair beside you? Let's look at the prosecution's arguments. For example, did you only get failing grades last year?

Tim: No, not only. I got a few passes too.

Therapist: OK, so not everything failed, because there were also tests where you did manage to get a pass mark.

Tim: Yes, that's true.

Therapist: (*Writes down:*) 'Tim also got some passing grades'.

(*The prosecutor's other arguments are also examined, and the therapist asks Tim about other events that show that there are things he succeeds at, which are noted down. Tim says from the defendant's chair that he feels 'small' and 'failed', and as a result he procrastinates or feels a lot of tension.*)

Therapist: Would you now like to tell the judge why you think the prosecutor is wrong in saying that everything Tim does is a failure?

Tim: He also got some passing grades … It's true that he pointed out the wrong tools, but his uncle is just one person who think this matters … His mother says that he can do anything if he really wants to … And a customer at the garage recently said that he had helped him very politely at the counter. When he plays football, he is often the one who scores. And the message that everything will fail causes him extra stress, so it's not surprising that he gets lower marks.

Therapist: Very good. Would you like to sit in the judge's chair now? In this chair, you can review all the arguments. (*The therapist lists all the arguments again.*) What do you think when you look at it this way? Who do you want to prove right, the prosecutor or the defence?

Tim: Well, I think the defence.

(The therapist discusses with Tim the reasons why he thinks so and asks him to formulate this in front of the empty chair of the defendant. The therapist then asks him to take a seat in the defendant's chair and imagine that the judge acquits him of the charge that everything he does fails. The therapist also asks Tim to say the judge's verdict out loud, using 'I' statements, in order to maximize the effect of the exercise. Tim says that this makes him feel a little lighter. The alternative thought that is formulated is: 'Some things don't work out, but there are also many things that do work out. I don't want to be discouraged in advance by the thought that something won't work out, but I want to go for it'. Tim writes this down on a flashcard.)

What if your client:

- ...cannot think of any counter-arguments from the defender's perspective?

  Ask questions about previous experiences or opinions of their loved ones. Help them broaden their perspective by asking about the arguments they could come up with if the defendant were someone other than themselves. If your client really can't come up with counter-arguments or voice them to the judge, you can take the defender's seat yourself. Let your client sit in the defendant's chair (focus on corrective emotional experience) or in the judge's chair (focus on cognitive restructuring).

- ...does not find the alternative belief credible?

  The alternative belief may be too strongly worded. Do not phrase it as the opposite of the original belief (e.g., 'I am valuable'), as this is too far removed from your client's experience and does not feel realistic. Stay close to your client's experience, but make sure to incorporate some nuance.

Variations

Towards the end of the middle phase and in the final phase, you can vary the exercise by playing the role of the prosecutor yourself and having your client directly contradict you in the role of the defence lawyer. In this way, you can challenge your client's Healthy Adult to oppose the inner critic mode.

In group therapy, group members can play the different roles and the 'court' can be expanded to include roles such as clerks, who write down the arguments of the prosecutor and defender, and a jury that advises the judge.

Chapter 32: Cognitive Technique – Pie Slice

Objective

To adjust punitive, guilt-inducing or demanding messages from inner critic modes about responsibility and guilt to more realistic assumptions.

Guidelines

Step 1: Identify the dysfunctional (critical) belief
Step 2: Rationale
Step 3: Score the credibility of the belief
Step 4: Come up with alternative interpretations
Step 5: Put all interpretations on a pie chart
Step 6: Re-evaluate and score credibility
Step 7: Homework

Explanation of the guidelines

Step 1: Identify the dysfunctional (critical) belief

Determine whether your client is taking on too much responsibility ('I have to keep my mother company every day'), feels excessively guilty ('It's my fault that the project failed') or otherwise draws conclusions about an event that take the form of self-criticism ('He doesn't talk to me because I'm worthless').

Step 2: Rationale

Depending on the nature of the critical belief (responsibility/blame for a 'disaster' versus a one-sided explanation of an event), you introduce the technique. In the case of guilt/responsibility, the approach will be retrospective, even if the 'disaster' did not actually happen (*'let's assume that this happened and look back, as an investigation team, and ask ourselves who and what was involved in bringing it about'*). The pie slices then represent the people or factors that contributed to this 'disaster'. In the case of a one-sided conclusion of a particular event, the starting question is: '*Your inner critic thought this, but what other explanations could there be?'* The pie slices then represent the alternative explanations.

It is important not to use this technique too early in therapy. From the middle phase onwards, your client will usually be able to look at their critical belief with some distance, which increases the chances of success for this technique.

Step 3: Score the credibility of the belief

Ask your client to score their dysfunctional (critical) belief on a credibility scale by assigning it a score between 0–100%.

Step 4: Come up with alternative interpretations

To come up with alternative interpretations of, or explanations for, a situation, it helps to ask your client what someone else experiencing this situation might think about it. This change of perspective allows your client to take a broader view instead of immediately drawing negative conclusions about themselves. Write down all alternative interpretations or explanations and, if necessary, introduce an option for 'other explanations' for those explanations that you may have overlooked. After this inventory, point out to your client that there were apparently several possibilities, possibilities that were not mentioned or seen at all by the inner critic mode. The reality is therefore much more complex than the inner critic mode suggested.

Step 5: Put all interpretations on a pie chart

Ask your client to estimate the size of the pie slice for each alternative factor or interpretation. Trace the circumference of the pie with your pencil and ask your client to say 'stop' when they consider the size of the pie slice to be appropriate. The size of the pie slice represents how likely the client thinks that factor contributed to the 'disaster', or how credible the client thinks the alternative interpretation of the event is. Discuss why your client estimates this size for each slice of cake. The size of the slices may need to be adjusted later, as your client gradually realizes that the factors or interpretations no longer fit into the cake (circle). After all, all pie slices together (including the original interpretation) must add up to 100%. By first estimating the pie slices for each alternative factor or interpretation separately, there will be one pie slice left at the end for the original interpretation (this is always estimated last).

Step 6: Re-evaluate and score credibility

Look at the pie chart together and discuss again that there are more interpretations or explanations than just the conclusion that your client's inner critic mode originally drew. Then ask again about the credibility of the original belief about themselves. Usually, because it has become clear that multiple interpretations are possible, the client's Healthy Adult will now score the credibility lower. It is not a problem if the difference with the original credibility score is not very large, as long as your client's perspective has broadened somewhat and they can see that other interpretations may also be correct. Finally, ask about their feelings: *How does it feel for you when you look at this pie chart now?*

Step 7: Homework

Together, think about how your client can practice this. For example, by making pie charts after events in which their inner critic mode became active. Or together, come up with a behavioural experiment that can further challenge the dysfunctional (critical) thought (see also Chapter 51: Cognitive Behavioural Therapy Techniques).

Example

Therapist: I can hear your Pointing Finger side kicking in again, saying that it's your fault that the project at work failed. Today, I'd like to do an exercise to see whether that's true, or whether there might be other reasons for the failure of this project.

Mary: OK.

Therapist: How strongly do you believe right now that the Pointing Finger is right, that it's really your fault that the project failed? If you had to score it from 0 to 100%?

Mary: Well, I think about 85%.

Therapist: (*Writes this down along with the statement.*) Good, let's take a look. Suppose this had happened to your friend, that she was the one who had worked so hard on a project that failed. What explanations could she come up witht?

Mary: Um … Maybe the preconditions weren't properly arranged by management?

Therapist: Yes, that sounds plausible. (*Therapist notes this down.*) What else?

Mary: Well, maybe the communication from the department wasn't good; the staff are already overworked and maybe couldn't handle this on top of everything else.

Therapist: I hear two other possible explanations there, is that right? Communication was not good and the staff are overworked?

Mary: Yes, I think so.

(The therapist notes these alternative explanations, and together they come up with a few more explanations, which are also written down.)

Therapist: What strikes you when you look at this list?

Mary: Well, that there may be more factors involved than just my fault.

Therapist: It's great that you see that! That Pointing Finger makes it seem like it's all your fault. But look at all the other explanations we've come up with in a short time. And we haven't even covered everything; there are bound to be more possibilities. Last time, you also said something about the financial basis not being right?

Mary: Yes, that's right.

(*Therapist and Mary gather more explanations.*)

Therapist: Look, I'm going to draw a pie chart here, and we can divide it among all the different explanations we've come up with. So, the greater the share of the factor in the explanation for the failure of the project, the larger the slice of the pie. We can write percentages next to them, and all the percentages together must add up to 100% so the pie is completely divided. How big do you think the share of the preconditions was that were not met by management? (*Therapist moves pencil over the pie.*)

Mary: Hm, I think 15%.

(*Therapist notes this down and all explanations are given their own slice of the pie.*)

Therapist: Then we still have this slice of the pie left, which I think is for the explanation of the Pointing Finger. So, your share can still be a maximum of 10%.

Mary: Hm, yes, that's right.

Therapist: So, you're experiencing an unpleasant situation: a project you've worked very hard on isn't succeeding. And the Pointing Finger immediately concludes that it's your fault! Very unfair, especially when you consider all the other possible explanations. They don't leave much room for you to have any real influence.

Mary: No, it's strange. I see it, and I understand it, but it still feels like it's my fault.

Therapist: How much do you still believe that, emotionally? At the beginning of the session, you said 85%. Has anything changed?

Mary: Yes, it has – it's less now. I think about 55%.

Therapist: I'm very pleased that this exercise has helped us to rein in your Pointing Finger a little. It will continue to draw these kinds of conclusions and try to drum them into you, but you don't have to listen to it, because it thinks in a very short-sighted way. The point is that at the moment it seems very credible that it is your fault, but we shouldn't be so quick to believe that inner critic. If we can now find out, with a little research, that the Pointing Finger is wrong, then that could very well apply to other situations in which the Pointing Finger initially seems credible. What do you think about that?

Mary: …Yes, that sounds logical, yes … But I think I still very often see it as my fault…

Therapist: Exactly, that inner critic is still very dominant and also credible to you. So, I'd like to ask you to try, over the next week, when you notice that your Pointing Finger is drawing another negative conclusion about you, to see if you can try to imagine what your friend might think in that situation. If you find it difficult, you can also ask her to actually think along with you. And write down all those explanations, even if you don't find them entirely credible. Then we'll work on that next time.

What if your client:

- **…cannot come up with any alternative interpretations?**

  Your client will be most successful in coming up with alternative interpretations when they can let go of some of their old beliefs. Therefore, use the role reversal technique: if someone else were to experience this (give an example of someone in your client's environment), what might that person think? If necessary, suggest alternative interpretations as hypotheses, or let your client ask others in their environment about this.

Variations

This technique can be applied not only to negative messages from inner critic modes, but also to other one-sided interpretations of situations (e.g., in the Vulnerability to Harm or Illness schema: *I have a lump, so I have cancer*).

When working with children and young people, you can make it a little more playful and not express probabilities in percentages. Instead, you can draw a pie chart and have them cut it into pieces according to the probability that an alternative interpretation is true, or divide a lump of clay among the different interpretations.

Chapter 33: Replacing Critical Messages with Realistic Ones

Objective

To help the client reduce the influence of critical messages. The critical messages are replaced by more nuanced, positive and helpful messages about themselves.

Guidelines

Step 1: Choose symbols for the inner critic and Vulnerable Child modes
Step 2: Cover the Vulnerable Child with critical statements
Step 3: Replace with positive messages to cover the inner critic mode
Step 4: Reflection

Explanation of the guidelines

Step 1: Choose symbols for the inner critic and Vulnerable Child modes

Ask the client to draw a picture of their inner critic and Vulnerable Child modes, or use mode cards for this purpose. The client may also choose from other materials. If so, ensure that these materials are small enough to be covered by sticky notes or other notes on which messages are written.

Step 2: Cover the Vulnerable Child with critical statements

Ask the client to write all demanding, punitive and/or guilt-inducing messages from the inner critic mode on separate sticky notes or pieces of paper. Each message is then stuck onto the Vulnerable Child, so that it gradually becomes buried. Make the client aware of this and the feelings that go with it: all those critical messages weigh heavily on the client, and they disappear beneath them. How does that feel?

Step 3: Replace with positive messages to cover the inner critic mode

Whereas in the previous step you asked how this *feels* (Vulnerable Child), now ask your client what they *think* about this (Healthy Adult side): do they want to allow themselves to be oppressed like this any longer? Tell them that together you are going to replace all critical messages with more nuanced, positive and helpful messages. This will strengthen the Healthy Adult and help the client to view themselves with compassion. Remove a critical message from the Vulnerable Child and, instead, ask the client to write a helpful counter-message on a new sticky note, which you will then stick on the inner critic mode. The critical message can be rejected in any way the client chooses, for example, by tearing it up, crumpling it and/or throwing it away. Let the client consciously reflect on this process: they are now distancing themselves from this critical message and accepting the new, helpful counter-message. Take the next critical message from the Vulnerable Child and repeat the procedure until all critical messages have been rejected. The Vulnerable Child is visible again, and now the inner critic mode is buried under positive, helpful messages.

Step 4: Reflection

Ask the client how they felt doing the exercise. Were any positive, powerful feelings released? Ask the client to locate these feelings in their body and to concentrate on them for a moment. The client can take the result home with them (in the case of a drawing) or take a photo of it (if materials were used that need to remain at the practice). A homework assignment could be that when the client notices that their inner critic mode is activated, they consciously take the time to replace the critical messages with positive, realistic and helpful counter-messages and write these down for themselves.

Example

Therapist: When you say that you have to work harder, that you don't have time for other things, which side do you think is speaking?

Mary: Ha, that's my Strict side, yes…

Therapist: Very good! You know this side well now, don't you? We've also practiced a lot with sending away this Strict side, so that you not only have more space to relax and do fun things, but also time to connect with others.

Mary: Yes, that works. I'm getting better at sending it away. But not always – sometimes I get so engulfed by it that I don't notice or I feel like I have no choice.

Therapist: Aha, that's a nice metaphor, that you're swallowed up by it. I can picture that the Strict side standing in front of Little Mary with its mouth wide open, as if it could swallow her up at any moment.

Mary: Yes, that's it!

Therapist: Would you like to draw that on this piece of A4 paper? Little Mary and the Strict side with its mouth open in front of her? (*Mary draws.*) Very good! Now, we've heard a lot of messages from that Strict side over recent weeks. Would you like to write them down, each message on a separate sticky note?

Mary: OK. So, for example: 'You have to work harder. You can do better than this. You can take on this task. Doing nothing is for lazybones.'

Therapist: Yes, exactly! Write it down and stick each message on Little Mary, because she's the one who keeps getting all these messages, right? (*Mary writes down all the messages and sticks the sticky notes on the drawing of Little Mary.*) Can you remember any other things that your Strict side says? Write those down too. Very good. What strikes you now?

Mary: I can't see Little Mary anymore.

Therapist: Exactly. She's completely buried under all those strict, unrealistic demands. How does it feel to see that?

Mary: It's so oppressive; it's as if I don't matter, as if I don't exist … All I have to do is run, run, run. I always feel stressed and rushed.

Therapist: How do you feel when you see Little Mary disappearing like that and you have this feeling of rushing, of stress?

Mary: Yes, it's actually very sad. I don't want that anymore!

Therapist: Shall we formulate a counter-message for every strict, demanding message? Take the first sticky note from Little Mary. Which one would you like to start with?

Mary: (*Takes the sticky note that says: 'Doing nothing is for lazybones'.*) This one, we talked about it last week.

Therapist: That's right, when we did that imagination exercise. At the end, we also wrote down a counter-message, didn't we? Do you remember?

Mary: Yes. 'Doing nothing is important for recharging your batteries, so you can work more efficiently at other times'.

Therapist: Excellent! Write that on a new sticky note and stick it on the inner critic. Now let's bury it under positive messages until it's no longer visible! What do you want to do with the message that doing nothing is for lazybones?

Mary: It can go in the bin, where it belongs! (*Mary tears up the sticky note and throws it in the bin.*)

Therapist: Fantastic! Free Little Mary from another unhealthy demand.

Mary: (*Picks up the sticky note that says: 'You have to work harder'.*) Well, what am I supposed to make of this, then? You don't have to work harder?

Therapist: Yes, you can. Do you believe that?

Mary: (*Laughs.*) No, not really.

Therapist: Well, let's formulate a counter-message that you do believe. Remember when we last talked about the things that are important to you in life? Working and achieving things was one of them, but there was much more. Like spending time with your friends, walking the dog, playing tennis and so on.

Mary: I could write down: 'There is more to life than work'?

Therapist: Yes, good!

(*The therapist and Mary continue formulating counter-messages until all the critical messages are in the bin and the Strict side of the drawing is buried under the positive counter-messages.*)

Therapist: How did you find doing this exercise?

(*A short debriefing and a homework assignment follow, which consists of reading the formulated counter-messages every day.*)

What if your client:

- ...is unable to formulate counter-messages?

  It may be too early for this exercise. Think carefully about the timing of this exercise and only use it when the client's Healthy Adult side has been sufficiently nourished by previous exercises. When the client no longer merges with the critical messages, can look at them from a distance and does not resist your counter-arguments as a therapist against the inner critic mode, it is possible to use this exercise. If you have already started the exercise, you can use the first two steps to create distance and give the client insight into the effect of the inner critic mode. The exercise is then useful for identifying those critical messages that need to be discussed in therapy. Do Step 3 yourself by countering the inner critic mode and, if necessary, switch to chairwork with the inner critic mode.

Variations

You can do this exercise using various materials, as described in Step 1. Tailor it to the client's (cognitive) abilities by writing down the messages yourself if the client has difficulty doing so. Or, when you express a critical message, place a stone on the symbol for the Vulnerable Child. For the positive counter-messages, you can use flowers, for example, to cover the inner critic mode.

In group therapy, all group members can participate in the exercise. Use a larger writing area for this, for example, on a whiteboard or flipchart. A variation could be to draw only the Punitive Critic, stick all the punitive messages on sticky notes around it and let the group crumple, tear, trample, etc. that sheet of paper, the Punitive Critic with all the punitive messages.

Final Phase

In the final phase, the aim is for your client to be able to combat the messages from their inner critic mode more independently. They know what is needed to do this and are increasingly able to send their inner critic mode away. At the same time, it is important in this phase to work towards a more realistic and nuanced view of the inner critic mode. Whereas in the initial phase you are mainly concerned with instilling healthy messages about self-image and sending away the inner critic mode, as the therapy progresses, the client will have to realize that this inner critic mode will always rear its head from time to time, even after the therapy. In this phase, you want to teach your client that they can turn a blind eye to this side, do not have to listen to the critical messages and certainly do not have to act on them. They can notice the inner critic mode and respond to it with a sense of humour (*'Oh well, there's that little shit again'*). This teaches your client that they do not have to take their inner critic mode so seriously. On the following pages, you will find guidelines for techniques you can use in the final phase to deal with your client's inner critic mode. However, please note that you can also use all the techniques described in the previous phases in the final phase, with the difference that you give your client more control in combatting or ignoring their inner critic mode.

Chapter 34: Imagery Rescripting – The Client Rescripts

Objective

To strengthen the Healthy Adult by allowing your client to independently fight the antagonist in the image using their Healthy Adult, and to provide for the core emotional needs of the child in the image.

Guidelines

Step 1: Rationale

Step 2: Visualizing the Healthy Adult

Step 3: Original memory from the child's perspective

Step 4: Rescripting from the perspective of a Healthy Adult

Step 5: Repeat rescripting from the child's perspective

Step 6: Debriefing and homework

Explanation of the guidelines

Step 1: Rationale

Explain not only the objective, but also briefly describe the procedure in that the client will experience the rescripting from different perspectives. Different perspectives will touch on different emotional needs, which can increase the effect of the exercise.

Step 2: Visualizing the Healthy Adult

It is advisable to start the exercise by visualizing the Healthy Adult, so that your client will have less difficulty connecting with that side of themselves during the schema-activating memory.

Step 3: Original memory from the child's perspective

If this is the first time you want to have the client practice self-rescripting, it is advisable to use a previously rescripted memory, so that the client can use your previous modelling and their previous experience as an example. If the client has done this before, it is advisable to 'script' the exercise less. After all, in life after therapy, memories that have not been rescripted before will be activated more often. This way, you prepare the client for that. Ask your client to empathize with the child's perspective and ask for sensory information: *Be that child. What do you see, hear and smell now? How do you feel now? What are you thinking?*

Step 4: Rescripting from the perspective of a Healthy Adult

When sufficient schema activation has taken place (the client is emotional, but can still [just] tolerate it), ask them to bring the Healthy Adult into the picture. Observing the Healthy Adult is followed by the instruction to empathize with the perspective of the Healthy Adult: 'Now *be* that Healthy Adult, the Big You who knows what is needed'. Address the Healthy Adult and coach them in addressing the antagonist and validating the needs of the child in the image. In this part of the exercise, the emphasis is on the need for self-expression (voicing arguments against the antagonist and showing compassion for the child) and on the client's competence (independently bringing about corrective emotional experiences). Asking further questions about such experiences helps to consolidate this corrective emotional experience.

Step 5: Repeat rescripting from the child's perspective

Then ask to rewind the image to the point where the Healthy Adult entered the image. Now ask the client to empathize with the child's perspective again. The rescripting is repeated from this child's perspective. In this section, the emphasis may be more on needs such as (safe) attachment ('I am seen and cared for'), but other emotional needs may also apply. Ask about such aspects of perception: *How does it feel that the Grown-up ... [client's name] stands up for you?* Here, too, asking questions about perceptions helps to consolidate the experiences.

Step 6: Debriefing and homework

In the debriefing, the most important conclusions are summarized and homework is agreed upon to help further consolidate the experience: listening to the recording of the exercise, writing down and rereading the most important conclusions, or making a separate audio flashcard. In this final phase of treatment, homework can also focus on behavioural change, such as actively practicing self-expression in daily life.

Example

The therapist and Sandra have agreed to return to a memory that they worked on earlier in the therapy, in which the therapist addressed the aggressive father.

Sandra: My father grabs a beer and then he sees me sitting there and shouts, 'What are you doing here? Don't get in my way! What do you look like, anyway? With a face like that, you'll never get a boyfriend!'

Therapist: OK, pause this image. Be that girl, that eleven-year-old girl with your father standing in front of you saying this to you. How do you feel?

Sandra: I want him to stop, to act normally…

Therapist: What emotions do you feel when you think about this?

Sandra: (*In a soft voice:*) Sad … but also angry…

Therapist: You really need help now. Would you like to bring Big Sandra in? The Sandra who is grown up, who has learned a lot, who can handle difficult situations? Can she come in, into the kitchen, with you and your father? Can you see her? (*Sandra nods.*) How does it feel to have her with you?

Sandra: Good.

Therapist: Step into the shoes of Big Sandra, be her completely, and sit down as she would sit. (*Sandra sits up a little straighter.*) You're Big Sandra now. And you're looking at that girl with her father who is so angry with her and speaks to her so harshly. What do you think about that?

Sandra: Stupid!

Therapist: What do you want to say? What does that girl need?

Sandra: I walk up to him and say (*in a firm voice:*), 'Are you stupid?! Have you gone completely mad to talk to your child like that?! Stop it now! This is the last thing she needs! She needs a father who is kind to her and doesn't put her down.

Therapist: How does your father react?

Sandra: Surprised. (*Smiles a little.*)

Therapist: How does it make you feel when he reacts with surprise?

Sandra: Yes, that's fine.

Therapist: And what do you want now? Do you want him gone? Do you want something else? Do you want to say anything else to him?

Sandra: 'Really, it's over, get lost, go away! Leave her alone! Just don't say things like that anymore, ever again!'

Therapist: And now let your father leave … Can you see him leaving? (*Sandra nods.*) Now look at that girl … What do you see?

Sandra: She's relieved, but also sad…

Therapist: What do you want to say to her?

Sandra: I want to sit with her, take her on my lap…

Therapist: Fine, go ahead … picture it. Hold her. Comfort her. How does that feel?

Sandra: Very good…

Therapist: Would you like to pause the image and rewind a little? Go back to the moment when Big Sandra arrives. Can you do that? (*Sandra nods.*) Empathize with that little girl. Be Little Sandra, eleven years old, scared and also a little angry and sad that her father says such nasty things. But now you also see Big Sandra standing there. And what is she doing? What is she saying?

Sandra: She says all the things I don't dare to say myself.

Therapist: How does that make you feel?

Sandra: It's nice that someone is standing up for me.

Therapist: Just watch how Big Sandra does that. What do you hear her saying?

Sandra: She says he's stupid and that he should stop it. And that he should be nice to me.

Therapist: And do you also see that Big Sandra is sending him away? That Big Sandra is in control? That she decides what happens?

Sandra: Yes, now she's sending him away and coming over to me.

Therapist: And how do you feel now that she is with you?

Sandra: (*Soft voice:*) Good, very safe.

Therapist: And where do you feel that sense of safety? (*Sandra points to her chest.*) Enjoy it … It's safe, hold on to that feeling, and slowly come to the end by letting the image fade and becoming more aware of where you are now. When you're ready, you can open your eyes again.

What if your client:

- ...is in the final phase, but is not yet able to rescript independently?

  During the exercise, you can coach more actively and possibly take over by also stepping into the image. In the debriefing, you can work with the client to identify the obstacles that made it difficult for them. Is the client still too overwhelmed by the experience of the Vulnerable Child? In that case, next time you can do the exercise from an observer's perspective, allowing the client to see from a distance how the Healthy Adult rewrites the image.

Variations

In a group, other group members can play the voice of the antagonist and the client can bring reinforcements into the image to help them fight the antagonist.

Some clients, such as adolescents or clients with mild intellectual disabilities, will also need coaching in this final phase to be able to rewrite memories themselves. It may then be helpful to discuss this prior to the exercise or to work with more scripted texts so that the client knows, or can read, what to say to the antagonist and the Vulnerable Child.

Chapter 35: Chairwork with an Inner Critic Mode in the Final Phase

Objective

To strengthen your client's Healthy Adult in resisting the messages of the inner critic mode.

Guidelines

Step 1: Rationale
Step 2: Therapist articulates the inner critic mode (schema activation)
Step 3: Client combats critical messages (corrective emotional experience)
Step 4: Reflection (consolidation)

Explanation of the guidelines

Step 1: Rationale

Explain that in this final phase of treatment, the client must prepare themselves for future situations in which the inner critic mode will become active again. Tell them that they will practice strengthening their Healthy Adult, whereby you will verbalize the messages from the inner critic mode and they will counter them from their Healthy Adult. Agree that your client will not only learn to resist the inner critic mode, but also learn to decide, at a certain point, to no longer pay attention to its negative messages.

Step 2: Therapist articulates the inner critic mode (schema activation)

Place a chair where the inner critic mode is always positioned. Sit on the chair (for demanding or guilt-inducing messages) or next to the chair (for the Punitive Critic, which causes a lot of insecurity). Express the critical messages, but do not express them at full strength right away: give your client the opportunity to successfully combat these messages.

Step 3: Client combats critical messages (corrective emotional experience)

First, ask your client to connect with the Healthy Adult. Discuss the arguments your client can use (at the beginning of the final phase) or ask your client to counter the critical messages you have just expressed without preparation (at the end of the final phase). Your client ultimately tells the inner critic mode that they will no longer listen to its messages and turns away.

Step 4: Reflection (consolidation)

Ask your client to reflect on the experience of standing up for themselves and fighting against the inner critic mode. Does it feel good? Where do they experience the good feeling in their body? Homework could be that as soon as your client notices the inner critic mode, they fight it but, at a certain point, stop paying attention to its critical messages.

Example

Therapist: I'd like to suggest using the last ten sessions to prepare you for difficult situations that are sure to arise in the future. I think that the Demanding Critic will continue to try to interfere with you.

Mary: Yes, I fear so too...

Therapist: The stronger your Healthy Adult becomes, the less that critical voice will be able to take hold of you. That's why today I want you to practice fighting that Demanding Critic independently, without my help. But I also want you to stop arguing with it endlessly and, at some point, decide to stop listening to it. Remember? There are two ways to fight: actively opposing what that side says, but, at some point, also turning your back on it.

(Mary nods.)

Therapist: I'll get the chair for the Demanding Critic. (*Places an empty chair where the Demanding Critic always sits.*) But this time, I'll sit in that chair. I'll express the messages from the Demanding Critic so that you can practice responding to them. Get your Healthy Adult ready.

(*While the therapist sits down in the chair of the Demanding Critic, Mary sits up a little straighter and makes contact with her Healthy Adult.*)

Therapist: Before we begin: I'll now play the Demanding Critic, so I'll use its words, but I want to emphasize that I'm only saying them, I don't mean them at all, you know that.

(*Mary nods.*)

Therapist: Mary, you really need to work harder. You can always rest later, but this work needs to be done now. Come on, just do it.

Mary: ...Yes, I find that difficult ...

Therapist: (*Remains silent and says after a few seconds:*) That's fine, take your time, think about what you want to say in response.

Mary: ...Well, maybe: there's nothing wrong with resting. I've already worked hard, and people need to rest too.

Therapist: Yes, but this is really important. If you just finish this first, you'll be able to enjoy your rest much more afterwards.

Mary: ...Yes, that's how it goes ... um ... (*The therapist remains silent and gives her the opportunity to practice pushing back.*) But that's not true. It's important that I rest now and don't push myself beyond my limits again. That's happened too often, and I don't want to end up completely exhausted again.

Therapist: Yes, but you did promise to finish that work ... They're waiting for it...

Mary: Phew, this is difficult ... (*Straightens up again.*) Yes, I promised, but it's not the end of the world if it takes a little longer. I want to and will pay more attention to my limits, and that means it's important that I get enough rest.

Therapist: Very good, Mary! You're doing really well. I can see that it takes effort sometimes, but you're doing it! Think about how long you want to continue with this, because I can go on forever down this path, but do you want to spend all your time talking to this Demanding Critic?

(*Mary shakes her head.*)

Therapist: That may be true, but this is a really important task, and it won't take long. If you could just for a moment...

Mary: (*Raises her hand in a stopping gesture.*) No, I'm stopping, I don't feel like doing this anymore. (*Mary then turns away.*)

Therapist: Well done! Wow … How do you feel?

Mary: A little shaky. You weren't easy, were you?

Therapist: No, sorry! It took some effort, but I think these are exactly the things that your Demanding Critic might say to you. At least, that's what I've heard you say many times.

Mary: Yes, that's right, those are exactly the things I think at times like this.

Therapist: And how can you make sure you remember what you just said, how you said it, and how it felt?

Mary: Maybe you could make another recording like that; that always helped me.

Therapist: Yes, I can do that, but I'd actually prefer it, and I think it would be more appropriate to this phase, if you made a recording yourself. Or, if you really find it unpleasant to listen to your own voice, you could write down on paper what you'd like to hear in such a recording. Would that be OK?

What if your client:

- …still finds it very difficult to come up with and express counter-arguments?

  You can coach more actively by discussing arguments together and encouraging your client to repeat those arguments more loudly. However, don't take over from your client too quickly: at this stage, the idea is that you, as a coach, remain on the sidelines and give your client the opportunity to learn to solve problems themselves.

Variations

In a group setting, a group member can sit in the inner critic mode chair with a piece of paper in front of them on which the inner critic mode is drawn. From behind that paper, they express the critical messages. Your client, with or without the support of other group members, can contradict those critical messages.

Chapter 36: Empathic Confrontation with an Inner Critic Mode

Objective

To make your client aware of their resignation to their inner critic mode and the consequences thereof, and then to encourage the Healthy Adult to take control of that inner critic mode.

Guidelines

Step 1: Preparation
Step 2: Name the behaviour
Step 3: Empathy
Step 4: Confrontation
Step 5: Consolidation

Explanation of the guidelines

Step 1: Preparation

Empathic confrontation is usually focused on coping modes, but the intervention can also be used with the inner critic or child modes (see Chapter 22: Empathic Confrontation with the Vulnerable Child). Consider for yourself which examples illustrate how your client shows resignation to their inner critic mode and which primary emotional and behavioural responses this evokes in you. These primary responses may also be exhibited by other people in your client's life. Consider whether it is the right time to confront your client with this resignation to their inner critic mode: this intervention is appropriate in the final phase of treatment, as there has already been sufficient time and support to learn to detach from that inner critic mode and resist it.

Step 2: Name the behaviour

Indicate that your client is resigning themselves to the inner critic mode by, for example, focusing all attention on self-criticism.

Step 3: Empathy

With compassion, bring your client back into their window of tolerance so that they can reflect on the inner critic mode: 'I understand how persistent it is.'

Step 4: Confrontation

Identify the feelings of frustration and impatience that you notice in yourself when your client seems to be merging with that inner critic mode again. Express your concern that others in your client's environment may also have these feelings. Explain that you helped your client in the early and middle phase of treatment to notice and fight the inner critic mode, but that it is important for your client to do this themselves now.

Step 5: Consolidation

Compliment your client when they are able to hear this message and tolerate it to some extent. Discuss together how your client can become more aware of and counter the inner critic mode themselves in the future.

PART V: Treatment Phase – Working with Coping Modes

Coping modes

A coping mode involves avoidance or inversion of the emotions, cognitions and behaviours associated with activated schemas. Avoidance may consist of your client completely avoiding schema-activating situations or not being in touch with the emotions and experiences evoked by activated schemas. With avoidance coping modes, you will generally see no emotion in your client: they feel flat, numb or alienated from themselves. With inverted coping modes, your client will feel, think and act in the opposite way to what the activated schema dictates: for example, they will act superior in situations that trigger their Defectiveness/Shame schema.

How do you recognize coping modes?

You have already identified the coping modes in the case conceptualization. During the session, you can further recognize and differentiate the coping modes from other mode categories by using four sources of information:

- ***What* does your client say?:** In an avoidant coping mode, your client makes statements that show that they feel little or even deny emotions altogether. They may also be silent or give only short answers to your questions. In inverted coping modes, your client makes statements that you feel are not consistent with their history, complaints or the schemas you have come to know. Sometimes coping modes can express emotions or experiences very strongly, such as the Attention and Approval Seeker. The difference compared with child modes is that a client will continue to do this without really responding to your attempts to validate their emotional needs.

- ***How* does your client say this?:** In an avoidant coping mode, your client sounds flat or emotionless, and sometimes a bit monotonous. Statements are often repeated without any depth. The latter can also apply to inverted coping modes. More emotional expressions in some inverted coping modes still serve the function of protection and therefore sound less primary than in child modes. In coping modes, your client may stubbornly cling to dysfunctional cognitions that justify the behaviour of the coping mode.
- **What is your primary *emotional response* as a therapist?:** Because coping modes hide your client's emotions and experiences, you are likely to feel distant from your client. You may also experience feelings of powerlessness because the coping modes cling so stubbornly to beliefs. In the case of transgressive coping modes, feelings of fear or inferiority on the part of the therapist are not uncommon. With inverted coping modes, you may also feel irritation, especially if there are exaggerated expressions, sullenness, manipulation or self-aggrandisement. With inner critic modes, you may also feel irritation, but because these are self-critical beliefs, you are more likely to feel vicarious indignation.
- **Pay attention to *contrasts* in the presentation:** Some coping modes are very similar to child modes because they seem to express or even emphasize emotions. For example, you may think that your client is in the Vulnerable Child mode when they say they feel bad but, at some point, you notice that they seem to repeat these statements emotionlessly without going into any depth. When their Vulnerable Child mode is active, you will see much more emotion and the client will also respond to your attempts to offer care and acknowledge of their emotional needs.

What is the goal in working with coping modes?

Your goal is always to connect with the Vulnerable Child, whose feelings and experiences are avoided. However, it is important to recognize the function and origin of the coping modes: your client has developed these modes for a reason. They often had an important (survival) function in the past and often still provide benefits in the present, at least in the short term. Your strategy is therefore to negotiate with the coping modes in order to move past them. This section describes methods and techniques that can help you in this negotiation.

Initial Phase

In the initial phase of therapy, the coping modes are often still very prominent and block your access to the Vulnerable Child. In this phase, the most important goal is for your client to learn to recognize their coping modes and gain insight into how these have helped them in the past, but how they still prevent your client's emotional needs from being met in the present. To do this, you need to make your client aware of the coping modes when they are active, because the client is often unaware of them. In the initial phase, you also play an active role in negotiating with the coping modes: you make the client aware that the underlying emotions are not being resolved by their coping mode and ask that mode for permission to make contact with the Vulnerable Child.

On the following pages, you will find techniques and methods for dealing with your client's coping modes in the initial phase of treatment.

Chapter 37: Empathic Confrontation with a Coping Mode

Objective

To offer the client insight into the interaction between you and your client, or between the client and others and the relevant mode, and thereby work towards modifying that mode.

Guidelines

Step 1: Preparation

Step 2: Name the client's behaviour

Step 3: Choose whether to start with confrontation or empathy

- a: Confrontation
- b: Empathy

Step 4: Alternate between confrontation and empathy

Step 5: Reflection

Explanation of the guidelines

Empathic confrontation is not so much a technique as an attitude within limited reparenting. There are many possible forms of empathic confrontation. Below, empathic confrontation is described as a planned intervention when there is dysfunctional behaviour that structurally interferes with the therapy and the therapeutic relationship.

Step 1: Preparation

Identify concrete, specific examples of your client's dysfunctional behaviour. What exactly does the client do or say that affects you, and how does the client do or say it? Identify your own primary emotions and (tendency towards) certain behaviour. Do not go into your 'caregiver mode' just yet, which may understand the client's behaviour. Your primary reactions will also be exhibited by others in your client's environment. Then, based on the case conceptualization, see if you can understand the origin and function of this behaviour and which mode of your client exhibits this behaviour. Finally, assess whether this is a good time for an empathic confrontation. In principle, you should not engage in an empathic confrontation immediately during the case conceptualization phase or the first treatment sessions, but if the behaviour interferes too much with your contact, it may be a good time after all.

Step 2: Name the client's behaviour

Introduce the empathic confrontation by saying, for example: '*Would you mind if I told you something I've noticed about our contact? I want to tell you this because I think it might be beneficial for you, even though it may be difficult to hear at first.*'

Then name the behaviour (including non-verbal aspects) that you observe in your client. For example: '*I notice that you say little and give short answers to my questions.*' After naming the dysfunctional behaviour, ask your client if they recognize it.

Step 3: Choose whether to start with confrontation or empathy

Whether you confront first or show empathy first, and where the emphasis lies, depends on a number of factors: 1) the client's 'window of tolerance' (Siegel, 2012); 2) the phase of treatment; and 3) the severity of the dysfunctional behaviour. If there is little emotional arousal (the client is low in their window of tolerance), starting with confrontation will lead to necessary schema activation, after which empathy can provide a corrective emotional experience. However, if there is already a lot of schema activation noticeable, it is advisable to start with empathy and only then confront. In the initial phase of therapy, there is more emphasis on empathy than in the final phase of treatment. However, in the case of more serious dysfunctional behaviour, you will use confrontation earlier in therapy and perhaps more forcefully.

a: Confrontation

In the confrontational part of your intervention, you tell your client how you feel when they display this behaviour and what you are inclined to do in response to this behaviour (self-disclosure): '*When you are so quiet, I feel … When I feel this way, I am inclined to [behavioural response].*' Indicate that their behaviour might also elicit this response in others. Self-disclosure is an important part of empathic confrontation and is characteristic of the limited reparenting attitude within schema therapy. Make sure you show sufficient empathy (Step 3b) and that you check with the client to see what effect the self-disclosure and confrontation have had.

b: Empathy

In this step, explicitly use mode language as a form of understanding and empathy: indicate that you see the dysfunctional behaviour as one side of the client, and that you realize that there are other sides to the client as well. Another form of empathy is explaining this mode on the basis of the past with unmet emotional needs: '*In the past, there was often no one who really listened to you and supported you. So, it makes sense that you now expect that I won't really be there for you either, and that touches on that old pain. I understand very well that this brings out your quiet side, which doesn't say much and withdraws, to ensure that you are not disappointed again.*' You can use gestures to point out this coping mode as if you are talking about another person sitting next to the client. This will help in the process of awareness and emphasizes once again that the confrontation does not concern your client as a whole.

If you do not yet fully understand the origin and function of the mode, present hypotheses to your client. Or ask your client questions to find out what the origin and function are. You can also choose to explore this in depth using chairwork (see Chapter 39: Chairwork with Coping Modes).

Step 4: Alternate between confrontation and empathy

During the conversation, pay close attention to the degree of emotional arousal (schema activation) and alternate between confrontation (Step 3a) and empathy (Step 3b) so that your client can continue to tolerate the emotions that are being evoked.

Step 5: Reflection

Reflect on what has probably been a new experience for your client: something negative has been discussed, but the relationship is still intact and so it feels (ultimately) like a positive experience. This reflection consolidates this corrective emotional experience.

To actually lead to behavioural changes, you will need to repeat the empathic confrontation more often. To support this process, you can also consider homework assignments, such as keeping a mode diary or, later in therapy, practicing skills to deal with schema activation differently.

Example

Therapist: I'd like to discuss something with you that I think is important for you, for how things are going between us. I notice that you're often quiet or give very short answers. Like just now, when I asked you about your week and how you had been feeling, and you became quiet. Do you recognize that?

Mary: (*Barely responds.*) Yes? Oh, well, I didn't really notice...

Therapist: ...Exactly, even now you're responding rather curtly and not really addressing what I just said.

(*Mary gives the impression that there is little schema activation; there is little emotional arousal. The therapist therefore decides to start confronting her.*)

Therapist: When you're so quiet, I notice that part of me feels uncomfortable. It's a feeling that what I say doesn't seem to matter. Can you imagine that?

Mary: Um, yes, I think so.

Therapist: It isn't just this once; I've noticed that this happens quite often. And if it continues to happen, I can imagine that this uncomfortable feeling might make me less inclined to say or ask much myself. Can you imagine that?

Mary: Yes, I understand that.

Therapist: My concern is that you don't just do this with me, but with others as well. Is that correct?

Mary: (*Now visibly nervous and tense.*) Well, sometimes, yes. It often happens automatically.

Therapist: (*Switches to empathy.*) People only see the Mary (*pointing to the space next to Mary*) who is silent. I know there's more to you than that silent side; I also know you as a very sensitive person, and I know that you experience a lot (*points to Mary's stomach*), but right now I mainly see that silent side. And if other people only see that quiet side too, they might, as I'm starting to notice, tend to ask or say less too. Can you imagine that?

Mary: Yes, there are often awkward silences in conversations with other people. I don't like that either, but then I just shut down even more.

Therapist: I think that Silent One actually wants to protect you. In the past, when you were being bullied, I think it was nice and very useful that she kept you out of the limelight a bit. How does it feel when we discuss it like this, that the Silent One tries to protect you by not saying much, but that the other person may also withdraw a bit, making it even more uncomfortable for you?

Mary: Yes, that's right. That feels good, accurate or something.

Therapist: Good. I think it's important to first notice in which situations the Silent One appears. Would you like to focus on that over the next week? Maybe you could write down the situations so we can look at them together next time?

What if your client:

- **...reacts angrily or sadly when you try to discuss the behaviour?**

  Emphasize empathy, and then gently move on to confrontation. Do not avoid empathic confrontation, because you are offering your client an important opportunity to learn to understand what happens in interactions.

- **...denies the behaviour or does not recognize the problem?**

  A coping mode may have been activated. It may be a signal that it is necessary to 'shake up' the client by emphasizing confrontation. Continue to alternate between confrontation and empathy, and observe carefully what effect this has on the client.

- **...responds with a lot of self-criticism? ('See, I can't do anything right, I'm such a loser.')**

  The inner critic mode has probably been activated. Acknowledge this, use hand gestures if necessary to 'bring this side into the room', as it were, and then put it aside so that you can continue with your empathic confrontation. If this does not work immediately, you may consider using another technique first to combat this inner critic mode.

Variations

Empathic confrontation is often used in cases of dysfunctional coping modes but, in principle, empathic confrontation can be used for any type of behaviour and can therefore also involve inner critic modes (see Chapter 36: Empathic Confrontation with an Inner Critic Mode) or child modes (see Chapter 22: Empathic Confrontation with the Vulnerable Child). To support your empathic confrontation, you can use mode cards, figurines or other materials.

Chapter 38: Acute Limit Setting for Bully and Attack Mode

Objective

To stop aggressive, threatening or intimidating behaviour. By setting limits in a personal way and then focusing on (restoring) contact, you offer your client a corrective emotional experience. By also making agreements about behaviour, you work specifically on behavioural change.

Guidelines

Step 1: STOP and say your client's name
Step 2: Describe the behaviour and effect
Step 3: Set personal limits and specify desired behaviour
Step 4: Invite them to share their feelings
Step 5: Reflect and make agreements about the future

Explanation of the guidelines

Step 1: STOP and say your client's name

When the Bully and Attack mode is active and your client is displaying bullying, threatening or intimidating behaviour, interrupt and literally say the word 'STOP', together with your client's name. Take up space by raising your hand(s) in a stopping gesture. Repeat this if necessary, until your client stops the behaviour.

Step 2: Describe the behaviour and effect

Describe the behaviour you are observing and, if applicable, mention the Bully and Attack mode if you have already agreed that this is part of your client's mode model. Describe the behaviour as concretely as possible so your client cannot argue about it. Tell your client what effect their behaviour has on you, making it clear that this behaviour is likely to achieve the opposite of what they need: *'When you shout at me and call me names like that, I feel very uncomfortable and I can't listen to you properly, even though I want to hear what you're angry about.'*

Step 3: Set personal limits and specify desired behaviour

Tell your client what you no longer want them to do and what you do want them to do, i.e., what you expect from them. Do this in a personal way (*'I don't want you to…'*; *'I need you to…'*; or *'I think it's important that…'*), and explain why. Also explain that if the behaviour continues to cross limits, you will pause or stop the conversation.

Step 4: Invite them to share their feelings

Let your client know that you think it is important to listen to them, even if they are dissatisfied with you or the therapy. After setting limits and extending this invitation, your client may switch to the Angry Child mode. If so, give your client space to rage (see also Chapter 15: Validating the Angry Child). Try to connect with the feelings of the Vulnerable Child. If your client does not express the feelings or needs of the Vulnerable Child themselves, offer suggestions based on your case conceptualization. What caused the Bully and Attack modes to activate at this particular moment? Did the current situation trigger old pain: which schemas were affected?

If your client displays threatening or intimidating behaviour again at any point, set limits again (Step 1) and briefly repeat Steps 2 and 3 to remind your client of what you expect from them.

Step 5: Reflect and make agreements about the future

Afterwards, it is important to look back with your client on what happened between you. Compliment them on being able to tolerate the boundary you set and adjusting their behaviour, even though you may have had to repeat it a few times. Ask your client how they feel now you're back in contact: *Does it feel better or not? Do they also feel that there is now more contact or connection between you?* Make them aware of this more comfortable feeling and discuss how you

can prevent aggressive or intimidating behaviour from occurring in the future, or what you'll do if it happens again (set limits again, possibly attaching a consequence if necessary; see also Chapter 41: Step-by-Step Limit Setting).

Example

Therapist: Hi Tim, you look angry. What's going on?

Tim: As if you don't know. Did you really think I wouldn't find out or something?

Therapist: I don't know what you mean.

Tim: (*Points his finger at the therapist and says threateningly:*) Don't pretend you don't know anything! I'm sick of you pretending to understand me and be on my side, but meanwhile telling my mother everything. You're just as nasty as all the others…

Therapist: Whoa, stop, Tim. (*Makes a stopping gesture.*) Tim, I really want to hear what you're so angry about, but… (*is interrupted by Tim*).

Tim: (*Leaning forward in a threatening posture.*) Yes, listen to me, because you're not really listening, you're just pretending… (*interrupted by therapist*).

Therapist: Stop, Tim, stop. When you talk in such a threatening way and swear at me, I can't listen to you properly. It makes me feel uncomfortable and I can't give you my full attention.

(*Tim is silent.*)

Therapist: I need you to tell me what's going on without swearing and without threatening language, otherwise we can't continue this conversation. And I would find that very unfortunate, because you're clearly very angry with me, and I want to talk to you about that.

(*Tim hums a little and leans back a little more.*)

Therapist: I appreciate you sitting back a little, and I would also appreciate it if you could speak at a normal volume so that I can really hear what you have to say. I want to hear what's bothering you, but I need you to do so at a lower volume and without swearing. Is that acceptable? Can we agree on that?

Tim: …OK then…

Therapist: Tell me what you're so angry about…

(*Tim recounts how he overheard a telephone conversation between the therapist and his mother. The therapist asks neutral questions so that Tim can express his anger before explaining what the conversation was about. The therapist explains the link with experiences from his childhood, in which both adults and peers were insufficiently reliable for him and he felt that people were talking about him and making decisions about him. Once his need for a safe attachment to others has been validated, Tim calms down.*)

Therapist: Well done for being able to tell me all this without shouting or swearing. How does it feel for you to tell me what was bothering you in this way?

Tim: Yes, I don't know, OK, I think.

Therapist: I really appreciated it, much more than when you were shouting at me. I was able to really focus on what was going on with you, instead of being preoccupied with your threatening attitude. Did you feel that too, that I was able to listen to you more attentively?

Tim: Yes, I did.

Therapist: And how does that feel for you, when I can listen to you attentively?

Tim: Yes, that's nice.

Therapist: Shall we see how we can ensure that we can do this in the future, instead of your Attacker taking over? What could help with that?

What if your client:

- ...does not stop their aggressive behaviour?

  You can repeat Steps 1 to 3 at any time if your client continues with the undesirable behaviour. If your client persists, you can announce a consequence and, if there is no improvement in behaviour, implement it immediately, such as pausing or stopping the session altogether.

Variations

This intervention can also be applied to other modes that exhibit aggressive behaviour, such as the Enraged Child. In this case, the emphasis is even more on Step 4; keep Steps 1 to 3 as short as possible. You can also use the intervention for other transgressive behaviour that needs to be stopped immediately. For example, sexually suggestive comments or flirtatious behaviour by your client. You can also use it to put a stop to highly disruptive, undisciplined or impulsive behaviour, such as constantly getting up or making unrestrained comments during the therapy session.

In group therapy, you make clear agreements about aggression at the start of the therapy, because such behaviour undermines the feeling of safety and thus disrupts the group process. If aggression does occur, it is important to discuss it carefully with the group.

Chapter 39: Chairwork with Coping Modes

Objective

To negotiate with the coping mode to connect with the Vulnerable Child and validate its emotional needs.

Guidelines

Step 1: Recognize the coping mode
Step 2: Name the mode
Step 3: Rationale
Step 4: Place the client on another chair
Step 5: Negotiate with the coping mode
Step 6: Place the client on the Vulnerable Child chair
Step 7: Validate relevant core emotional needs
Step 8: Summary, reflection and homework

Explanation of the guidelines

Step 1: Recognize the coping mode

The coping mode can be recognized by the fact that few to no primary, vulnerable emotions are shared, either verbally or non-verbally. In addition, there is likely to be little contact with your client when they are in this mode.

Step 2: Name the mode

Describe your client's verbal and non-verbal behaviour. Use gestures by pointing to a place next to your client when describing their behaviour, almost as if you were describing another person.

Step 3: Rationale

In this initial phase of treatment, briefly explain the purpose and procedure of the chairwork. Explain that the technique not only helps to better understand what causes your client to be in these coping modes, but also to make them feel better. If necessary, offer reassurance and control by saying, for example, that your client has control over the technique and can stop at any time.

Step 4: Place the client on another chair

Next, place an extra chair in the spot you indicated earlier and ask your client to sit there and 'be' in their coping modes on that chair. Don't be afraid to be directive; this will provide clarity.

Step 5: Negotiate with the coping mode

Address your client directly in coping mode, i.e., in the second person ('you').

- Recognize the benefits of the coping mode by asking how it helps your client (point to your client's original chair). Take your time and explicitly express your recognition and appreciation for its historical and possibly still current protective function.
- Make your client aware that their problems have not gone away because of this coping mode: ask, for example, whether the emotions they are trying to keep at bay as a coping mode have also been resolved.
- Offer hope: trust that by validating emotional needs, your client will certainly fare better than by simply (temporarily) suppressing their emotions.
- Ask permission to connect with the Vulnerable Child: offer reassurance and control when you ask your client to sit in the Vulnerable Child chair.

Step 6: Place the client on the Vulnerable Child chair

Give your client clear instructions to leave the coping modes behind in the chair when they get up. When your client is sitting in the Vulnerable Child chair (the original chair or an extra chair, depending on your preference), ask explicitly about those suppressed feelings and schema-activating situations. This schema activation with the accompanying feelings is necessary in order to provide a corrective emotional experience.

Step 7: Validate relevant emotional needs

You offer that corrective emotional experience by explicitly expressing understanding and recognition of how both the current context and the past have activated these feelings. Then validate the relevant need, for example, safe attachment to others or space for self-expression. Ask your client to focus their attention on the experience when you validate emotional needs by asking, for example, 'Is this a pleasant or unpleasant feeling? Where do you feel that in your body?'

Step 8: Summary, reflection and homework

The corrective emotional experience needs to be further consolidated by addressing your client's Healthy Adult side. This can be done in the chair where your client is sitting, but an alternative is to ask your client to stand up and, standing next to the therapist, look at the chairs. This debriefing is concluded by agreeing on homework.

Example

Therapist: I'm curious to know how you've been feeling over the past week.

Sandra: Normal, I think, nothing special … normal, I think.

Therapist: It seems that, as you're sitting there now (*the therapist gestures to a place next to Sandra*), you don't seem to be feeling very much. I know that you (*therapist gestures towards Sandra*) are capable of feeling a great deal, but as you are sitting there now (*therapist gestures again towards the spot next to Sandra*), I seem to see mainly that non-feeling side that we discussed in the previous session.

Sandra: Yes, that could be, I'm not sure…

Therapist: Then I suggest we do an exercise to help us better understand why that non-feeling side is so active today. At the same time, it's also an exercise that will help us change something, so you ultimately leave the session feeling better. OK?

Sandra: Yes, I think that's fine.

(*The therapist stands up and pulls up an extra chair.*)

Therapist: Then I'd like to ask you to sit on that other chair now.

(*Sandra moves to the extra chair.*)

Therapist: Just be the Non-feeler here on this chair, and I'll address you that way. I don't think you're here by chance. I think it's better for you to sit here as the Non-feeler than to sit there and feel all of Sandra's emotions. Is that right?

Sandra: Yes, this is much calmer … without all that sadness … I don't even want to think about it…

Therapist: So, you're actually protecting her from those feelings of sadness?

Sandra: Yes, actually, yes…

Therapist: And how do you do that? You say, 'I don't really want to think about it'. Is that what you do, not think about it?

Sandra: Yes, exactly, just flip a switch.

Therapist: OK, so you have your ways of not letting her feel that sadness. And that makes sense: if she feels so miserable, and you can suppress those feelings a little, then you do that.

(*Sandra nods.*)

Therapist: And what happens to that sadness then? Is it resolved?

Sandra: No, not resolved … but for now, I don't feel it.

Therapist: That's the only downside to you, that you can't really get rid of the sadness. I do think it's possible that she feels better. How does it sound if I make her feel a little better: positive or negative?

Sandra: Yes, positive, of course.

Therapist: Good, Sandra, can you come and sit on this chair next to me? But when you get up from that chair, I want you to leave the Non-feeler behind, stuck to it.

(*Sandra stands up and sits down on the chair next to the therapist.*)

Therapist: (*In a softer voice:*) She (*gestures to the chair of the Non-feeler*) was just talking about sadness. What are you feeling sad about?

Sandra: …Well, I just feel lonely … I haven't seen anyone this past week and I felt very lonely … (*Tears well up in her eyes.*) On Saturday evening, I heard people laughing outside; they were going to town or coming back from town, I don't know. But then I felt really awful…

Therapist: I can imagine that, Sandra. You're alone and it doesn't feel good when you hear other people having fun together. But then I remember that you know that feeling of loneliness very well. It reminds me of the girl I saw in the photos from your childhood. That girl often felt alone and lonely, didn't she?

(*Sandra nods.*)

Therapist: It's very understandable that you felt so miserable when there was so much old pain involved. Is what I'm saying about right?

Sandra: Yes, exactly. I thought: 'Here I am, alone again…'

Therapist: How does it feel to hear that I understand you? Is that a nice feeling or an unpleasant one?

Sandra: It feels nice, yes.

Therapist: Where in your body do you experience that nice feeling?

(Sandra puts a hand on her chest.)

Therapist: Keep your hand there for a moment. And 'taste' that pleasant feeling for a moment; is it more a feeling of being alone or of being together?

Sandra: More together.

Therapist: Finally, I'd like to explore with you how we can ensure that you don't forget this pleasant feeling. Perhaps I could make a recording of the things I just mentioned, so you can listen to it again after this session. Would that be acceptable?

Sandra: Yes, that would be nice, yes…

(See also Chapter 45: (Audio) Flashcard)

What if your client:

- …sees no disadvantages to the coping mode?

  Remind your client of the reason for the therapy.

- …cannot connect with the Vulnerable Child?

  As a therapist, explain what you think those feelings are from the perspective of the Vulnerable Child.

- …says they do not find the care provided pleasant?

  Explain that they need to get used to that care, because they did not receive normal care in their childhood.

Variations

If your client still cannot feel anything in the Vulnerable Child chair, you can help them connect with the emotions by 'charging' the chair with feelings. For a description of this variation, see Chapter 24: Chairwork with the Demanding Critic.

In a group, another group member can play the coping mode while the client sits in the Vulnerable Child chair behind the coping mode. This allows your client to experience the advantages and disadvantages of the coping mode.

Chapter 40: Visualizing the Coping Mode

Objective

To distance yourself from the coping mode by visualizing it from an observer's perspective. The exercise can also be used to negotiate with the Protector and imaginatively pass it, thereby gaining access to the Vulnerable Child.

Guidelines

Step 1: Recognize the coping mode
Step 2: Prepare for the imagery exercise
Step 3: Client visualizes the coping mode
Step 4: Therapist enters the image
Step 5: Negotiate with the coping mode
Step 6: Offer care to (the Vulnerable Child of) the client
Step 7: Reflect and consolidate

Explanation of the guidelines

Step 1: Recognize the coping mode

Notice that a coping mode is active and name it. Try to describe the mode to your client in behavioural terms as concretely as possible. For example: '*Now that I am trying to address this topic, I notice that you are slumping down and no longer answering my questions.*'

Step 2: Prepare for the imagery exercise

Tell your client that you want to do an imagery exercise, but that this time it is not about a specific memory that you want to work on. Explain that you want to help them form an image of their coping modes in the exercise. The aim is to then give more space for what they feel and experience.

Step 3: Client visualizes the coping mode

Ask your client to close their eyes and focus on the feelings and thoughts they are experiencing now while the coping mode is active. What do they notice in their body when they try to stay away from the emotions of the Vulnerable Child? For example, a cramp or, conversely, a feeling of emptiness? Have your client concentrate on this and then ask them to form an image of this coping mode: *What does it look like?* This can be an abstract image, a person, an animal, a fantasy figure or simply themselves as they are sitting there now. Examples of visualizations by clients include a suit of armour, a wall, a mask, a bunker, a thick coat, etc. Ask your client to also place their Vulnerable Child in the image. Is the Vulnerable Child visible or is it completely hidden from view by the visualized coping mode?

Step 4: Therapist enters the image

Next, ask your client to place you in the image. Ask them where they see you in relation to the visualized coping mode and their Vulnerable Child. *Does anything happen in the image when you step into it? For example, does the visualized coping mode become larger / more protective, or not?*

Step 5: Negotiate with the coping mode

Let your client watch while you negotiate with the visualized coping mode and try to pass it. You keep asking your client as *an observer* what the coping mode says or does (observer perspective), not to *be* the coping mode (first-person perspective). After all, the aim of the exercise is for your client to distance themselves from the coping mode. During the negotiation, express your appreciation for the protective function of the visualized coping mode, but also indicate that you are concerned about the Vulnerable Child, who is not being given any space and may need some closeness, support or comfort (for more examples of the negotiation, see Chapter 39: Chairwork with Coping Modes). Ask permission to come a little closer: for example, ask if the hatch of the armour can be opened a little, or if the wall can be moved a little, etc.

Step 6: Offer care to (the Vulnerable Child of) the client

As soon as the coping modes allow some space, offer care to the Vulnerable Child in the image. Validate their feelings and needs, help them to put them into words where necessary, and offer support, comfort and safety (or whatever else is needed in terms of emotional needs; use your case conceptualization as a guideline). Ask your client what they see happening in the visualized image, both in the coping modes and in the Vulnerable Child. How do they think the Vulnerable Child feels about the validation by the therapist? How do they feel as an observer? The observer perspective can help your client stay within their window of tolerance when the therapist triggers unusual and therefore uncomfortable experiences by validating the emotional needs of the visualized child.

Step 7: Reflect and consolidate

Ask your client to let the image fade and open their eyes. Look back on the exercise together. How did they feel about doing this exercise? How do they view the coping modes now compared to the beginning of the exercise? Are the thoughts and feelings of the coping modes still as strong, or have they diminished? What things did the therapist do or say in the image that contributed to this? Write these things down or incorporate them into a flashcard that the client can take home.

Example

(*Therapist suggests looking at a photo of Little Tim.*)

Tim: (*Looks at the floor, crosses his arms.*) Well, I'm definitely not going to do that today, I don't want to feel awful again later.

Therapist: I notice that your attitude is becoming more closed off. You're no longer looking at me and you're sitting with your arms crossed.

Tim: Yes … I don't know. I feel like I don't want to do this.

Therapist: I'd like to explore this feeling with you, perhaps with an imagery exercise. We won't work with memories from the past, but rather with this feeling you have, that 'I don't want to do this'. Is that OK?

Tim: Yes, I think so.

Therapist: How exactly does that feel, that 'not wanting to work with those memories' today? Is it a kind of tense feeling? Or anger?

Tim: A tense feeling, I think…

Therapist: Close your eyes so you can concentrate on it properly. Where in your body do you notice that feeling?

Tim: In my chest.

Therapist: If you focus on that tense feeling in your chest, that feeling of 'I don't want to do this', and consider that this is a part of you, that 'I don't care' side, then I'm curious to know how you see that side when you close your eyes. What comes to mind, what does that side look like?

Tim: Like barbed wire … Yes, the barbed wire is around a gate.

Therapist: OK, there's the gate with the barbed wire. It's tightly closed. I can't see through it. Is Little Tim behind it?

Tim: I can't see him.

Therapist: OK. Can you put me in the picture? I'm walking towards the gate with the barbed wire.

Tim: Er, OK.

Therapist: Just watch me walk calmly towards the gate. I hesitate a little, because the gate looks quite threatening with all that barbed wire. But I keep walking, because I know that Little Tim must be here somewhere. I say, 'Hey, Gate, how nice of you to protect Tim so well with all that barbed wire. You've learned to keep people at a distance so they can't disappoint Tim, so they can't hurt him. That's important work you've done.' Tim, how does it feel for you when I say this to the gate?

Tim: Eh, I don't know. I do like it when you say something nice about the gate, because usually I hear that I should behave differently.

Therapist: Aha, yes, I'm glad you feel that way. Gate, I also appreciate everything you've done for Tim. I notice that sometimes you make sure that I also keep my distance. Even though I'm actually looking for Tim, because I want to help him. But you're so closed off now that I can't even see him. Whereas there have been moments in therapy when I did see him. I liked that – then I could really connect with him. Tim, how does that feel for you?

Tim: Hm, well, I don't know.

Therapist: 'Gate, I understand that you're not letting me in right now; you don't have to. But could you maybe open the door a crack so I can say hello to Tim?'

Tim: OK, a crack is fine.

Therapist: 'That's great, thank you'. Tim, can we see Little Tim now?

Tim: Yes, he's sitting a little further away, in the grass.

Therapist: What do you see in him?

Tim: He's not feeling very well.

Therapist: No, I can see that. I want to ask him: 'Hey Little Tim, how are you feeling?' How does he respond to that?

Tim: ...He feels lonely ... no one understands him...

Therapist: How sad to hear ... and at the same time, I understand where that feeling comes from. It's always been that way – he's always been so alone...

Tim: ...Yes...

Therapist: So, I want to say to him: 'Little Tim, I want you to know that I'm here. I'm here for you ... and I want to help you...' Is that a good or a bad feeling, that I want to help Little Tim, that I'm there for him?

Tim: ...I don't know ... good ... a little...

Therapist: Do you notice any of that good feeling in your body?

Tim: ...My chest, it feels lighter.

(The therapist concludes the exercise and allows Tim to open his eyes. The exercise is discussed, and they write helpful messages from the exercise on a flashcard.)

What if your client:

- ...doesn't let you bypass the coping mode?

  Remain respectful of the coping modes, because they are there for a reason. Re-emphasize the importance of validating and expressing the feelings and needs of the Vulnerable Child. You can also try to address the Vulnerable Child through the coping mode, as it were. For example: *'OK, Gate, you stay closed, but I hope that Little Tim, behind you, can still hear me. Little Tim, I want to tell you that ...'* Realize that the exercise is already successful: your client is observing the coping mode instead of completely merging with it.

Variations

With children or young adolescents, this can be played out in a game and various materials can be used. In group therapy, the coping modes and the Vulnerable Child can be vividly portrayed and fellow clients can contribute ideas about ways to bypass the coping modes and get more in touch with the Vulnerable Child. In later phases of therapy, your client can also enter the image themselves, as a Healthy Adult, to negotiate with the coping modes and provide care to the Vulnerable Child.

Middle Phase

By now, your client will be able to recognize the moments when one of their coping modes becomes active and will be aware of the dysfunctional effect this has on their feelings and needs. You can therefore take a more confrontational approach when identifying the coping mode: in empathic confrontation, for example, there will be more emphasis on confrontation than on empathy. In the middle phase, the goal is for your client to gain more control over the coping modes, so that they can negotiate with them more independently and know how to set them aside. You can help them with this by adopting a coaching approach and challenging cognitions in a more direct manner, for example, with cognitive techniques. You can continue to apply the methods and techniques described in the initial phase. In addition, the following chapters describe several other techniques that are suitable for working with coping modes in the middle phase.

Chapter 41: Step-by-Step Limit Setting

Objective

To stop the undesirable behaviour by setting limits in a personal way.

Guidelines

Step 1: Preparation
Step 2: Personal explanation of limits
Step 3: Set limits and identify desired behaviour
Optional Step 4: Repeat Steps 2 and 3 and announce the consequences
Optional Step 5: Repeat Steps 2, 3 and 4 and implement increasing consequences

Explanation of the guidelines

Step 1: Preparation

Aggression or other forms of behaviour that cause (a feeling of) insecurity must be set limits in an acute, direct manner (see Chapter 38: Acute Limit Setting for Bully and Attack Mode). Many other forms of behaviour may also need to be limited. Not so much because they make the situation unsafe, as because they are annoying behaviours that undermine the therapist's motivation. Examples of such behaviours include frequently arriving late, frequently interrupting the therapist and frequently seeking contact between sessions. Often, it is a combination of behaviours; choose one behavioural pattern to set limits for in the coming period.

You decide which behaviour you are going to limit and when – limits are personal, and no one can tell you what your boundary is. The freedom to set your own limits comes with the responsibility of being aware of your limits. After all, limit setting is the final step in all the other interventions you have tried to stop the behaviour.

Ask yourself why this behaviour pattern bothers you; what feelings does it evoke, what consequences does the behaviour have for you or your work? If you find it difficult to set limits, you can prepare for the session by visualizing your own Healthy Adult (see also Chapter 47: Visualizing the Healthy Adult).

Step 2: Personal explanation of limits

Make sure you have enough time in the session to discuss the boundary you want to set. Announce that you want to discuss something and indicate that you need a moment to get your message across. Name the behaviour that you want to set limits for. Explain in a personal way why this behaviour bothers you. Using reciprocity is a simple way to explain this personally: 'When you do that, I feel tense and uncomfortable. Just as I want you to be relaxed in the sessions, I too need to be able to relax.' Also explain that you have already tried many other ways to break this behaviour pattern, but they haven't been effective enough.

Step 3: Set limits and identify desired behaviour

Clearly indicate which behaviour must stop. Also clearly state what you do want your client to do.

Optional Step 4: Repeat Steps 2 and 3 and announce the consequences

If the behaviour continues, explain your limits again, with more emphasis. Announce that the next time the behaviour occurs, there will be a consequence. Consequences do not only include taking away something valuable, such as ending the session early. Other examples of consequences include having the client do something useful for the therapy, such as extra homework, or taking responsibility for crossing the boundary, such as offering an apology. The basic principle of consequences for boundary violations is that when your client crosses a boundary, they experience a negative consequence or have to do something that requires extra effort. What that is can be different for each client.

Optional Step 5: Repeat Steps 2, 3 and 4 and implement increasing consequences

If the undesirable behaviour is repeated, keep repeating what the boundary is and add increasingly severe consequences each time the boundary is crossed again. Continue to do this consistently: explain and announce, and only implement the consequence if the behaviour occurs again. As a final consequence, you can pause or stop the therapy.

Example

Since the start of therapy, Sandra has regularly arrived late for sessions. This varies from five to fifteen minutes. Early on in therapy, this behaviour was linked to her Detached Protector. During the sessions, attempts have been made to change this behaviour by discussing it and negotiating with that Protector using chairwork, and several empathic confrontations have already taken place. Nevertheless, Sandra continues to arrive late on a regular basis. In this session, too, she storms in almost ten minutes late.

Therapist: Welcome, Sandra, please take a seat.

Sandra: Yes, sorry, I'm late again, but it was really busy and then I also had to...

Therapist: Wait a minute, Sandra, I appreciate you acknowledging the fact that you're late again, but I'd like to say something about that first. I won't take too much time, but I really need to discuss something with you calmly. Agreed?

Sandra: ...Yes, OK...

Therapist: You said it yourself: you're late. And this isn't the first time. We've talked about this before. In fact, we've been talking about this since the beginning of therapy, that there's this side of you that causes you to be late a lot. We've done exercises with chairs, and I've also told you a few times that I feel uncomfortable when I don't know when you're coming. But it hasn't changed much; you're still often late. And I'm starting to find that really bothersome. When you're late, I don't know when you'll arrive, or whether you'll be here at all. That means I have to keep checking to see if you're in the waiting room. I don't like it when you are late, and then I have to keep walking back and forth. I'm starting to find that restlessness really annoying. Just as you should be able to feel relaxed and comfortable in the room, I too would like to feel relaxed and comfortable when we have an appointment together. Do you understand that?

(Sandra nods.)

Therapist: So, I need you to be on time from now on. Of course, if there are circumstances beyond your control, such as an accident or sudden illness, then it may not be possible. But those are exceptions, and I need you to make it a rule to be on time. Do you understand?

Sandra: Yes, but like now, the roads were really busy, and I was delayed with the shopping. I really tried to be on time!

Therapist: I believe you, and I can see how rushed you are when you come in. And if it had been just this once, I wouldn't have made a fuss about it. The problem is that every time there's something else that prevents you from arriving on time. And again, I want you to realize that I don't feel comfortable with that. Just as I want you to take your feelings and needs seriously, I do the same. That's why I need this to change. Can we agree that from now on you'll arrive on time?

Sandra: (*A little sulkily.*) Yes, OK then.

Therapist: Very good. Well, now I'm very curious to hear how your week has been.

(*Sandra arrives late for the next session again, five minutes late this time.*)

Therapist: Welcome, Sandra, take a seat ... As you know, you're a little late again.

Sandra: Yes, but it was only a few minutes this time, which is much better than before, isn't it?

Therapist: Certainly, it's not as bad as it has been. But you're still late, and once again I find myself wondering what time you will arrive today, or whether you'll come at all. And I noticed again that this made me feel a bit stressed and irritated. And I don't want to feel irritated when we have an appointment, Sandra. I explained that, just like you, I want to feel relaxed when we have an appointment, so that I can give you my full attention. I explained that I really need you to be on time, to respect my boundaries. And that's why I want to agree with you that if you're late again, we'll use the rest of the session to explore why you weren't able to be on time. Agreed?

Sandra: Well, I'm a little shocked: you sound really angry or something, very different from usual...

Therapist: I think you can tell that I don't feel comfortable with this. To be honest, I'm glad about that, because I think it makes it more likely that you'll try even harder to be on time next time. What do you think?

Sandra: Yes, you're not very pleasant when you're like that, so I'd rather not have it happen again, no...

Therapist: Fine, well, if that helps you to be on time next time, then I'm very happy.

What if your client:

- …desperately tries to explain how they just can't seem to change their behaviour?

  Remember that this boundary is the final piece of many other interventions. Now that none of those have worked, you appeal to the Healthy Adult to take more control. By setting a boundary, you are sending the message: '*Captain, one of your crew members is bothering me, and I need you to do something about it.*' Your client's message that they are unable to change appeals to the therapist's understanding. However, realize that you have shown a great deal of understanding for a long time and that your boundaries are not unreasonable. So, stick to your boundary.

Variations

In a group setting, there are often general group rules that are supported by all therapists. It may be that it is not necessarily your personal boundary that is being crossed, but one of the group rules. In that case, it is useful to think about why that rule is there and how you, as a therapist, can also support it.

Chapter 42: Chairwork with Coping Modes in the Middle Phase

Objective

To teach your client, with your guidance, to use arguments from their Healthy Adult to counter the coping modes, to connect with their Vulnerable Child and to validate its emotional needs.

Guidelines

Step 1: Rationale

Step 2: Client in the chair of the coping mode

Step 3: Client in the chair of the Healthy Adult

Step 4: Coach the client in negotiating with the coping modes

Step 5: Coach validation of the Vulnerable Child's needs

Step 6: Reflection

Explanation of the guidelines

Step 1: Rationale

Explain that your client will learn to bypass the coping modes and validate the needs of their Vulnerable Child, and that you will take the role of a coach rather than doing it for them.

Step 2: Client in the chair of the coping mode

Place a chair where the coping modes are always located in the room. Ask your client to express the thoughts, experiences and behavioural responses of the coping modes from that chair.

Step 3: Client in the chair of the Healthy Adult

Then ask your client to sit next to the Vulnerable Child on the chair of the Healthy Adult (possibly your therapist's chair). Sit on the other side of the Vulnerable Child yourself. First, ask your client to connect with their Healthy Adult (see Chapter 47: Visualizing the Healthy Adult).

Step 4: Coach the client in negotiating with the coping modes

Discuss which arguments your client can use in the negotiation with the coping modes. Ask open questions that encourage self-expression and autonomy, appropriate to this middle phase. Ask your client to voice the arguments aloud to the coping modes. Discuss what objections it might have and, if necessary, let your client respond to them.

Step 5: Coach validation of the Vulnerable Child's needs

Coach your client in expressing compassion for the Vulnerable Child. Encourage them to identify the relevant emotional needs, for example: '*Your opinion matters, and it is good to express it.*'

Step 6: Reflection

Ask your client to reflect on the experience of negotiating and validating independently. Agree on homework to further consolidate these insights and experiences, for example, by noting down the most important arguments against the coping modes.

Example

The therapist and Mary sit on either side of the Vulnerable Child's chair. On that chair is a photo of five-year-old Mary. Opposite is a chair with her Compliant Surrenderer (the Pleaser).

Therapist: Just tell your Pleaser what you want them to hear.

Mary: I know you're trying to help, but it's important that I listen to my own needs and do what I want…

Therapist: Very good! I can see that you still find it a bit scary because you don't go along with what others want?

Mary: (*A little nervous.*) Yes, I'm afraid they'll get angry.

Therapist: I think you're feeling her fear (*gestures towards Little Mary's chair*). We understand why she finds this scary, don't we? (*Mary nods.*) Can you tell her that you understand?

Mary: (*Turns to Little Mary.*) Of course you find it scary.

Therapist: Because...

Mary: Because you've learned that people get angry when you want something different, like when Dad gets grumpy.

Therapist: (*Speaking softly:*) Very good. And maybe now you can say that it's OK to want things for yourself? That autonomy is an important emotional need?

Mary: (*Softly:*) Yes, it's good to want and do things for yourself. Everyone is allowed to make their own choices...

Therapist: Very good, say that again, now twenty per cent louder.

Mary: (*A little louder:*) It's OK to make your own choices, that applies to everyone, including you!

Therapist: Good. How does it feel to say this?

Mary: Exciting.

Therapist: Just exciting, or is it also nice in some ways to say that you're allowed to make your own choices in life?

Mary: ...A little bit...

Therapist: Where do you feel that in your body?

(*Mary points to her chest.*)

Therapist: Let's practice again, so that little bit can grow.

What if your client:

- ...keeps merging with the coping mode?

  Consider an empathic confrontation, in which you place more emphasis on confrontation at this stage to encourage your client to change.

Variations

Your client can read prepared arguments aloud from a piece of paper. Use a symbol for the coping modes to mark the distance from that mode.

Final Phase

By now, your client will be able to negotiate with their coping modes within the session and, with some help from you, will usually be able to put them aside. In the final phase, the goal is for your client to become even more independent in this and to break through patterns of avoidance and inversion of schemas outside of the sessions, in everyday life. You will therefore increasingly encourage your client to express emotions, stand up for themselves and do things that give them satisfaction. Give brief instructions where necessary, ask open questions and give your client the space to make their own choices with regard to healthy coping. In this final phase, behavioural techniques will become more important, such as behavioural experiments that the client can perform more and more independently. In the next chapter, you will find an addition to the chairwork in this final phase.

Chapter 43: Chairwork with a Coping Mode in the Final Phase

Objective

To teach your client to conduct the inner discussion with their coping modes more and more independently and to stay in touch with their feelings and needs.

Guidelines

Step 1: Rationale
Step 2: Identify a future problem situation
Step 3: Client in the Healthy Adult chair
Step 4: Therapist in the coping mode chair
Step 5: Client negotiates with the coping mode
Step 6: Reflection

Explanation of the guidelines

Step 1: Rationale

Explain that this exercise is intended to prepare your client for future schema-activating situations that may trigger the coping modes.

Step 2: Identify a future problem situation

You can focus the exercise on specific situations that trigger this coping mode (e.g., receiving criticism, setting limits or expressing anger). You can also choose to keep the exercise more general and focus only on the known beliefs of the coping modes.

Step 3: Client in the Healthy Adult chair

Ask your client to sit in the chair that symbolizes the Healthy Adult, which may also be their original therapy chair. Ask them to connect with their Healthy Adult.

Step 4: Therapist in the coping mode chair

Take a seat in the coping mode chair. Start the dialogue with a typical statement from this coping mode, based on previous sessions.

Step 5: Client negotiates with the coping mode

As a Healthy Adult, your client gives arguments as to why the coping modes are wrong or react too extremely. At the beginning of the final phase, you can still provide support by making suggestions. As the end draws nearer, it becomes important to challenge your client more. You can do this by asking more probing questions as the coping modes or by offering typical counter-arguments (*'Just avoid it, lock yourself up at home, then nothing will happen that you find difficult'*). This helps your client to remain firmly in their Healthy Adult state in the future, even without your presence.

Step 6: Reflection

In the debriefing, you explore together what your client has experienced and what this means. Ask your client to note down the most important arguments, insights or helpful experiences and to repeat them regularly between sessions.

PART VI: Treatment Phase – Working with Healthy Modes

Healthy modes

The category of healthy modes not only includes the Healthy Adult, but also the Happy Child (which may also be classified in the category of child modes). These modes involve positive schemas (see Chapter 1: Introduction). The Happy Child is characterized by the ability to respond naturally and spontaneously, by playfulness, and by having fun and creativity. Within the Healthy Adult, the International Society of Schema Therapy (2024) distinguishes between eight categories of qualities:

- **Metaconsciousness:** Is your client able to reflect on themselves and others?
- **Contact with emotions:** Is your client open to emotions, able to experience them and respond to emotional pain and uncertainty with self-acceptance and compassion?
- **Reality orientation:** Can your client make decisions based on reality and act accordingly?
- **A coherent sense of identity:** Can your client maintain a coherent sense of who they are (personal beliefs, norms and values, motivation)?
- **Assertiveness and reciprocity:** Can your client stand up for themselves, while respecting others and their needs?
- **Agency and responsibility:** Can your client take responsibility for their own decisions and actions, and their consequences?
- **Caring for others:** Is your client able to show concern for others and society as a whole?
- **Hope and meaning:** Is your client able to find and maintain confidence even in the face of adversity?

How do you recognize healthy modes?

In your case conceptualization, you described the characteristics and behaviour associated with your client's Happy Child and Healthy Adult. During sessions, you can further recognize healthy modes by using four sources of information:

- ***What* does the client say?:** In their Healthy Adult mode, your client will make realistic statements and be in touch with their emotions. Other modes may also make statements that seem realistic, such as a Demanding Critic that says it is important not to procrastinate. However, if you probe further, there is usually an unrealistic component to such a statement, because it turns out that this hard work comes at the expense of other emotional needs. The Happy Child mainly makes statements that show spontaneity and pleasure. You can distinguish the Happy Child from an Undisciplined or Impulsive Child because it does not cross boundaries and, although carefree, does not display unruly behaviour.

- ***How* does the client express this?:** In healthy modes, your client will generally display spontaneity and a lively or balanced attitude. For example, the Healthy Adult will weigh things up, seeing the importance of themselves but also that of others, identifying pros and cons and focusing on meeting their own emotional needs in a healthy way. This does not mean that their statements are always very nuanced: even a Healthy Adult can be emotional, but your client does show some reflection and self-awareness ('Excuse me for talking so loudly, but I really think what you're saying is stupid!').
- **What is your primary *emotional response* as a therapist?:** When your client's healthy mode is active, you experience contact with your client and cooperation is possible, even if it is sometimes difficult. A Healthy Adult also evokes compassion with their emotional experiences. Finally, it is possible to have fun together when your client is in a healthy mode.
- **Pay attention to *contrasts* in the presentation:** Although coping modes, such as the Detached Protector or the Compliant Surrenderer, appear very well adjusted, your client is not in touch with their emotions or emotional needs in these modes and is more likely to present themselves as purely rational or docile. When your client's Healthy Adult is active, you will have more insight into their perception of the world and feel a sense of equality in exploring what your client really needs.

What is the goal in working with healthy modes?

The goal is to strengthen the healthy modes by making room for relaxation, play and fun, by allowing your client to connect with their own emotions and by enabling them to adequately strive to fulfil their emotional needs.

Initial Phase

In the initial phase of therapy, your client's healthy modes are often largely absent. You will therefore mainly focus on modelling and actively fulfilling core emotional needs, so that your client can gain corrective emotional experiences and internalize healthy messages. In doing so, you build positive schemas. In addition, reinforce every quality or characteristic of your client's Healthy Adult or Happy Child when they show themselves, even if only minimally. In this way, you work towards *shaping* healthy coping and playfulness.

Of course, all methods and techniques targeting child modes, inner critic modes or coping modes also strengthen the Healthy Adult. The following pages contain guidelines for methods and techniques that specifically target the healthy modes in the initial phase.

Chapter 44: Mode Sequence

Objective

To recognize modes and underlying needs (initial phase), and to contribute to behavioural change (middle and final phases).

Guidelines

Step 1: Identify the schema-activating situation
Step 2: Rationale
Step 3: Discuss the situation in detail
Step 4: Discuss and note down the modes
Optional Step 5: Interaction with the other person's modes
Step 6: Reflection *(Optional: Emotional needs and healthy behaviour)*

Explanation of the guidelines

Step 1: Identify the schema-activating situation

Your client talks about a recent situation that triggered intense emotions, thoughts and/or feelings. You suspect that one or more schemas have been activated and that different modes have followed each other. Sometimes, it will not be about one specific situation, and various situations will overlap. In such cases, select one situation that you will discuss in detail.

Step 2: Rationale

Explain that you want to use the schema-activating situation you have chosen as practice material to explore which of your client's modes played a role in it. In this initial phase of therapy, this contributes to learning to recognize the modes and what your client actually needed. If the therapy is in the middle or final phase, and therefore more of the Healthy Adult is present, you can then discuss how your client can ensure that their emotional needs are met in a healthy way. The information from the mode sequence can be used as input for a safety plan.

Step 3: Discuss the situation in detail

Let your client describe the situation in detail, as if you were conducting a behavioural or topographical analysis. So, what exactly did your client do, say, think and feel at each moment, and what exactly did someone else do or say?

Step 4: Discuss and note down the modes

During or after Step 3, discuss with your client which modes you recognize in the analysis. Draw this sequence of modes or use mode cards or figurines to represent them. Visualizing the mode sequence gives your client an overview and a point of reference. See Figure 44.1 which relates to this chapter's

Example

Figure 44.1: A mode sequence.

Optional Step 5: Interaction with the other person's modes

When your client describes a situation with another person, you can choose to include hypotheses about the other person's modes in the mode sequence. This is particularly helpful when that other person is involved in the therapy (e.g., a partner, parent, other family member or fellow client in group therapy or clinical admission) or when you yourself are the other person. In the latter case, you are examining an interaction between the two of you in the therapeutic relationship, in which something you said or did triggered your client's schemas and modes. Mapping the interaction between your client's modes and those of another person provides insight into each other's patterns and needs.

Step 6: Reflection
(Optional: Emotional needs and healthy behaviour)

In the initial phase, you mainly reflect on the insights your client has gained by creating the mode sequence. You also try to consider with your client what they actually needed at those moments (emotional needs) when each mode was active. In the middle and final phases, you will increase focus on strengthening their Healthy Adult. Looking back, what could they have done to ensure that their emotional needs were met in a healthy way? When others are involved, what can they do in such moments? This information can be used in a safety plan and, during the final phase, in the relapse prevention plan. The healthy alternatives mentioned can be practiced during sessions (e.g., through roleplay) and in daily life.

Example

Therapist: Shall we examine that situation at your internship to see how it ultimately came to the point where you pushed your colleague and went home? (*Tim nods.*) Would you like to tell me in detail what happened?

Tim: I was working on a car with a colleague. I was allowed to help with the repairs, and then another colleague called me to come and help him. That made me angry.

Therapist: OK, wait a minute, let's go through it step by step. So, first you were allowed to assist with repairing the car. How did you feel about that?

Tim: Yes, I liked it. I like doing something real instead of just having to vacuum the cars or top up the windscreen washer fluid.

Therapist: OK, so the situation is that you're in the service workshop (*writes down the situation*). And when you're working on the car, it sounds like you feel happy and enjoy being able to really help out. I think that's your Happy Child side (*points to the Happy Child mode card*), is that right?

Tim: Yes, I think so.

Therapist: OK, let's put that on the board. (*Attaches the Happy Child mode card to the board with a magnet, with an arrow pointing from the situation to this card.*) And then, what happened while you were assisting?

Tim: My colleague, who was on the other side of the room, shouted my name across the entire workshop.

Therapist: What went through your mind?

Tim: Oh no, he wants something from me again. He always wants me to do his dirty work for him. I didn't feel like it, so I pretended I didn't hear him and just kept assisting.

Therapist: Aha, OK, that sounds a bit like the rebellious 'Screw it' side of you, I think.

Tim: (*Chuckles.*) Yes, that's possible.

Therapist: (*Sticks the Undisciplined Child card on the board and draws an arrow to it from the Happy Child card.*) OK, and then? What did your colleague do?

Tim: He started shouting louder and said, 'Hey, are you deaf or something? Why don't you listen when I call your name?'

Therapist: How did that make you feel?

Tim: I got angry. Who does he think he is? He's just a trainee mechanic himself. I don't have to put up with him, do I? He acts like he owns the whole workshop. And because I'm an intern, he thinks I should just listen to him. I'm not his dog!

Therapist: I hear your Angry Child side here, and maybe also a little bit of Little Tim, who feels small and humiliated?

Tim: Yes, maybe a little. Mainly angry.

Therapist: And how did you react then? Could the others see that you were angry?

Tim: No, I held back. But I did put him in his place by saying that I was still assisting my other colleague and he shouldn't act like he's all-important, that he should just wait until I was finished.

Therapist: Which side of you do you think that was?

Tim: Just my Healthy side.

Therapist: Can you demonstrate how you said that? As if I were your colleague?

(*Tim demonstrates with a haughty tone and attitude.*)

Therapist: Could it be that this was perhaps the Great One, the side that puts itself above others? To make it clear to him that you won't let him belittle you? (*Therapist points to the Self-Aggrandizer card.*)

Tim: Yes, maybe, but he deserved it.

Therapist: (*Therapist sticks the Self-Aggrandizer card on the board and draws an arrow to it.*) You felt belittled by him, and the Great One came to your aid by reversing the roles, by placing yourself above him.

(*They work through the situation until the entire mode sequence is on the board.*)

Therapist: If you now look at the sequence of your different sides in this situation, you'll see that it's possible to replace each one with your Healthy Adult side. This gives you several opportunities to prevent situations like this from getting out of hand. We'll look at that more closely later in the therapy. For now, I think it's especially important that you learn to recognize when and in which situations different sides of you come to the fore. Would you like to pay attention over the next week to when the Great One and the Attacker become activated and why?

What if your client:

- ...considers a mode or behaviour of the other person to be more dysfunctional than you suspect it actually was?

  Try to stay as close as possible to your client's experience, but also offer alternatives. For example: you are analysing a situation between you and your client, in which your client says that you responded to them in your Self-Aggrandizer mode, while you think it was your Healthy Adult mode. Ask your client what makes them think this was your Self-Aggrandizer. *How did you come across to them? What was your tone of voice or attitude?* Acknowledge their experience (and reaction to it), and name any real aspects of it that you also recognize. Then compare this with your own experience and explain what your intention was. Do not get into a discussion about which side of you it was, as this is generally not that relevant.

Variations

If you use figurines, you can create arrangements of (parts of) the mode sequence, which can be moved around.

When interactions between the client on the one hand and a partner, parent or other close relative on the other are analysed, this can be done separately or jointly with that other person. If you opt for joint sessions, it is important that both parties have some access to their Healthy Adult modes to ensure that the conflict does not flare up again. Working out mode sequences together in a joint session can lead to greater mutual understanding and better attunement to each other's needs. Clashes or collusions between modes of partners, family members or members of a group therapy may be worked out experientially in role plays, in which the steps of the historical role play (see Chapter 29: Historical Role Play) can be followed to create this mutual understanding and to practice healthy responses to each other. Chairs can also be used to work out interactions between the modes of the different parties. Getting up from those chairs, shifting the position of the chairs and observing that arrangement from a distance can all contribute to greater insight and discussion of options for how the Healthy Adult can learn to handle such interactions.

Chapter 45: (Audio) Flashcard

Objective

To consolidate corrective emotional experiences gained by repeating healthy messages from the session at home.

Guidelines

Step 1: Name the feeling and/or behaviour
Step 2: Psychoeducation about the origin of the mode(s)
Step 3: Compassion
Step 4: Cognitive restructuring
Step 5: Name the corrective emotional experience
Step 6: Healthy behavioural instruction

Explanation of the guidelines

Step 1: Name the feeling and/or behaviour

Choose which pattern you want to create the (audio) flashcard for: the overwhelming experiences of the Vulnerable Child, the critical self-evaluations of the inner critic mode, the behavioural patterns of a coping mode or a combination of these. First, make sure the flashcard matches your client's experience by specifically naming the feeling or behaviour that your client often struggles with.

Then indicate that this feeling or behaviour is a pattern; it is not the first time that your client feels anxious/sad/angry or has the tendency to shut down/walk away/numb themselves. Based on the specific descriptions, you can now identify the relevant mode. This is an important step in the change process, namely the defusion of an overwhelming experience into an awareness of that experience.

Step 2: Psychoeducation about the origin of the mode(s)

Explain that the mode(s) is/are a logical consequence of a history of unmet emotional needs, a history full of learning experiences that have developed into this side of your client.

Step 3: Compassion

Show explicit and extensive compassion for the emotions and behavioural tendencies felt. Take the time to explain, for example: '*Of course you feel [sad / anxious / angry], because not only is this a difficult situation now, but also for you it is yet another time that you are missing out on the fulfilment of … [name the emotional need(s)].*' Take your time with this, knowing that compassion has a calming, soothing effect on schema activation.

Step 4: Cognitive restructuring

Give explicit reasons why the activated schemas/modes are incorrect. Give personal arguments to counter those old beliefs, in line with the personal therapeutic relationship you are striving for within limited reparenting.

Step 5: Name the corrective emotional experience

Name the pleasant feelings your client experiences when validating emotional needs. Use your client's own words to do this. Explicitly focusing attention on the positive emotions your client experiences when validating emotional needs is an important way to consolidate those experiences.

Step 6: Healthy behavioural instruction

End the flashcard with healthy behavioural instructions, offering an alternative to the behavioural tendencies arising from coping modes. For example, give the instruction to read or listen to the flashcard again the next day.

Example

Therapist: You've worked very hard during our session today, and I'm pleased to see that you're now a little calmer than at the beginning of the session, right?

Sandra: Yes, I feel much calmer. I felt so miserable because of all that stuff with Mark, the arguments, but now things are better.

Therapist: I'm glad to hear that. And actually, I'd like you to experience more moments of peace like this in the coming week. That's why I want to give you something that might help you with that. I'd like to record a message on your phone, in which I say some things that are important for you to hear and remember. And when you listen to that recording over the next week, perhaps hearing my voice and those words will help you experience that feeling of peace again. How does that sound?

Sandra: (*Smiling.*) Yes, that sounds nice, yes…

(*The therapist asks Sandra to take out her phone and starts recording. The therapist says the following:*)

'As you listen to my voice now, Sandra, I want to start by complimenting you. I think it's great that you've taken a moment to sit quietly and listen to this recording. That is a moment of self-care. Perhaps you need that care right now, because you're not feeling very well. Perhaps you're feeling that sadness and anger again, that pain you can feel so strongly in your stomach. And perhaps you're having those thoughts again that you aren't doing anything right, that you're stupid.

I know that those kinds of thoughts are common and that at times like these, you feel like they're true, like you really are stupid.

But you know, Sandra, what you hear at those moments isn't the truth – it's only your father's punitive messages again. He could get so angry and criticize you. He told you those things so often, with and without words. And when you feel so bad about yourself, you're actually listening to your father's voice again.

And when that Punitive Critic of you is raging again, of course you feel sad and angry. I would too, if someone told me I was stupid. That's a very normal feeling to have. And it's completely understandable that you feel so sad and angry, because this is the umpteenth time you've heard that message. What you feel at such moments is actually the sadness and anger of that little girl you used to be. You feel that little Sandra inside you again, with all her sadness and pent-up anger.

Sandra, I really disagree with your father. It's nonsense: you are not stupid. I think you're very good and valuable. There's so much to be proud of: you're intelligent; I know that you sometimes find that hard to believe, but it's true. I think you're sensitive, and I find that a very beautiful quality in you. I know that this can cause you pain, but I think your ability to feel deeply is something very beautiful about you. You're a go-getter; you have a lot of strength in you. I also think you have a great sense of humour; I really like that about you too.

And I think it might feel a little uncomfortable when you listen to my words now, because it's so unusual to hear them. But I know that you can also get a nice feeling, that warm feeling in your stomach when you hear this kind of healthy message. That's that nice, warm feeling that makes you feel more connected. Perhaps you could place a hand on your stomach right now so that you can consciously experience that feeling again.

And I know that sometimes, when you have felt so much anger and sadness, you have the tendency to withdraw, to shut yourself off, but I don't want you to let your Protector take over completely. I actually want you to contact your friend Debbie and talk to her for a while, so that you are literally not alone anymore. And finally, I want to tell you that you can listen to this recording again tomorrow, so that you give yourself the opportunity to feel calmer and more positive about yourself.

(*The therapist hands the phone back to Sandra, who stops the recording.*)

Therapist: How did you feel hearing what I recorded?

Sandra: Yes, that was nice…

Therapist: I'm glad to hear that. Please listen to this message whenever you like; give yourself the chance to carry those nice words with you. You can do that when you're having a hard time, but you can also take another quiet moment to sit down and listen to it. It's important that you hear those healthy messages more often, as a counterbalance to your father's punitive messages.

What if your client:

- ...says that the recording doesn't affect them that much, or that they won't listen to the whole thing?

  Do not take these comments too personally, and take a moment to consider which mode you are listening to at that moment. There is a chance that you are listening to a coping mode. Of course, they may not feel much and may criticize the recording, but that does not mean that you have done something wrong and should stop making such recordings. It is important that your client hears healthy messages, in which emotional needs are validated, and can hear them more often.

Variations

The flashcard can be processed in written form and in an audio file. In the initial phase of therapy, the audio flashcard has the advantage that the attachment process is reinforced by limited reparenting through repeatedly listening to the therapist's voice. The flashcard does not have to be recorded during the session itself, but can also be recorded before or after the session. As a therapist, choose the moment that feels best for you.

In the middle phase, cognitive arguments take centre stage, which may be a reason to use more written flashcards. In the final phase of therapy, your client can make flashcards themselves. Clients often prefer written flashcards because hearing their own voice activates all kinds of schemas.

Chapter 46: Cognitive Techniques – Circle Diary

Objective

To learn to recognize the activated modes and calmly reflect on the automatic assumptions and associated behavioural responses. Your client can also learn healthy modes to validate needs.

Guidelines

(See Figure 46.1)

Top of the circle: Situation

Step 1: What is happening? Describe the situation

Right side of the circle: Primary responses

Step 2: What do I feel in my body?

Step 3: How do I feel?

Step 4: What am I thinking?

Left side of the circle: Awareness

Step 5: Which mode is this?

Step 6: What are the facts?

Step 7: What would I like to happen?

Inside the circle: Change

Step 8: What did I do in that situation?

Step 9: What was the effect of what I did?

Step 10: What do I need now (emotional need)?

Step 11: What can I do to get what I need?

Explanation of the guidelines

There are many variations of the circle diary, of which this is one (adapted from van der Wijngaart and van Genderen, 2024). See Figure 46.1.

Top of the circle: Situation

Step 1: What is happening? Describe the situation

Try to describe the chosen problem situation as concretely and specifically as possible. Choose the specific moment when your client felt triggered ('I hear that woman say, "You're not cleaning properly"') and do not describe the entire context (e.g., 'Cleaning at that critical woman's house last Monday').

Right side of the circle: Primary responses

The conditioned physiological, emotional and cognitive responses are described on the right-hand side of the circle. The order of these responses may vary depending on the version of the cognitive circle you have. The common goal of all these versions is to first identify the expressions of schema activation.

Step 2: What do I feel in my body?

Note down the physiological aspects of schema activation here. Ask specific questions about the physical reactions your client noticed at the selected moment (*What did you feel in your body when you heard that woman say, 'You're not cleaning properly?'*).

Step 3: How do I feel?

Ask your client about their emotions at the moment of schema activation. Sometimes, you will need to help them put words to the feelings that arise at such moments (*What emotion did you feel when she said that? Were you afraid, angry … perhaps a little sad?*).

Step 4: What am I thinking?

Clients find it difficult to answer the question of what was going through their minds at that moment. They often respond in the form of a question ('Why is she saying that now?'). It is not the question, but probably their own answer to that question that makes them so angry, afraid or sad ('She thinks I'm stupid'). Therefore, ask directly about the reason for the emotional reaction (*What were you angry / sad about or afraid of at that moment?*).

Left side of the circle: Awareness

On the left-hand side, you ask your client to reflect on the reactions in the situation. After writing down the primary reactions, the goal now is for your client to become more aware of the activated modes and the actual circumstances, and to start considering the underlying needs.

Step 5: Which mode is this?

Based on the experience in the situation, with all subsequent feelings and thoughts, the active mode can be identified. However, keep in mind that no matter how specifically the situation is described, multiple modes may have been active. Therefore, choose the mode you want to focus on this time; perhaps you have already talked a lot about an inner critic mode in previous sessions and today you want to use the cognitive circle to focus more on a coping or child mode.

Step 6: What are the facts?

Ask your client to describe the actual circumstances (*Who said what? What exactly happened?*). This will help your client to develop more realistic thoughts about the schema-activating event.

Step 7: What would I like to happen?

In the process of learning to think more realistically, the first question is what your client would have liked to see happen (differently) in the situation. Keep in mind, however, that wishes can still be influenced by the active modes and that *wishes* are not automatically the same as *needs*.

Inside the circle: Change

In this part of the circle, you actively appeal to your client's Healthy Adult. Instruct your client to activate it: *'Let's take a good look at this situation together and how you can deal with it. These are questions I really want to address to your Healthy Adult. So now be that Healthy Adult, the captain of your ship, for a moment.'*

Step 8: What did I do in that situation?

As a Healthy Adult, your client can reflect on the behavioural responses that dominated the situation and that may have resulted from the activated coping modes.

Step 9: What was the effect of what I did?

In this step, the Healthy Adult is invited to realistically examine how the activated modes often produce the opposite effect to what is actually needed. You can facilitate this process by asking questions: *Did it help you get what you wanted by doing … [behaviour]?*

Step 10: What do I need now (emotional need)?

This is an important step in which your client is invited to become/remain aware of the relevant emotional needs. Some early questions could therefore be: *What is an important need for you to keep an eye on? What do we know about this from the assessment phase? Could this need also be relevant in this situation?*

Step 11: What can I do to get what I need?

In this final step, the Healthy Adult is invited to develop different, healthier behaviour patterns by thinking about healthy ways to fulfil needs in the situation described.

Example

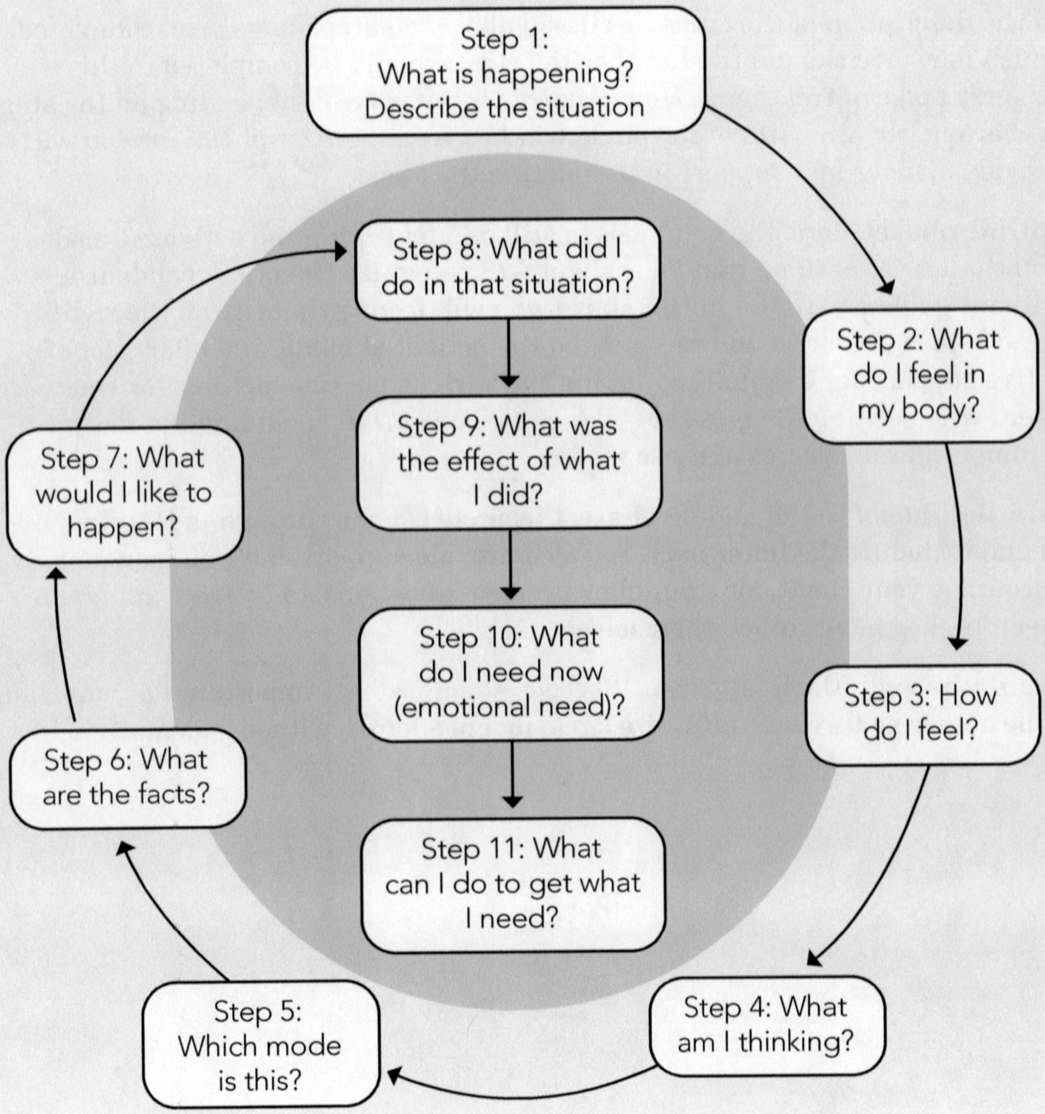

Figure 46.1: Circle Diary

Variations

In the description of the circle discussed above, all steps have been completed, which may give the impression that the circle should be completed in this way at every stage of treatment. However, this is not correct; depending on the stage of therapy, certain parts of the circle will be given more emphasis, or you will provide more or less support in completing the steps.

Initial phase: Here, the emphasis is still on identifying the activated modes. You cannot yet assume that your client will recognize them independently, without guidance. In the initial phase, you will focus primarily on the right-hand side of the circle and recognizing the activated mode. You offer a lot of active support, for example, by listing the various possible options for your client when asking the question, *'Which mode is this?'*, including the most common characteristics of those modes.

Middle phase: In the middle phase, the circle is gone through more often, up to and including the inner part. You still provide support, but you increasingly encourage your client, for example with open questions, to actively apply the insights they have gained themselves.

Final phase: In the final phase, it becomes increasingly important for your client to be able to go through the entire circle independently, without too much help.

Middle Phase

In the middle phase, your client's Healthy Adult has already grown somewhat and your positive messages are beginning to compete with your client's dysfunctional cognitions. You will therefore increasingly address your client's Healthy Adult. Your role becomes more coaching-oriented, helping your client to rewrite their own stories in imagery exercises, for example, and to negotiate more independently with coping modes and fight against inner critic modes in chair exercises. You will increasingly work with cognitive techniques and begin to encourage your client to make actual behavioural changes.

On the following pages, you will find techniques that you can use in the middle phase to further strengthen your client's Healthy Adult.

Chapter 47: Visualizing the Healthy Adult

Objective

To teach your client what Healthy Adult behaviour means and to help them form an image of their own Healthy Adult.

Guidelines

Step 1: Explain the Healthy Adult
Step 2: Give a personal example of a Healthy Adult being active
Step 3: Rationale
Step 4: Imagine the Healthy Adult
Step 5: Debriefing and homework

Explanation of the guidelines

Step 1: Explain the Healthy Adult

Clients often have a distorted view of the concept of 'Healthy Adult'. For example, some clients think that healthy means that they will not be affected by anything at all, while that perspective seems to fit better with a coping mode. Or your client may see being healthy as having everything perfectly under control and never making mistakes again. That perspective seems to fit better with a Demanding Critic. In this step, you explain that the 'Healthy Adult' mode entails that you can still be emotionally affected, but that you can deal with the emotions and the situation that these emotions evoke in a healthy way. The image of a parent holding a child's hand can support this explanation: the child can be affected, and although the parent notices this and takes it seriously, the parent does not merge with the child. The parent can handle the emotions, as well as the situation that caused them.

Step 2: Give a personal example of a Healthy Adult mode being active

By setting a personal example, you make clear what may be realistic expectations of therapy: even as a therapist, there are situations in which you are affected by old pain and it sometimes takes some effort to deal with those emotions and the situation. In addition, the example makes you more human after a phase in which your client may have placed you on a pedestal, unsolicited and unintentionally, with the associated unrealistic ideas about your abilities as a Healthy Adult. Such personal examples also allow for more autonomy for your client, just as children in puberty learn that parents are not omniscient and omnipotent.

Step 3: Rationale

Explain that you want to do a visualization exercise in which your client learns to form an image of their Healthy Adult. You will ask your client to become aware of all the characteristics of that Healthy Adult, because this awareness can help to activate this mode: they serve as 'keys' to open the door to the Healthy Adult. Then explain that your client can often find the image of that Healthy Adult in memories of challenging situations that they managed to handle well. These are often memories that your client looks back on with a certain satisfaction, or even pride.

Step 4: Imagine the Healthy Adult

Ask your client to close their eyes and recall an image of such a memory. First, let your client focus on the schema-activating elements of that memory and become aware of the Vulnerable Child that became palpable. Then ask your client to empathize with the healthy handling of the situation and the emotions it evoked. Try to make your client aware of the different aspects and modalities of the Healthy Adult: *How does it feel to be that Healthy Adult? Where do you feel that in your body? What do you look like in this state? What words does that Healthy Adult radiate?* Such questions help to reinforce the image and experience of the Healthy Adult.

Step 5: Debriefing and homework

Further consolidation of the Healthy Adult takes place in the debriefing about important aspects of that mode and the experience associated with it. Homework consists of visualizing the Healthy Adult more often, initially in neutral practice situations but, during the middle phase of treatment, also in situations in which schemas are activated.

Example

Therapist: Now that we're in the middle phase of the therapy, I think we can start working on your Healthy Adult, the captain of your ship. Ultimately, the goal of your treatment is for that captain to be strong enough to manage without therapy, even though life can sometimes be difficult and challenging. I'm curious to know what image you have of such a Healthy Adult side?

Sandra: ...I think I won't be so emotional anymore? That I'll have more control?

Therapist: Yes, that's partly true: being a Healthy Adult does indeed mean having more control over your life. But it's also good to realize that as a Healthy Adult, you can still be affected by things. When I look at myself, there are plenty of moments when I feel upset, sad or angry. So being a Healthy Adult doesn't mean you're never affected by things anymore, but it does mean you're no longer completely overwhelmed by such feelings. It's like you're holding that little child's hand, and you notice that she's being affected, but at such moments you aren't that child; you remain the adult, who is able to listen to those feelings and needs, but also to handle the situation. How does that sound to you?

Sandra: Yes, I understand, that makes sense.

Therapist: It helps to have a good picture of that Healthy Adult mode in you. The better you know that side of yourself, the easier it becomes to bring it out. (*Sandra nods.*) An exercise to help you with this is to think back to a memory of a situation in which you had a difficult time, but in which you still managed to handle all those feelings and the situation reasonably well. In other words, a memory that you look back on with a certain satisfaction. Shall we give it a try?

(*The therapist asks Sandra to close her eyes and prepare for the exercise, and then to visualize such a memory.*)

Sandra: ...I'm thinking of a situation at work, when I was cleaning for that woman who always criticizes me...

Therapist: Just be there and look at that woman. What happens now?

Sandra: ...She's watching me dust and then she says, 'You shouldn't do it like that, you're doing it completely wrong; let me show you how it's done.'

Therapist: And what are you feeling now?

Sandra: Angry, I get irritated immediately.

Therapist: Where do you feel that in your body?

(*Sandra points to her stomach and chest.*)

Therapist: Take a moment to check in with yourself: is this the first time you've felt this way, or are you familiar with this feeling?

Sandra: I know this feeling very well, I've had it many times in my life.

Therapist: OK, then realize that what you're feeling now is old pain; this is Little Sandra. Now I want to ask you to fast forward in the image. Go to that moment when you're handling the situation quite well. What do you see now?

Sandra: ...Well, I take a few deep breaths, and then I say: '...I know you think it should be done differently, but this is a great way to dust. This is how I do it, and it works fine for me.' And then I continue with what I was doing.

Therapist: How do you feel now?

Sandra: (*Smiles a little.*) Yes, good, powerful, but calm, not as angry as I can sometimes be.

Therapist: And where do you feel that calm, powerful feeling in your body?

(*Sandra points to her chest.*)

Therapist: Put your hand on your chest for a moment and connect with that calm, powerful feeling. (*Sandra puts her hand on her chest.*) And concentrate on that feeling. Let it flow, so that this calm, powerful feeling flows through you completely...

(*Sandra sits up a little straighter and takes a few calm breaths in and out.*)

Therapist: And realize, Sandra, that what you are feeling now is the Healthy Adult side of you, the captain of your ship. How does that feel?

Sandra: (*Smiling.*) Yes, it feels good...

Therapist: Let's form an image of that healthy side. Can you zoom out for a moment, as if you were a camera looking at Sandra in this state of mind from a distance. Can you see her?

Sandra: ...Yes.

Therapist: Just look at her, there you see Big Sandra. Is she standing or sitting?

Sandra: She's standing, firmly, with both feet on the ground.

Therapist: And how can you tell that she is the Healthy Adult?

Sandra: The way she stands, but also the way she looks, so confident.

Therapist: What words would appear as subtitles for this Sandra?

Sandra: ...Confident ... I can handle this ... Yes, that...

Therapist: There she is, that's the Healthy Adult side of you. Maybe now is a good time to really step into her shoes again. Be her now, be that healthy, Big Sandra you just saw. And being her, enjoy the feeling of strength, of confidence ... And take that feeling with you, even when we calmly finish the exercise in a moment...

What if your client:

- ...says they have no image of their Healthy Adult?

  Actually, everyone has moments when their Healthy Adult side takes more control: the choice to leave a bad relationship, to go to university despite the temptation to go out, etc. If your client says they have no memories, it may be that they have too high expectations of what such memories should be. So be alert to inner critic modes that set high standards, and make suggestions based on normal, everyday experiences with the Healthy Adult.

Variations

You can expand the exercise further by asking your client to become aware, as the Healthy Adult, of the Vulnerable Child they encountered earlier in the memory. *Where is that little child? To your left, to your right, or on your lap?* You can ask them to focus their attention on that child for a moment and, in doing so, also focus their attention on all the feelings that arise when the schema is activated. Then ask them to look away again and concentrate on the experience as a Healthy Adult. In this way, you practice an important goal of therapy: learning to reconnect with the Healthy Adult when schemas are activated.

Chapter 48: Practicing Setting Boundaries

Objective

To learn that it is safe to set boundaries, and that this produces positive feelings.

Guidelines

Step 1: Rationale

Step 2: Client sets a boundary with rope

Step 3: Check: Is the boundary correctly positioned?

Step 4: Client adjusts where necessary

Step 5: Client formulates a message for themselves and for the other person

Step 6: Practice

Step 7: Reflection

Explanation of the guidelines

Step 1: Rationale

Explain to your client that you want to practice setting boundaries. Discuss which modes of your client find it difficult to set boundaries, and summarize why it is important to do so (as discussed in the earlier phases). By practicing this in therapy, your client can experience that they can set boundaries without being rejected, ignored or punished. Your client can also learn that they can experience a sense of power, healthy self-reliance/competence, peace and space when they set boundaries.

Step 2: Client sets a boundary with rope

Give your client a piece of rope, a long scarf or a strip of fleece, and ask them to use it to mark out their personal space. If your client feels they have a lot of personal space and freedom to set boundaries, the rope will form a large circle around them. If they feel they have little space to set boundaries, the rope will form a small circle around them.

Step 3: Check: Is the boundary correctly positioned?

Tell your client that you are going to walk slowly towards them, up to the boundary. As you walk towards them step by step, ask them how it feels (pay attention to body signals). Do they notice any changes as you get closer to their boundary? If your client feels uncomfortable before you reach the boundary, suggest that they may have created too little space for themselves. This is already an important insight, so let your client reflect on it: there is a side to your client that apparently acts modestly and takes up little space.

Step 4: Client adjusts where necessary

Invite your client to shift their boundary so that they have sufficient personal space. Repeat Steps 2 and 3 until they feel comfortable with the boundary.

Step 5: Client formulates a message for themselves and for the other person

Before your client practices expressing that boundary to another person, you want to activate your client's Healthy Adult (see Chapter 47: Visualizing the Healthy Adult). Activating the Healthy Adult can also be done by having your client formulate and write down a helpful, motivating message for themselves. For example: 'setting boundaries is healthy' or 'I am allowed to stand up for myself'. Make sure that the motivating message is an appropriate antidote to the schemas that are activated in situations where your client allows their boundaries to be crossed. In addition, work with your client to formulate a message that they can give to the other person who is approaching the boundary. Start this message with the word 'Stop'. For example: 'Stop, this is my boundary!', or: 'Stop, this is as far as you go!'

Fold a sheet of paper so that it can be placed as a sign at the boundary. On one side of the sign, your client writes the message for themselves (so that they can read it from their side of the boundary), and on the other side of the sign, they write the message for the other person (so that the person approaching the boundary can read it).

Step 6: Practice

Prepare your client to practice expressing their boundary. Walk slowly towards your client and ask them to say the message to you before you reach their boundary. Repeat this several times, asking them each time if they can say it a little louder or more convincingly. Compliment your client after each time and continue to coach them.

Step 7: Reflection

Ask how it felt to do the exercise. When did they feel most powerful? Where did they feel that in their body? Let your client reflect on this and draw a conclusion ('So, when you set boundaries with others, you feel a powerful and open feeling in your chest'). Explore with your client how they can evoke that feeling in their daily life and how they can use it to practice setting boundaries outside of the sessions.

Example

Mary: I just didn't dare say 'no' to my colleagues. I was afraid they would think I was exaggerating if I said I already had too much work.

Therapist: And who do you recognize in that, in not being able to say no …?

Mary: Yes, that's my Pleasing side.

Therapist: It's good that you recognize the pattern. But it's difficult to set boundaries, so today I want to do an exercise in which your Healthy Adult side can practice doing that.

Mary: OK.

Therapist: Come on, let's stand up. You can use this rope on the floor to mark out an area for yourself. (*Therapist gives Mary a long rope.*) That is your own personal space, where no one is allowed to enter.

Mary: (*Places the rope in a small circle around herself.*) Like this?

Therapist: Let's see. I'm going to walk very slowly towards you until I reach the rope. See what happens when I walk towards you. (*Therapist takes a few steps towards Mary.*) What do you notice?

Mary: This is OK. (*Therapist takes a few more steps towards the rope.*) Now I feel a little uneasy.

Therapist: (*Stops walking immediately and points to the rope.*) Could it be that you haven't marked out enough space for yourself? Perhaps your Pleasing side is also active here? See if you want to move the boundary a little, so that you have enough space and it feels OK when others walk up to that boundary.

Mary: (*Moves the rope a little further away.*) I think that's better. (*Therapist walks towards the rope again.*) Yes, that's good.

Therapist: OK, I have a sign here to mark the boundary. On one side of the sign, we're going to write an encouraging message that will help you to clearly communicate your boundaries to others. Last week, you told me about a situation where you said 'no' to your friend who wanted to call you late at night when you were very tired, remember? She reacted well when you suggested calling her the next day, and you were proud of that. Would you like to close your eyes for a moment and go back to that moment, to the pride you felt? Can you feel it now?

Mary: (*With eyes closed:*) Yes, I feel it here, on my chest.

Therapist: With this situation in mind, that feeling of pride in your chest: what do you believe about yourself and about setting boundaries? Are you allowed to do that?

Mary: Yes, it's good for me to set boundaries, because then I feel better.

Therapist: Great, that's a wonderful statement! Open your eyes and write that statement on the board. (*Mary writes the statement.*) And what should be written on the other side of the board? A message that the other person can see, so that they know that this is your boundary?

Mary: Um … Maybe something like, 'Will you respect my boundary?'

Therapist: Yes, good. Shall we make it a statement instead of a question? A question can elicit an answer you don't really want to hear. Someone might say, 'No, I don't want to'. But it's your boundary, so you're allowed to set it and enforce it.

Mary: Yes, that's true. So: 'Respect my boundary!'

Therapist: Perfect! Write it down, and shall we start with 'Stop!', so that it is clear that the other person really has to stop there? (*Mary writes it down and places the sign at the boundary.*) Very good. Now let's practice actually saying the boundary out loud. I will walk slowly towards you. Before I reach the boundary, stop me by saying: 'Stop! Respect my boundary!' And in the meantime, look at what is written on the sign for yourself: 'It is good for me to set boundaries, because then I feel better!'

Mary: (*Therapist walks slowly towards Mary. Mary says softly:*)
Stop. Respect my boundary.

Therapist: Very good! Let's do it again. Connect with that proud feeling in your chest. And now try to speak ten per cent louder, so that the message really gets through to me. (*This is repeated several times. Mary speaks the message louder and more powerfully each time.*) Fantastic! Well done! Let's sit down again.

Therapist: (*After general discussion of the exercise and consolidation of the positive, powerful feeling.*) We started today's session with the situation with your colleagues, where your Pleasing side had taken over. Now that we've done this exercise, what can you take from this to the next situation with your colleagues? Or perhaps you'd like to reconsider your commitment to take on that task?

What if your client:

- ...has a lot of trouble setting boundaries in Step 6?

  Try to time the exercise well: your client must already be aware of their pleasing pattern, and there must be agreement on the importance of setting boundaries. If your client still has a lot of trouble setting boundaries, you can discuss in advance what they can say. In fact, your client only needs to say the message out loud to the other person, and you can then encourage them to convey this message more powerfully.

- ...sets the boundary very far away at the start or in Step 3 and creates too much space for themselves?

  Ask whether their need for connection can still be sufficiently met if people have to stay so far away. Repeat Steps 2 and 3 until the boundary feels comfortable for your client and is realistic.

Variations

In a group setting, group members will notice that everyone has their own boundary and that these can differ. This is a good opportunity to emphasize that a boundary is personal and that no one can tell you what your boundary is, that you have the freedom to determine it based on your feelings. In a group setting, an important aspect of the exercise is learning to respect everyone's boundaries, even if they differ from your own.

Chapter 49: Evaluating Treatment with the Line Exercise

Objective

To promote a realistic view of progress in therapy, emphasizing (small) successes. There is also an opportunity to adjust goals where necessary and to set out concrete actions to take another step towards the final goal in the coming period.

Guidelines

Step 1: Introduction to the line
Step 2: Looking back at the start of therapy
Step 3: Placing learning experiences on the line
Step 4: Reflecting on progress so far
Step 5: Setting goals for the end of therapy
Step 6: Set out actions for the coming period

Explanation of the guidelines

Step 1: Introduction to the line

Tell your client that in this session you want to evaluate the therapy and their progress towards their goals. Lay a piece of string or clothesline on the floor and explain that this line symbolizes the therapy from start to finish. Mark the place (in time) where today's session is located. If you are halfway through the estimated number of sessions in the treatment plan, place a symbol representing today's session halfway along the line.

Step 2: Looking back at the start of therapy

Walk with your client to the beginning of the line and ask them to remember how they were when they started therapy. What bothered them most at the time? What did they need help with? Let your client empathize with that version of themselves for a moment, possibly with their eyes closed. How did they feel then? Discuss the goals you set at the time, perhaps using the treatment plan, and write them down on the whiteboard if necessary.

Step 3: Placing learning experiences on the line

Ask your client what learning experiences they have gained during therapy. What have you been working on? Which modes and schemas have already changed during therapy? Use the mode model as a guide. For each change or learning experience your client mentions, choose a symbol (e.g., from material used earlier in therapy) or write a short note on a piece of paper, which you place on the line.

Step 4: Reflecting on progress so far

Walk with your client to the point on the line where the current session is. Together with your client, look back at the starting point and at all the symbols/notes that are now on the line. What does your client experience when they look at what they have already learned and possibly changed? Let your client reflect on this experience, and reinforce every learning experience and change, no matter how small. If there are also goals or modes where no learning experiences or changes have yet occurred, discuss whether the goals need to be adjusted or what is needed to pay more attention to them in the coming period.

Step 5: Setting goals for the end of therapy

Then walk with your client to the end of the line to determine what the (possibly adjusted) final goals are. Let your client reflect on this for a moment (perhaps with their eyes closed) and imagine the moment when the therapy is over and the goals have been achieved. How will your client feel then?

Step 6: Set out actions for the coming period

Walk back to the point on the line representing today's session. What needs to happen in the coming period to achieve those goals? You can discuss this in broad terms for a longer period, but you can also make it more specific: What concrete steps can your client take in the coming week to get one step closer to their goal?

Example

Therapist: We're about halfway through the therapy. That seems like a good moment to look back at what we've done, what insights you've already gained and what we can work towards and focus on in the coming period.

Tim: OK. I don't think much has changed yet, because I'm still having problems with my mother.

Therapist: OK, let's take a look. I've drawn a line here that runs from the beginning of therapy (*points to one end of the line*) to the end of it (*points to the other end of the line*). Because we're halfway through, we're now in the middle. This stone symbolizes today's session. (*Therapist places stone in the middle of the line.*) Now let's go back to the beginning of therapy. (*Tim and therapist walk to the beginning of the line.*) Do you remember the first time you came here? How did you feel then?

Tim: Well, I didn't feel like it at all. My mother and the youth probation officer kept saying I had to go, but I didn't want to.

Therapist: Yes, I remember that very well. At that time, I was mostly talking to your 'I don't care' side.

Tim: (*Laughs.*) Yes, that's right.

Therapist: That part of you still comes out sometimes in our sessions, doesn't it? But something has changed, right?

Tim: Yes, back then it was just automatic. Now, I'm more aware of when I'm acting angry or grumpy and don't feel like doing anything. Especially when you want to talk endlessly or do an exercise.

Therapist: Yes, you now know that that side of you wants to protect you from difficult feelings, which arise, for example, when we talk about something or do an exercise. I think it's great that you've already noticed that yourself, that you recognize it in those moments.

Tim: But I can't always do anything about it. I can't just put it aside. Sometimes I can, but often I can't.

Therapist: That's right, and it's perfectly fine. The fact that you recognize it now is very important, because without that recognition, you certainly won't be able to put it aside. So, Step 1 has already been taken! Let's mark that down. Shall we put the mode card from your 'I don't care' side on the line? I'll write a note on it: 'I can recognize this!' (*Therapist places mode card with note on the line.*) What else have we been working on recently?

Tim: Um … we talked about the arguments with my mother.

Therapist: Indeed! (*Therapist discusses with Tim what they have already discovered about this – for example, which modes of Tim and his mother can clash and that they have already tried to interact with each other in a different way. This is also written down and placed on the line with mode cards. They continue in this way until various learning experiences and changes have been presented on the line.*)

Therapist: (*Walks with Tim to the middle of the line, near the stone representing the current session.*) You said at the beginning that not much has changed yet, but look at everything we've done! You've already gained a lot of insights, and you've managed to change a few things! How does that feel when you look at it now?

Tim: Yes, it's more than I thought, definitely.

Therapist: How does that make you feel?

Tim: It feels good.

Therapist: Let's walk to the end of the line, as if we were at the end of the therapy. (*Therapist and Tim stand at the end of the line.*) Imagine that we're there, that you've finished the therapy. What's changed?

Tim: I won't argue with my mother as much anymore. At least we won't shout at each other anymore and I won't see black spots when I'm angry.

Therapist: Can you pause for a moment and reflect on that? Close your eyes for a moment. Imagine you're there: you have more control over yourself when you're angry, and you and your mother generally treat each other calmly and respectfully … How does that feel?

Tim: Yes, that feels really good. That would make a big difference.

Therapist: Yes, it would. Let's go back to where we are now in therapy and see how we can get a step closer to that goal, that nice feeling you can experience. What could you do in the coming week to get a little closer to that – when it comes to dealing with your anger, for example?

Tim: Um … I was thinking of buying that punching bag, so that every time I get angry, I can hit it for a while, so that it doesn't build up so much.

(*The therapist and Tim discuss this further and also look at the broader context of what they want to focus on in therapy in the coming period. At the end of the session, the therapist asks Tim how he felt about evaluating the therapy using the line. It helped him to see that things have changed more than he realized. He takes a photo of the line to show his mother at home.*)

What if your client:

- ...finds that nothing has changed yet in Step 3?

  By talking about the learning experiences or insights your client has gained during the therapy sessions so far, it usually becomes clear that something has indeed been achieved. You can, of course, also mention the changes you see in your client. These changes are often more visible to the therapist than to your client. Mention the small changes too, because they also make an important contribution to your client's sense of increased competence. For example, your client may already be able to recognize their inner critic mode, even if they are not yet able to dismiss it. Evaluate each goal or mode in the mode model to bring some structure to this.

Variations

Various materials can be used to indicate learning experiences. If the learning experiences, insights or changes are written on notes, you can collect these notes afterwards and make a chain out of them or attach them to a key ring so that your client can keep them and read them again at home. In group therapy, you can use to map out shared learning experiences and changes and identify what will be needed in the coming period.

Chapter 50: Mode Meeting

Objective

To learn to view a problem situation from all modes and then respond to it using the three steps of the Healthy Adult.

Guidelines

Step 1: Define the problem or dilemma

Step 2: Rationale

Step 3: Let each mode speak from an extra chair

Step 4: Connect with the Healthy Adult

Step 5: From their Healthy Adult:

- a: ...your client shows compassion for themselves
- b: ...your client offers themselves cognitive restructuring
- c: ...your client gives advice for behavioural change

Step 6: Reflection and homework

Explanation of the guidelines

Step 1: Define the problem or dilemma

Try to recognize the different modes when your client presents a problem or dilemma. Indicate that you understand that they are facing a problem and that different sides of them have different opinions about it. You can already link these different modes to specific places in the room with gestures, where you will later place chairs.

Step 2: Rationale

Explain to your client that you want to do an exercise in which all the sides of them that have something to do with this problem or have an opinion about it are given a voice. You will organize a meeting in which each mode is allowed to have its say. Your client will then, from their Healthy Adult, be the chair of the meeting, who has the final say and is authorized to make decisions. Explain that this is a way to train yourself to look at a problem from different sides, but ultimately decide for yourself what you really need and how you are going to make sure you get it.

Step 3: Let each mode speak from an extra chair

Add an extra chair each time to allow a new mode that has something to do with the problem or has an opinion about it to speak. You can make an inventory of all modes in advance and set up the required number of chairs (stick notes or mode cards on them so you know who sits where) or do this as you go along. In any case, make sure that the Vulnerable Child always gets a chair, because it must always be heard and seen. Let your client in each other chair respond (briefly) to the problem from the relevant mode.

Step 4: Connect with the Healthy Adult

Once all modes have had their say, ask your client to return to their original chair. Leave all the other chairs around them and, if necessary, briefly repeat what the modes think of the problem or how they think your client should deal with it. Tell your client that now, as chair of the meeting, they can start to consider about what they actually think about it. Ask them to connect with their Healthy Adult (see also Chapter 47: Visualizing the Healthy Adult).

Step 5: From their Healthy Adult:

a: ...your client shows compassion for themselves

First, let your client show compassion for themselves and the problem. You can make this extra vivid by having your client address the chair of the Vulnerable Child, on which you may place a mode card or symbol for this mode. Help your client to acknowledge that this is a difficult problem, that it is logical that the Vulnerable Child does not know what to do about it, and that the problem (and the comments from all the other chairs) evokes all kinds of emotions that your client is familiar with, not only in the present, but probably also from the past.

b: ...offer your client cognitive restructuring

Then ask your client to say aloud which statements or arguments from the different modes they find valid and appropriate, and which they do not. In this middle phase, your client will already be able to do this to some extent, but support them where necessary and help them to explain this. Then ask them to focus on the modes on the chairs that made these statements or arguments.

c: ...give your client advice for behavioural change

Finally, help your client to formulate an appropriate conclusion to the meeting. Given the problem and the needs and feelings of the Vulnerable Child, what is now needed to meet those needs in a realistic way? How does your client want to deal with this problem?

Step 6: Reflection and homework

Ask your client how they experienced the exercise. What was it like to let all modes have their say and then, from their Healthy Adult, look at themselves with compassion, reframe unrealistic thoughts and form a conclusion about how to deal with it now? Let your client reflect on how this makes them feel, that they are taking control of all other modes in a healthy way and then making a decision. Then discuss what they need from you or others in order to be able to carry out this decision. Make sure this is realistic and achievable, so that your client has a successful experience.

Example

Therapist: So, you're facing a problem *(points to a spot on the floor)*. You realize that you no longer enjoy your work, and you'd like to do something completely different in another sector. But now you've been offered a new role at your current workplace and you don't know what to do. I just heard a few people here who already have an opinion on this, and I'm sure there are others who have something to say.

Mary: Yes, it's such chaos in my head...

Therapist: I suggest holding a meeting with all those sides of you. Because they're all giving their opinions right now, which is confusing you. Let's give them a chance to speak one by one. And then, as the chair of the meeting, you can use your Healthy Adult side to see what YOU really think, what you really need and how you want to deal with this problem.

Mary: OK.

Therapist: Have you already recognized sides of yourself that say something about this problem or how you should deal with it?

Mary: Yes, the Strict side, I think, and the Hider. And the Yes-man, that's there too.

Therapist: Indeed. And then we also have Little Mary, who feels all kinds of things about this. (*The therapist fetches extra chairs and places them in a circle with mode cards on them.*) Is there one of your sides that is shouting the loudest about what you should do when it comes to this problem?

Mary: Yes, I think the Hider.

Therapist: Shall we let Mary speak first? Go and sit on the Hider's chair. (*Mary sits on that chair.*) Now be the Hider. Hello Hider, tell us what you think about Mary's problem and how she should deal with it.

Mary: (*In the role of the Hider:*) Well, she'd better not do anything about it. Then she can't do anything wrong. Just don't make a decision. Maybe don't go to work at all, then she won't be confronted with it. Otherwise, it will only make her panic.

Therapist: OK, clear. Mary, would you now like to leave the Hider on that chair and sit on the next chair?

Mary: (*Sits down on the chair representing her Strict side and immediately starts talking.*) Yes, I think I do have to make a decision, and right now.

Therapist: Aha, as the Strict side, you think that Mary should decide right now.

Mary: Yes, because she's not the youngest anymore. She needs to take action right now and figure everything out; she needs to know now.

Therapist: OK, that's a clear opinion, Strict side. (*Mary then takes a seat in the chair of the Yes-man, who believes that Mary should accept the job offered by her current employer, because otherwise she will disappoint her colleagues and they may no longer like her. After that, in the chair of Little Mary, she reflects at length on the feelings that the problem and the statements and advice of all the modes evoke in her.*)

Therapist: Mary, would you like to sit back down in your own chair, where you started the session? We've now heard from all your different sides, and they all give different advice, so I can imagine that this is confusing you. But let's first look at what Little Mary feels.

(*The therapist helps Mary go through the three steps of the Healthy Adult, see also Chapter 52: Chairwork with the Three Chairs of the Healthy Adult. At the end of the exercise, Mary decides to give herself the next six months to calmly explore what she would like to do. In the meantime, she wants to discuss with her employer whether she could possibly try out the task on a temporary basis.*)

What if your client:

- ...finds it difficult to empathize with all the different modes or does not know what they say or think about the problem?

  In this middle phase, you can expect your client to recognize their different modes and to have practiced sufficiently with 'getting into the skin' of their different modes in previous chairwork. However, your client may become somewhat confused by the many chairs when using this technique. Stick notes or place mode cards on the chairs to make it clear which mode is sitting where, and help your client empathize with the mode when they sit in that chair (for example: '*Which posture fits this mode again? Just adopt that one.*').

Variations

You can also do this exercise in the final phase, where your client can practice actively and directly negotiating with the coping modes, rejecting or ignoring unrealistic statements from inner critic modes, and setting appropriate limits for, for example, undisciplined, impulsive or transgressive Angry Child modes.

When working with young clients or clients with mild intellectual disabilities, the multitude of chairs can cause confusion. In that case, involve fewer modes in the exercise and summarize briefly at regular intervals. You can also choose to work through the modes one by one. So, after your client has given their opinion on the problem from an extra chair, ask them to return to their original chair and form an opinion from their Healthy Adult side about what the dysfunctional mode said about the problem.

If you do this exercise in a group, other group members can step into the shoes of your client's different modes and represent them on the different chairs. A real meeting can then be played out, with your client in the role of Healthy Adult leading the entire meeting and maintaining control. Of course, you ensure that the group members play the modes in such a way that your client's Healthy Adult is stimulated and slightly challenged, but not overwhelmed.

Chapter 51: Cognitive Behavioural Therapy Techniques

Objective

The aim of cognitive behavioural therapy (CBT) techniques is to achieve cognitive restructuring and structural behavioural change. These techniques can be used from the initial phase of treatment, but they are even more effective in the middle and final phases. Cognitive restructuring and interventions aimed at behavioural change are incorporated into most of the techniques described in this book, and some chapters are devoted entirely to a cognitive technique. In this chapter, you will find guidelines for various other techniques that you can use to further strengthen your client's Healthy Adult.

Historical test

Because your client sees things through the lens of their negative schemas (e.g., 'I can't do anything') or beliefs (e.g., 'If I show emotion, people will laugh at me'), they tend to interpret events in a way that fits those schemas or beliefs. They will often pay more attention to and better remember events that prove a schema or belief than one that proves the opposite. With the historical test, you let your client focus on events that contradict their negative schemas or thoughts:

1. Formulate the negative schema or negative belief.
2. Make a list of relevant previous experiences (*Has nothing ever worked out for you in your life?, Have you ever cried and no one laughed?*).
3. Ask follow-up questions: *What kind of situations were they, and how often did they occur?* If necessary, look up information with your client (e.g., old school reports) and ask them to inquire with others.
4. Analyse the data and weigh up the evidence.
5. Formulate an alternative, helpful thought.

Example

Therapist: Have you ever cried and no one laughed?

Tim: I never cry when anyone is around. I stopped doing that a long time ago.

Therapist: When was the last time?

Tim: When I was about eight, when my dog died. My parents were there. My father laughed at me; he said I shouldn't make such a fuss.

Therapist: And your mother, did she laugh too?

Tim: No, she was sad, just like me. She hugged me.

Therapist: What does that mean for your assumption that you'll be laughed at if you show your emotions?

Tim: Maybe it was mainly my father who always laughed when that happened.

Therapist: Has it ever happened since then that you became sad or had tears in your eyes when someone other than your father was present?

Tim: Yes, I have. When I broke my arm last year, I really did have tears in my eyes.

Therapist: Who was there?

Tim: A few friends and people who happened to be nearby.

Therapist: And how did they react? Did they laugh at you?

Tim: No, they helped me.

Socratic dialogue

The starting point of Socratic dialogue, based on Socrates' conversational approach, is that your client already has the answers and that you ask questions to help them find those answers. So, don't give answers, but use your questions to help your client examine whether their assumptions are realistic:

1. **Identify the client's assumption.**
2. **Reason logically: if what the client assumes is true, then … [they will have evidence for this/does this also apply to others/do they already have experience with this, etc.].**
3. **Ask questions about this (*What are those experiences / indications?*). Listen carefully to your client's answer and try to identify the assumption.**

Repeat Steps 2 and 3 until it is clear whether the original assumption is confirmed or whether it can be adjusted to a different, more realistic conclusion.

Example

Therapist: You just said that you no longer feel like continuing with the therapy. I wonder: what makes that feeling so strong today?

Tim: It's pointless anyway.

Therapist: You sound very certain. What do you base that on, do you think?

Tim: Nothing is changing.

Therapist: What makes you think nothing is changing?

Tim: I'm still arguing with my mother.

Therapist: So, those arguments continue. And I can imagine that weighs heavily on you. But I'm not so sure … does that automatically mean that nothing has changed at all?

Tim: Well … maybe not absolutely nothing. But the arguments with my mother were the most important thing.

Therapist: Interesting. So, it seems to be different than we thought at first. Then it seemed simple: therapy is pointless because nothing changes. But now we know: things may have changed, but the arguments with your mother haven't. And those arguments are the most important thing for you. What makes them so important?

Tim: Well, they bother me the most.

Therapist: So, that one thing – the arguments with your mother and the distress they cause you – actually makes the difference in how meaningful all this feels?

Tim: Yes, I think so.

Therapist: And I'm curious: if one thing hasn't changed yet, can that make the rest feel pointless too?

Tim: Yes, that's how it feels.

Therapist: Would you say that to someone else? If therapy does produce results, but one thing doesn't change, even though it's an important issue, does that make the whole therapy pointless?

Tim: Hm...maybe not.

Therapist: So, it's not as black and white as you first thought. Something has changed, just not that difficult part yet – but that doesn't mean the whole therapy is pointless. Is that about right?

Tim: Yes ... that's about right.

Motivational interviewing

Whereas Socratic dialogue mainly involves exploring together how the client feels about something and asking critical questions with the aim of helping the client to think realistically, motivational interviewing (Miller and Rollnick, 2023) guides your client towards intrinsic motivation for behavioural change:

1. Connect with your client's perception of reality (summarize what they say, listen reflectively).
2. Explore ambivalences and elicit change talk (*What makes you think about change?, How important is change to you on a scale of 0–10, and why not a lower score?*).
3. Deepen change language (ask follow-up questions, summarize and reflect in a way that emphasizes arguments for change).
4. Work towards concrete steps towards change.

Example

Therapist: I just heard you say that you sleep better when you've been smoking weed, but also that you wake up feeling less rested. That sounds contradictory to me; how do you see it?

Tim: I fall asleep more easily, but then I have a kind of after-effect the next day.

Therapist: How does that feel?

Tim: I feel a bit sluggish and I can't concentrate very well.

Therapist: That seems difficult, because I know you already find it hard to focus at school. On a scale of 0–10, how important is it for you to have more energy during the day, so that you can concentrate better?

Tim: Um ... a 7, I think.

Therapist: Why not 3 or 4?

Tim: Because I notice that I can't keep up with the work at school, and I'm tired of feeling so worn out.

Therapist: What could be a small, achievable first step towards having more energy during the day?

Tim: Maybe not smoking weed one evening to see if that makes a difference. But I'm afraid I won't be able to sleep, and then it won't make any sense.

Therapist: If we could find other ways to help you fall asleep, would you be willing to try them?

Tim: Yes, if there are ways to help me sleep then I could try not smoking weed one evening.

Exposure

Clients tend to avoid situations that cause anxiety or only endure them with the help of safety behaviours. The aim of exposure is to break through this avoidance or safety behaviour by exposing your client, with their explicit consent, to a conditioned stimulus (in the absence of the unconditioned stimulus) that causes anxiety. Discuss the rationale for exposure carefully with the client so that they understand how it can help them: by exposing them to situations that make them anxious, they learn that these situations are not dangerous in themselves (*inhibitory learning*) and that their anxious expectations do not come true (*expectancy violation*), allowing them to adjust their expectations (*expectancy change*). They will also notice that their fear diminishes through habituation and they gain self-confidence by performing the exercises (*self-efficacy*). Recent research shows that all these factors can explain the effects of exposure (Kooistra et al., 2025; Pittig et al., 2022; Treanor et al., 2025). Guidelines for performing exposure are:

1. Discuss the rationale.
2. Identify the trigger situations and the most feared outcome.
3. Ask about the probability of the feared outcome.
4. Devise exercises in which the client is exposed to the conditioned stimulus. Vary stimuli and context so that your client can retrieve the new information later and generalize it to different contexts.
5. Consolidate the newly acquired learning experience (*Did your expectations come true?*, *What did you learn?*).

Example

Tim is very triggered by loud voices (especially male voices) or shouting and expects that he will not be able to tolerate this and that he will run away or become aggressive. After explaining the rationale, an exposure plan is drawn up with Tim's consent, consisting of various exercises (in random order):

- listening to audio recordings of women shouting in the therapy room;
- listening to audio recordings of men shouting in the therapy room;
- going to the market where market traders are shouting;
- watching and listening to a video in the therapy room in which men are shouting at each other;
- watching and listening to a man shouting at him in the therapy room with virtual reality (VR) glasses;
- walking around the canteen of the mental health institution while male colleagues of the therapist shout (staged);
- walking around late at night in an entertainment district accompanied by an uncle who has been informed about the exercise.

Behavioural experiment

A behavioural experiment allows your client to test whether their dysfunctional belief is true. It helps if they can already view the mode that belief has with some distance or if there is already some ambivalence about the credibility of the belief. That is why behavioural experiments are used from the middle phase onwards and in the final phase of treatment. Set up an experiment together and act like a true researcher:

1. Identify the negative belief.
2. Describe as concretely as possible which outcome proves that the belief is correct and which outcome proves that the belief is incorrect.
3. Set up an experiment whose outcome can only coincide with one of these two descriptions.
4. Have your client carry out the behavioural experiment.
5. Draw your conclusion and formulate an alternative, helpful thought.

You can also gradually increase the difficulty level of behavioural experiments.

Example

Middle phase of therapy: Tim

Hypothesis: If I say I'm nervous about something, someone will laugh at me.

Experiment: I'm going to tell my mentor at school in a short conversation that I'm a little nervous about the test.

Outcome 1: Mentor laughs and says I shouldn't be so silly.

Outcome 2: Mentor reacts normally and perhaps even supportively.

Final phase of therapy: Tim

Hypothesis: My friends think I'm weak when I show that something bothers me.

Experiment: This afternoon, while playing football, I'm going to say that I get annoyed when I miss a ball, that it frustrates me.

Outcome 1: My friends laugh at me or tell me not to be so dramatic.

Outcome 2: My friends react neutrally or say something about their own frustration.

Final Phase

In the final phase, the client gradually becomes more able to access and embody their Healthy Adult. You will increasingly take a coaching role from the sidelines, giving the client ample space to meet their own emotional needs and address problems independently. At the same time, you prepare the client for life after therapy, in which they continue on their own. You prepare your client for future schema-activating situations and help them to deal with these in an appropriate manner. You work towards saying goodbye to you and to the therapy itself. Be aware that this can evoke emotions and activate schemas. On the following pages, you will find guidelines for methods and techniques you can use to prepare your client's Healthy Adult for life after completing therapy.

Chapter 52: Chairwork with the Three Chairs of the Healthy Adult

Objective

To strengthen your client's Healthy Adult by practicing the three steps: self-compassion, cognitive restructuring and behavioural modification.

Guidelines

Step 1: Explore the problem situation

Step 2: Rational for the exercise and place three chairs

Step 3: Place client in first chair – Self-compassion

Step 4: Place client in second chair – Cognitive restructuring

Step 5: Place client in third chair – Behaviour modification

Step 6: Client receives messages in the original therapy chair

Explanation of the guidelines

Step 1: Explore the problem situation

The exercise can be used to explore a situation that has recently occurred or one that is expected to arise in the near future. Identify the schema-activating triggers, the emotional responses of the child modes, any negative self-reflections of the inner critic mode and any signals from the coping modes. During the exploration, give each of these modes its own place in the room, possibly with the help of materials such as mode cards.

Step 2: Rational for the exercise and place three chairs

Explain that you want to strengthen the Healthy Adult. You may have already explained the three steps of the Healthy Adult, but if not, do so now. A healthy way of dealing with schema-activating situations is to remain kind to yourself (self-compassion), then think calmly, fighting critical aspects and negotiating with coping modes (cognitive restructuring), and finally determining your response and taking action (behavioural modification). Place three chairs opposite your client and explain that each chair now represents one of these steps. In the exercise, you will coach your client in practicing these three steps.

Step 3: Place client in first chair – Self-compassion

In this chair, you ask your client to connect with their Healthy Adult. Your client can use the visualization exercise (see Chapter 47: Visualizing the Healthy Adult) to do this. Next, ask your client to express self-compassion aloud for the emotional responses in the problem situation. Make sure that your client not only shows understanding for the emotional reactions to the current trigger, but also for the fact that they are feeling old pain as well. Ask your client how it feels to have self-compassion, because awareness of this experience helps to consolidate it.

Step 4: Place client in second chair – Cognitive restructuring

In the second chair, invite your client to come up with arguments against the inner critic mode and arguments as to why the coping mode is not the best way to handle the situation. Ask your client to voice these arguments aloud against these critical and coping modes. Again, invite your client to be aware of how it feels to independently combat the inner critic mode and negotiate with the coping modes.

Step 5: Place client in third chair – Behaviour modification

In the third chair, you and your client discuss what healthy behavioural instructions could be to deal with the problem situation. Think of very practical things such as: *'don't react immediately, but let it sink in first'* or *'look away from the schema-activating trigger to give yourself a chance to think calmly'*. Try to get your client to come up with behavioural instructions that match their relevant emotional needs. Again, ask your client to say these instructions out loud, as a form of self-talk (*'What you need to do now is first take a few deep breaths and look away, and then …'*). Finally, ask your client to consciously experience what it is like to give such healthy behavioural instructions.

Step 6: Client receives messages in the original therapy chair

Optionally, you can now have your client sit back down in the original chair and empathize with the discussed schema-activating situation again. The therapist repeats the messages from the three different chairs and asks your client how they feel about receiving these messages now.

Example

Therapist: So that phone call from your mother brought up all sorts of feelings for you (*talking about the situational context, the therapist gestures towards a spot on the floor*). You said you were angry and sad because your plans with your friend couldn't go ahead (*talking about the emotional response, the therapist gestures towards Mary's stomach*). But then all kinds of thoughts came to mind, such as: 'If I say I can't make it now, they'll feel bad and have such a problem, and it will be my fault.' Is that right? (*Therapist holds up the inner critic mode card.*)

Mary: Yes, they are old, and they already have such a hard time, so it's only a small effort for me to help them, isn't it?

Therapist: Exactly, your inner critic was so convincing that you decided to help. (*Mary nods.*) Shall we use this situation to get some practice with using your Healthy Adult side? (*Mary nods.*)

Therapist: For the exercise, I first want to get three chairs (*places three chairs opposite Mary*) to practice the different steps you can take as a Healthy Adult. First of all, you can remain kind to yourself; that's especially important in difficult situations like this. You're going to practice that on the first chair. The second task you have as a Healthy Adult is to think calmly for a moment – for example, about whether that inner critic is giving you the reaction you really need. You'll practice this on the second chair. And in the third chair, you'll consider what is best to do in such a situation. Because no matter how kind you remain to yourself and how calm and reasonable you remain in your thinking, ultimately you do need to do something about your parents' request. Shall we give it a try?

(*Mary nods.*)

Therapist: Good, sit down on that first chair. (*Mary does so.*) First, make contact with the Healthy Adult side of yourself on this chair. Close your eyes to recall that image of your Healthy Adult side.

Mary: (*With her eyes closed:*) Then I see myself standing there again, on that mountain during the holiday, feeling so free, with the wind in my hair. With the thought that this is my life, and I can choose for myself what I do and don't want.

(*Mary smiles.*)

Therapist: I can hear her again, that healthy side of you, that Mary who is free and makes her own choices. Stay in touch with her. Now open your eyes, and let's look back together at what Mary said on that chair over there. (*Gestures towards the original chair.*) How did Mary feel when her mother asked her to come and help?

Mary: Sad, angry...

Therapist: Exactly, and I think you and I can understand why she felt all those things, can't we? (*Mary nods.*) Can you express that understanding out loud? Can you say to her: 'Of course you feel sad and angry, and also a little guilty, because ...' Tell her.

Mary: (*Turns to the empty chair and says in a soft voice:*) 'Of course you feel sad and angry, because you were really looking forward to that appointment with Chantal, and yes, it's not nice when that can't happen.

Therapist: And could you perhaps also explain why those are understandable feelings, given everything Mary has been through in the past?

Mary: Yes ... 'Of course, you feel sad and angry, because very often something got in the way when you wanted something for yourself...'

Therapist: Very good! How do you feel now that you've said that?

Mary: Yes, it feels soft, here in my chest.

Therapist: You're doing very well. Go and sit on that second chair, because you still have a task as a Healthy Adult. (*Mary sits down on the second chair.*) Sit on this chair and think calmly about that inner critic that came out when Mary felt so sad and angry. What did it say again? (*Therapist holds up the inner critic mode card.*)

Mary: That I really couldn't refuse, that it's my fault they feel bad...

Therapist: Let's think about this calmly for a moment: What do we actually think about this? Are you not allowed to refuse a request? Would you say the same thing to your friend, that she shouldn't refuse?

Mary: ...Well, no, I would tell her that she's allowed to do something for herself and that you're also allowed to say no when asked a question.

Therapist: Exactly, so what do we actually think about the inner critic saying that you're not allowed to refuse?

Mary: Well, that's not really right ... I actually think that's stupid.

Therapist: So, what do you want to do about that inner critic?

Mary: It has to stop.

Therapist: Can you say that again, to that inner critic, but a little louder this time?

Mary: (*In a slightly louder voice:*) You have to stop!

Therapist: Great! What do you want to do with the inner critic, throw it away? (*Mary laughs, picks up the card and throws it away.*) Great! How does it feel to go against it like that?

Mary: Good! Powerful, I could feel it all in my shoulders and arms.

Therapist: Very good! There is one more step you have to take as a Healthy Adult. Now sit down in the third chair. (*Mary moves.*) Here you can think about what Mary could do best in such a situation. What would you advise Mary?

Mary: ...Well, my friend always says that I shouldn't respond immediately to such a question.

Therapist: What great advice! Like, 'Well, I'll think about it and call you back in a moment'?

Mary: Yes, something like that.

(The therapist helps Mary realize that she can reflect on her own needs and call her friend to ask her to help her think things through. He asks Mary to say this out loud to the original empty chair and finally asks her to sit back down in that original chair, whereupon he repeats all the messages from her Healthy Adult.)

What if your client:

- **...is unable to take one or more steps?**

  If your client is doing this exercise for the first time, it is often also a measuring moment: Which of the three steps need further practice? With that knowledge, you can focus on the step that still needs practice in the following sessions. In the session itself, you can coach more actively.

Variations

In a group setting, other group members can participate by portraying the Healthy Adult from the different chairs and thus practicing the relevant step themselves. At a later stage of the treatment, instead of three chairs, you can use one extra chair for the Healthy Adult. An even later step is for your client to practice the three steps of the Healthy Adult within themselves.

Chapter 53: Future-Oriented Imagery

Objective

To prepare your client for expected schema-activating situations in the future. Your client can practice recognizing schema activation, connecting with the Healthy Adult and dealing with the evoked feelings and the situational context in a healthy way.

Guidelines

Step 1: Preliminary discussion

Step 2: Visualizing the Healthy Adult

Step 3: Visualizing a future problem scenario

Step 4: Connecting with the Healthy Adult

Step 5: Rescripting future problem situations

a: Rescripting from a first-person perspective

b: Rescripting from an observer's perspective

Step 6: Debriefing and homework

Explanation of the guidelines

Step 1: Preliminary discussion

Explain that visualizing healthy behaviour in future situations contributes to actually being able to perform that behaviour in those situations. Preparing for this exercise takes some time, because a number of choices have to be made in advance:

- Which problem situation are you going to use?
- How difficult will you make the situation?

- What exactly will your client be practicing: awareness of schema activation, self-compassion, realistic thinking, actual behavioural change or a combination of these options?

Step 2: Visualizing the Healthy Adult

The exercise begins with visualizing the Healthy Adult, so that later in the exercise, when the schema is activated, your client can more easily connect with that side of themselves. (see Chapter 47: Visualizing the Healthy Adult).

Step 3: Visualizing a future problem scenario

Ask your client to visualize the most difficult part of the problem situation from a first-person perspective: *'Now, gently bring to mind an image of such a difficult situation. It hasn't happened yet, but you know these situations from the past. What might it look like if you were to … [receive criticism] again?'* Let your client really empathize with the problem situation, so that the schemas are activated.

Step 4: Connecting with the Healthy Adult

The best time to let your client connect with their Healthy Adult is when there is increased emotional arousal (schema activation) or at the pre-identified most difficult moment. Ask your client to pause the image and connect with the Healthy Adult.

Step 5: Rescripting future problem situations

Now, ask your client to apply what has been discussed beforehand (self-compassion, realistic thinking, behavioural change or a combination of these). Do this rescripting twice: once from the first-person perspective and then again from the observer perspective. Research has shown that the observer perspective in particular seems to be linked to behavioural change ('I can see myself doing it') (Libby et al, 2007; Landkroon et al, 2022).

a: Rescripting from a first-person perspective

Ask your client to apply the agreed skills from the perspective of the Healthy Adult. Keep asking about the experience: *How does it feel to say / do this?, Where do you feel that in your body?* Questions like these, help to consolidate the experience.

b: Rescripting from an observer's perspective

When the rescripting is complete, ask your client to rewind the image to the beginning of the rescripting. Now ask your client to zoom out and describe the rescripting as if they were a fly on the wall. Ask your client to not only observe carefully whether the schema activation is visible, but also to describe in detail how the Healthy Adult then handles that schema activation and the situation well.

Step 6: Debriefing and homework

In the debriefing, you again pay explicit attention to the experience of handling this problem situation well as a Healthy Adult. The awareness of that experience, the repetition in the debriefing and the further repetition in the form of homework (in which your client visualizes the rescripting again) contribute to the further consolidation of these skills.

Example

Therapist: You've worked very hard, Sandra, and I think we both agree that a lot has already changed. But understandably, there are still situations that can affect you quite deeply. I'd like to practice with you how you can best handle such situations in the future. What situations do you think are still difficult for you?

Sandra: ...Well, I still find it very difficult when people criticize me.

Therapist: It's good that you're aware of that. What kind of difficult situations involving criticism are you still likely to encounter?

Sandra: Well, I still clean for that woman who comments all the time, so that's bound to happen again.

Therapist: Today, let's use an imagination exercise to explore how you, as a Healthy Adult, can deal with that situation. You told me that you tend to ignore her criticism at first, but that you often get angry and snap at her. How would you like to handle it in the future? And that's a question for you as a Healthy Adult, the captain of your ship.

Sandra: ...Well, that reminds me of what you always say, that you should take a moment to calm down and then tell the other person that you find something annoying, but mainly by pointing out their behaviour and how it makes you feel. And that it's better to look away when you do that, because I can stay calmer if I don't have to see her disparaging look all the time.

Therapist: You already have some very clear and wonderful ideas about what you'd like to achieve. Let's get started with that. Close your eyes and connect with your Healthy Adult ... Tell me how you do that.

Sandra: ...Well, I always sit up a little straighter (*sits up straighter*) and then I breathe in and out calmly a few times ... And then I always think of my friend Debbie, somehow that makes me feel calmer, more powerful.

Therapist: Good, now let that image fade away ... Now think about cleaning that woman's living room and the comments she might make ... It may not have happened yet, but when it comes to that criticism, what do you see in front of you now?

Sandra: ...Well, it always happens when I'm busy in the living room; she sits there on that chair and follows everything I do, which I find annoying.

Therapist: So, you see her sitting in the living room now? Let it play out until the moment she criticizes what you're doing...

Sandra: I'm dusting, near the television, and I'm doing it carefully because I know she's watching everything. But then suddenly I hear her voice behind me, telling me to wrap the duster around a ruler and dust under the television as well.

Therapist: And how does her voice sound?

Sandra: As if she's telling me off...

Therapist: What do you feel when you listen to her voice now?

Sandra: Irritated, I feel tense (*points to her chest*).

Therapist: What do you want to say or do?

Sandra: That she should stop commenting all the time! She's just so compulsive! Of course, I don't say that, but I do feel that I'm really angry.

Therapist: OK, so you notice that you're being affected and that your angry side wants to take over. Take a moment to bring back the Healthy Adult... (*Sandra sits up a little straighter and takes a few deep breaths.*)

Sandra: Yes, I feel a bit calmer, more powerful.

Therapist: Say what you want to say, as the healthy, Big Sandra that you are now.

Sandra: ...Madam, I understand that you want me to clean properly, but I do. I do my best, and I think I do it well. I find it quite annoying that you criticize me all the time.

Therapist: Very good! How do you feel when you say this?

Sandra: A little tense ... but also calm and powerful. It feels good to say this without immediately starting to shout.

Therapist: Very good. Where do you feel that calmness and strength in your body? (*Sandra puts her hand on her stomach.*) Stay in touch with that feeling. Is it a warm or a cold feeling?

Sandra: A little cool, powerful.

Therapist: Good ... Stay in touch with that feeling ... And now rewind the image to the moment when that woman criticizes you ... And now I want you to zoom out, as if you were looking at this situation from behind a camera. So, you see that woman, and you see Sandra. Where do you see them?

(*The therapist lets Sandra observe from an observer's perspective how she is criticized, how this makes her angry, but then she takes a moment to calm down and tells the woman that she doesn't like it.*)

Therapist: And how does Sandra's voice sound?

Sandra: Calm ... Powerful.

Therapist: Let her say it again and look closely at her. What is she saying now?

Sandra: She says, 'Madam, I'm doing my best, and I may be doing things a little differently than you're used to, but I know I'm doing a good job. I don't like getting comments from you all the time.'

Therapist: When you see her saying that, what do you think of her?

Sandra: I think she's tough, but in a powerful and calm way.

Therapist: So, you see a calm, powerful Sandra. She can handle this situation; she can manage her feelings in this situation very well. Do you see her doing that?

Sandra: Yes, I can see her doing that.

Therapist: And that Sandra is you ... How does it feel to realize that you are that powerful, calm Sandra?

Sandra: (*Smiling.*) That feels good, that feels nice.

Therapist: Then take that pleasant feeling with you, and hold on to it as you slowly let the image fade away ... Move your hands and feet, and when you're ready, you can open your eyes.

What if your client:

- ...becomes overwhelmed by the schema activation and is no longer able to practice the healthy behaviour discussed beforehand?

  First of all, it is a compliment that you have succeeded in making the visualization so realistic. It may just be a little too successful, perhaps. In that case, it may help to visualize the scenario immediately from an observer's perspective, so that there is more distance and your client is less overwhelmed.

Variations

In a group, instead of future-oriented imagination, you can also do future-oriented role-playing, in which group members participate in the exercise and someone plays the role of the woman who criticizes, for example.

You can vary the exercise by sketching different reactions from the antagonist, making the exercise more difficult and challenging. In this way, you can further strengthen the Healthy Adult.

Chapter 54: Concluding Therapy – Relapse Prevention Plan and Saying Goodbye

Objective

To ensure that the process of ending therapy proceeds in a healthy manner, even though it can be painful and trigger schema activation.

Guidelines

Step 1: Plan the end of therapy
Step 2: Discuss the results of therapy
Step 3: Identify what remains to be done
Step 4: Formulate a relapse prevention plan
Step 5: Saying goodbye to the therapist
Step 6: The farewell itself

Explanation of the guidelines

Step 1: Plan the end of therapy

Predictability is an important condition for ensuring that the farewell goes smoothly. Therefore, at the start of therapy, be as clear as possible about how long the treatment will last (see Chapter 11: Setting Goals and Creating a Treatment Plan). Announce the end of treatment in good time during the middle and final phases of therapy. At first, this will just be a comment that the therapy will not last indefinitely, but towards the end of treatment, you will give increasingly specific information about how long the treatment will last and how many sessions you have left.

Step 2: Discuss the results of therapy

Invite your client to reflect on the lessons learned during therapy and put them in writing. As a therapist, you should also make a similar overview of the changes that you believe the therapy has brought about. Discuss these experiences in detail; this is a form of consolidation of those experiences.

Step 3: Identify what remains to be done

Discuss with your client which complaints have not yet changed sufficiently. It is a pitfall to think that all presenting problems can be treated in therapy. Discuss realistic expectations regarding the possibilities and limitations of therapy. If necessary, make a selection of the complaints you still want to work on in the remaining time of the therapy. What else is needed to get to the point where the client can continue the change process that has been set in motion after the therapy has ended? Given the limited time available, you will need to draw up a concrete treatment plan for this.

Step 4: Formulate a relapse prevention plan

Ending therapy also means preparing your client for the time after treatment. Together, formulate a concrete plan that can help your client to deal with future problem situations independently. An example of a visual relapse prevention plan can be found in Appendix 7: Relapse prevention plan. This relapse prevention plan contains the guidelines and insights that helped your client during treatment. You can also make specific plans for those problem situations that you know your client will have difficulty with.

Step 5: Saying goodbye to the therapist

Pay attention to the process of detaching from the therapist, not just the process of detaching from the therapy. You have put a lot of energy and effort into forming an attachment relationship, so detachment requires attention and care. Prepare yourself and your client for the fact that saying goodbye can evoke all kinds of emotions, from sadness to anger. Ask your client what they will miss about you. Recognizing loss, being aware of it, is the first step in working towards a healthy farewell. However, also ask your client what else they would like to say to you. Be aware that this may also include irritations or frustrations; encourage them to express these.

Step 6: The farewell itself

Use rituals for the farewell itself. Part of this ritual can be accepting and/or giving small gifts. Examples of such gifts are a card, letter, plant, mineral or crystal, book or something you have made yourself. In the letting go process, as a therapist, you will delve less and less deeply into the problem situations described, based on the realization that, as a coach, you are on the sidelines and it is now really up to the player on the field.

Example

Unlike the other chapters, the example described below does not represent a dialogue from a single session, but rather pieces of dialogue from different sessions in the context of the completion of therapy.

Therapist: I hear you talking about the different sides of yourself, and I hear you paying much more attention to what you were feeling at that moment and what you actually needed. I think that's really great to hear. We're clearly no longer at the beginning of the therapy, do you recognize that too?

Sandra: (*Looks and sounds a little suspicious.*) ... Well ... What do you mean?

Therapist: Well, you seem to have learned a number of things, things that weren't at all clear to you when we began. For example, how about those different sides of you, right?

(*Sandra nods.*)

Therapist: That's good to realize, because it's obviously not your goal to remain in therapy for the rest of your life. We're now in a different phase of the treatment. As I see it, I think we're in the middle phase: you've learned a lot of things, and your Healthy Adult side can already take care of a number of things on its own. At the same time, you still need support with some things, and that's perfectly fine at this stage. Ultimately, of course, we're moving towards a phase of treatment in which you'll be able to manage more and more things yourself. But let's look back at the situation you described. How would you like to deal with your inner critic the next time it makes itself heard?

(*After this session, Sandra was quite upset. In the following sessions, she was more irritable and also more anxious. The therapist does not talk about the end of therapy in such concrete terms for a while, but brings it up again after some time.*)

Therapist: Well done! Well, Sandra, once again, when I hear how you've tried to listen to your own feelings, I think you've really grown enormously. I said a while ago that a fundamental goal of therapy is to learn to listen better to your needs, so that you can continue to do so independently, after the therapy has ended and we've said goodbye. Perhaps we can think about how long we want to take for that final phase of treatment.

(*Sandra's face tenses up and she becomes a little quiet.*)

I notice that you react immediately when I say something like that. I don't think you like this at all, do you?

Sandra: No, I immediately become tense and start wondering why you're saying this. Lately, I really feel like you want to get rid of me…

Therapist: OK, so when I talk about ending the therapy, you interpret that as a message that I want to get rid of you. I wonder who you're actually hearing … It can't be me, because I don't want to get rid of you at all, so who am I actually hearing, which side of you?

(*Following this conversation, the different modes are worked on again. The therapist continues to mention occasionally that the final phase will have to be shaped. A few weeks later:*)

Sandra: I've felt really miserable all week.

Therapist: Oh, would you like to tell me a bit more about that?

Sandra: Yes, I notice that lately you keep talking about the end of therapy and everything we've achieved. But there are still so many things that really bother me, and it almost seems like you don't see any of that!

Therapist: It's very good of you to say that. So, because I talked about the end of therapy and because last time, we looked at everything you've learned, it seemed as if I think there are only positive things to report, while you feel that there are still all kinds of things that aren't going well. Is that right?

Sandra: Yes, exactly.

Therapist: Well, I think it's very good that we're focusing on the problems that are still present in your life. At the same time, I also realize that therapy can't solve everything. That may sound a bit unpleasant to hear, but the reality is that we can't change everything we might want to. Life will always be complicated and difficult to some extent. That applies not only to you, but to all of us. I certainly think that these are very serious issues, and today I want to work with you to find the best way to deal with them. There will also be things that you'll have to find your own way with. I'm confident that you can do that, but today I want to help you think about how you can best go about it.

Sandra: But you can't help me with that…?

Therapist: Well, I don't think I'm really helping you if we just continue with the therapy. I know it doesn't always feel that way, but your healthy side is strong, and I want to use this last phase of therapy to put it even more firmly at the helm. That means I'm going to be a little less active in helping you, so that you can gain more and more confidence that you can do it yourself. By now, you can recite my words in your sleep, right?

Sandra: Yes, you're pretty much stuck in my head, almost to the point of annoyance!

(Sandra laughs.)

What if your client:

- **…still has many complaints that they say they cannot resolve on their own?**

  The temptation will be great to extend the treatment and offer extra help and support. However, research shows that it is advisable to stick to the treatment plan and end the therapy (Bamelis et al., 2014). In the final phase of therapy, and the two years after its completion, a further reduction in complaints is visible.

Variations

Your client can write down the results of the therapy in the form of a 'warm letter' to themselves, or perhaps to the Vulnerable Child. During the session, ask your client to read this letter aloud. By expressing the changes aloud, with the compassion you would use when speaking to a Vulnerable Child, the 'ownership' of those changes is further consolidated.

Flashcard Schema Therapy

In this section you will find a concise summary of the most important aspects of schema therapy.

Concepts

- The key concepts are emotional needs, schemas, coping and modes.
- The most important concept of schema therapy is 'core emotional needs'.
- Deficiencies in the fulfilment of emotional needs lead to negative schemas: emotional wounds.
- Schemas ('traits') are emotional experiences; coping responses or coping styles are the ways you deal with them.
- Schema + coping response = mode ('state')

There are four types of modes:

- **Child modes:** emotional sides with childlike thoughts and behaviours (resignation to schemas)
- **Inner critic modes:** negative self-reflections (resignation to schemas)
- **Coping modes:** protective sides (avoidance or inversion of schemas)
- **Healthy Adult mode:** able to handle context and needs

The therapeutic relationship: Limited reparenting

Objective:

Providing corrective emotional experiences by validating core emotional needs

Form:

Personal attachment relationship within the framework of professional practice

Guiding question:

'What would I do if this were my foster child?'

1. provide care
2. provide guidance
3. use empathic confrontation
4. use limit setting

Limited reparenting throughout the phases of therapy:

- **Initial phase:** demonstrating (providing guidance)
- **Middle phase:** doing together (coaching)
- **Final phase:** encouraging (coaching from the sidelines)

Treatment plan

How long will the therapy take?

What are the relevant needs for this client?

Each session

What are the relevant needs of this client?

What phase of therapy is this?

What kind of 'parent' should I be for this client in this phase of therapy?

Which mode do I have in the room? Which mode do I hear in the client's story?

Strategy:

- *negotiating* with coping modes to move past them
- *fighting* against the inner critic modes
- *validating* the emotional needs of the Vulnerable Child
- *strengthening* the Healthy Adult

Each session is a corrective *emotional* experience.

Techniques

Use methods and techniques that follow the path of thinking–feeling–doing.

Frequently use imagery rescripting and chairwork.

Delve Deeper into Schema Therapy

This book has provided you with guidelines for delivering schema therapy interventions with your client. Would you like to learn more? Here are some tips to help you explore the subject further. This list is not intended to be exhaustive. For more books, see the website of the International Society for Schema Therapy (https://schematherapysociety.org).

Books

General

- Arntz, A., & Jacob, G. (2013). *Schema therapy in practice: An introductory guide to the schema mode approach.* Wiley-Blackwell.
- Arntz, A., & van Genderen, H. (2021). *Schema therapy for borderline personality disorder* (2nd ed.). Wiley Blackwell.
- Behary, W. (2013). *Disarming the narcissist: Surviving and thriving with the self-absorbed* (2nd ed.). New Harbinger.
- Behary, W. T., Farrell, J. M., Vaz, A., & Rousmaniere, T. (2023). *Deliberate practice in schema therapy*. American Psychological Association.
- Brockman, R., Simpson, S., Hayes, C., van der Wijngaart, R., & Smout, M. (2023). *Cambridge guide to schema therapy* (Cambridge Guides to the Psychological Therapies). Cambridge University Press. https://doi.org/10.1017/9781108918145
- Heath, G., & Startup, H. (2020). *Creative methods in schema therapy: Advances and innovation in clinical practice*. Routledge.
- Jacob, G., van Genderen, H., & Seebauer, L. (2015). *Breaking negative thinking patterns*. Wiley-Blackwell.
- Reubsaet, R. (2018). *Schema therapy: A phase-oriented approach.* Pavilion Publishing and Media Ltd.

- van der Wijngaart, R. (2021). *Imagery rescripting: Theory and practice.* Pavilion Publishing and Media Ltd.
- van der Wijngaart, R. (2023). *Chairwork: Theory and practice.* Pavilion Publishing and Media Ltd.
- van der Wijngaart, R., & van Genderen, H. (2024). *Schema therapy for cluster C personality disorders: Treating Dependent, Avoidant and Obsessive–Compulsive clients*. Pavilion Publishing and Media Ltd.
- van Genderen, H. (2026). *Break your negative patterns in five steps: A systematic plan to change unwanted feelings, thoughts and behaviour*. John Wiley & Sons Ltd.
- van Vreeswijk, M., Broersen, J., & Nadort, M. (2012). *The Wiley-Blackwell handbook of schema therapy: Theory, research and practice*. Wiley-Blackwell.
- Young, J. E., & Klosko, J. (1994). *Reinventing your life*. Plume.
- Young, J. E., Klosko, J., & Weishaar, M. E. (2003). *Schema therapy: A practitioner's guide*. Guilford.

About schema therapy with children and adolescents

- Loose, C., Graaf, P., Zarbock, G., & Holt, R. A. (2020). *Schema therapy for children and adolescents: A practitioner's guide*. Pavilion Publishing and Media.
- Loose, C., Graaf, P., Zarbock, G., & Holt, R. A. (2026). *Contextual Schema therapy for Children and adolescents: Working with Diagnosed Populations and Their Differences.* Pavilion Publishing and Media.

About group schema therapy

- Farrell, J. M., & Shaw, I. A. (2012). *Group schema therapy for borderline personality disorder: A step-by-step treatment manual with patient workbook.* Wiley-Blackwell.
- Farrell, J. M., Reis, N., & Shaw, J. (2014). *The schema therapy clinician's guide: A complete resource for building and delivering individual, group and integrated schema mode treatment programs*. Wiley-Blackwell.

Audiovisual material

Available from www.dutchschematherapy.com.

- Schema therapy, step by step. Remco van der Wijngaart & Hannie van Genderen
- Schema therapy with children and adolescents, step by step. Marjolein van Wijk-Herbrink & Remco van der Wijngaart
- Schema therapy, working with modes. Remco van der Wijngaart & David Bernstein
- Fine tuning imagery rescripting. Remco van der Wijngaart & Chris Hayes
- Fine tuning chair work. Chris Hayes & Remco van der Wijngaart
- Schema therapy for the avoidant, dependent and obsessive–compulsive personality disorder. Remco van der Wijngaart & Guido Sijbers

Materials

Available via http://www.psykey.nl/en.

- Mode cards: Modes in Focus (various sizes) – set of twenty mode cards plus an overview card.
- Mode figurines: Modes in Focus – set of 20 figurines, each representing a mode.
- Free downloadable formats for a case conceptualization model (including a workbook for your client), safety plan, relapse prevention plan, flashcards and mode sequence.

References

Arntz, A., & Bögels, S. (2000). *Schemagerichte cognitieve therapie voor persoonlijkheidsstoornissen. [Schema therapy for personality disorders.]* Bohn Stafleu van Loghum.

Arntz, A., & van Genderen, H. (2021). *Schema therapy for borderline personality disorder* (2nd ed.). Wiley Blackwell.

Arntz, A., Rijkeboer, M., Chan, E., Fassbinder, E., Karaosmanoglu, A., Lee, C. W., & Panzeri, M. (2021). Towards a reformulated theory underlying schema therapy: Position paper of an international workgroup. *Cognitive Therapy and Research, 45*(6), 1007–1020. https://doi.org/10.1007/s10608-021-10209-5

Bamelis, L. L. M., Evers, S. M. A. A., Spinhoven, P., & Arntz, A. (2014). Results of a multicenter randomized controlled trial of schema therapy for personality disorders. *American Journal of Psychiatry, 171*(3), 305–322.

Brockman, R., Simpson, S., Hayes, C., van der Wijngaart, R., & Smout, M. (2023). *Cambridge guide to schema therapy* (Cambridge Guides to the Psychological Therapies). Cambridge University Press. https://doi.org/10.1017/9781108918145

Dweck, C. S. (2017). From needs to goals and representations: Foundations for a unified theory of motivation, personality and development. *Psychological Review, 124*, 689–719. https://doi.org/10.1037/rev0000082

Farrell, J. M., & Shaw, I. A. (2012). *Group schema therapy for borderline personality disorder: A step-by-step treatment manual with patient workbook.* Wiley-Blackwell.

Giesen-Bloo, J., van Dyck, R., Spinhoven, P., van Tilburg, W., Dirksen, C., van Asselt, T., Kremers, I., Nadort, M., & Arntz, A. (2006). Outpatient psychotherapy for borderline personality disorder: Randomized trial of schema-focused therapy vs transference-focused psychotherapy. *Archives of General Psychiatry*, *63*(6), 649–658. https://jamanetwork.com/journals/jamapsychiatry/fullarticle/209673

International Society of Schema Therapy (2024). *Case conceptualisation form and instruction guide.* https://schematherapysociety.org/

Kip, A., Schoppe, L., Arntz, A., & Morina, N. (2023). Efficacy of imagery rescripting in treating mental disorders associated with aversive memories: An updated meta-analysis. *Journal of Anxiety Disorders*, *99*, 102772. https://doi.org/10.1016/j.janxdis.2023.102772

Kooistra, M. J., Schoorl, M., Oprel, D. A. C., van der Does, W., & De Kleine, R. A. (2025). Maximizing expectancy violation and exposure outcomes in patients with PTSD. *European Journal of Psychotraumatology, 16*(1), 2447183. https://doi.org/10.1080/20008066.2024.2447183

Kroener, J., Hack, L., Mayer, B., & Sosic-Vasic, Z. (2023). Imagery rescripting as a short intervention for symptoms associated with mental images in clinical disorders: A systematic review and meta-analysis. *Journal of Psychiatric Research, 166*, 49–60. https://doi.org/10.1016/j.jpsychires.2023.09.010

Landkroon, E., Meyerbröker, K., Salemink, E., & Engelhard, I. M. (2022). Future-oriented imagery rescripting facilitates conducting behavioral experiments in social anxiety. *Behaviour Research and Therapy*, *155*, 104130. https://doi.org/10.1016/j.brat.2022.104130

Libby, L. K., Shaeffer, E. M., Eibach, R. P., & Slemmer, J. A. (2007). Picture yourself at the polls: Visual perspective in mental imagery affects self-perception and behavior. *Psychological Science*, *18*(3), 199–203. https://doi.org/10.1111/j.1467-9280.2007.01872.x

Loose, C., Meyer, F., & Pietrowsky, R. (2018). *Dusseldorf Illustrated Schema Questionnaire for Children (DISC)* [Database record]. APA PsycTests. https://doi.org/10.1037/t69949-000

Loose, C., Graaf, P., Zarbock, G., & Holt, R. A. (2020). *Schema therapy for children and adolescents: A practitioner's guide*. Pavilion Publishing and Media Ltd.

Louis, J. P., Wood, A. M., Lockwood, G., Ho, M. R., & Ferguson, E. (2018). Positive clinical psychology and schema therapy (ST): The development of the Young Positive Schema Questionnaire (YPSQ) to complement the Young Schema Questionnaire 3 Short Form (YSQ-S3). *Psychological Assessment, 30*(9), 1199–1213. https://doi.org/10.1037/pas0000567

Miller, W. R., & Rollnick, S. (2023). *Motivational interviewing: Helping people change and grow* (4th ed.). Taylor & Francis.

Morina, N., Lancee, J., & Arntz, A. (2017). Imagery rescripting as a clinical intervention for aversive memories: A meta-analysis. *Journal of Behavior Therapy and Experimental Psychiatry*, *55*, 6–15. https://doi.org/10.1016/j.jbtep.2016.11.003

Nadort, M., Arntz, A., Smit, J. H., Giesen-Bloo, J., Eikelenboom, M., Spinhoven, P., van Asselt, T., Wensing, M., & van Dyck, R. (2009). Implementation of outpatient schema therapy for borderline personality disorder with versus without crisis support by the therapist outside office hours: A randomized trial. *Behaviour Research and Therapy*, *47*(11), 961–973. https://doi.org/10.1016/j.brat.2009.07.013

Pittig, A., Heinig, I., Goerigk, S., … & Wittchen, H. (2022). Change of threat expectancy as mechanism of exposure-based psychotherapy for anxiety disorders: Evidence from 8484 exposure exercises of 605 patients. *Clinical Psychological Science 11*(2), 199–217. https://doi.org/10.31234/osf.io/khezc

Reubsaet, R. (2018). *Schema Therapy: A phase-oriented approach.* Pavilion Publishing and Media Ltd.

Roelofs, J., Muris, P., & Lobbestael, J. (2016). Acting and feeling like a Vulnerable Child, an Internalized "Bad" Parent, or a Healthy Person: The assessment of schema modes in non-clinical adolescents. *Journal of Personality Disorders*, *30*(4), 469–482. https://doi.org/10.1521/pedi_2015_29_209

Santos, L., Vagos, P., & Rijo, D. (2018). *Brief Form of the Young Schema Questionnaire for Adolescents (B-YSQ-A)* [Database record]. APA PsycTests. https://doi.org/10.1037/t74449-000

Siegel, D. J. (2012). *The developing mind: How relationships and the brain interact to shape who we are* (2nd ed.). Guilford Press.

Treanor, M., Zbozinek, T. D., Rosenberg, B. M., Sewart, A., Sandman, C. F., Ruiz, J., & Craske, M. G. (2025). A randomized controlled trial comparing two processes of exposure therapy: Extinction learning and habituation. *Journal of Consulting and Clinical Psychology, 93*(10), 705–717.

van der Wijngaart, R. (2021). *Imagery Rescripting: Theory and Practice.* Pavilion Publishing and Media Ltd.

van der Wijngaart, R. (2023). *Chairwork: Theory and practice.* Pavilion Publishing and Media Ltd.

Vereniging voor Schematherapie [Dutch Association for Schema Therapy] (2024). *Visiestuk: Wat is schematherapie [Conceptual paper: What is Schematherapy].* https://www.schematherapie.nl/home

Vuijk, R., Turner, W., Zimmerman, D., Walker, H., & Dandachi-FitzGerald, B. (2024). Schema therapy in adults with autism spectrum disorder: A scoping review. *Clinical Psychology & Psychotherapy*, *31*(1), e2949. https://doi.org/10.1002/cpp.2949

Yakın, D., Grasman, R., & Arntz, A. (2020). Schema modes as a common mechanism of change in personality pathology and functioning: Results from a randomized controlled trial. *Behaviour Research and Therapy*, *126*, 103553. https://doi.org/10.1016/j.brat.2020.103553

Young, J. E., Klosko, J., & Weishaar, M. E. (2003). *Schema therapy: A practitioner's guide*. Guilford Press.

Young, J. E., & Brown, G. (2005). *Young Schema Questionnaire-Short Form; Version 3 (YSQ-S3, YSQ)* [Database record]. APA PsycTests. https://doi.org/10.1037/t67023-000

Young, J. E., Arntz, A., Atkinson, T., Lobbestael, J., Weishaar, M. E., van Vreeswijk, M. F., & Klokman, J. (2007). *The schema mode inventory.* Schema Therapy Institute.

Appendix 1: Rationale for schema therapy

The following text can be used as a guideline when explaining the rationale for schema therapy to a client. Of course, many variations are possible. Make sure you at least briefly mention the different concepts of schema therapy (emotional needs, schemas and modes). You can give a general explanation or choose to personalize your explanation for your client, for example, by incorporating their presenting problems into it. The intention is not that you read the following sample text aloud in its entirety. Instead, select parts of it and give your client space to respond and ask questions in between.

Indication for schema therapy

'What has become clear to me is that your presenting problems are patterns rather than temporary problems. You have been experiencing these problems for a long time. When it comes to patterns that have crept into your personality, there are broadly speaking two options: treatment can focus on support, reinforcing what is going well and learning to deal with those patterns in a healthy way; or treatment may focus on change, with the aim of really breaking those patterns. I understand that you mainly want the latter. The form of therapy that is suitable for this is called psychotherapy. There are different forms of this; for you, I think schema therapy will be helpful.'

Emotional needs

'In schema therapy, we assume that every child has core emotional needs. For example, it is important that a child grows up in a safe and connected environment, where warm eyes are focused on that child, so that they experience that their feelings and needs matter and may be expressed. From there, a child explores the world, discovering what they like and dislike and what they can and cannot do, in order to develop a sense of autonomy and competence. And, of course, in that process, a child will encounter the limits that inevitably exist in life; not everything you want is possible. But those limits should be fair, and provide room for play and spontaneity, for enjoying life. And if all those emotional needs are sufficiently met, things then start to make sense: a child learns to understand itself and the world around it.'

Schemas

'When you have experiences in which core emotional needs are violated, you suffer 'emotional wounds'. You then start to view yourself, others or the world in a certain way. For example, if you lacked safe attachment to others you may have learned to expect that others cannot be trusted or that you are worthless. Such expectations are called schemas, hence the term schema therapy. Your expectations or schemas influence the way you interpret information in the here and now; you look at situations through the lens of those schemas, as it were. Because those earlier experiences have caused wounds, old pain resurfaces in the here and now. That is why you can sometimes react so strongly that other people, or you yourself, do not understand why it happens.'
[Give an example that the client can relate to.]

Modes

'In order to deal with these intense emotions, people develop different sides to themselves, which we call modes in schema therapy. Sometimes, we resign ourselves to these emotions and feel deeply depressed, while at other times it may feel as if difficult situations do not affect us. Or we may numb our emotions by, for example, eating them away or scrolling through our phones for hours on end. Some of us may ... [give other examples that your client can relate to, e.g., project a sense of greatness to inverse the inner feeling of smallness]. These are a few examples of the different sides that people can have. These sides come to the fore at different times, depending on our situation or mood.'

Assessment phase

'In the next five to seven sessions [specify duration of the assessment phase], I would like to explore with you which sides *you* have, which expectations or schemas are associated with them and which emotional needs were not sufficiently met in your childhood, causing these schemas to develop. Once we have mapped this out properly, we can formulate goals together and I can draw up a concrete treatment plan for you. I will then also be able to tell you how long I expect the therapy to take. After this exploratory phase, you can reconsider whether you want to embark on this journey. You do not have to say 'yes' to the entire treatment straight away.'

Treatment phase

'If you agree to the treatment, we will then work on changing your different sides and expectations so that your presenting problems will be reduced. The therapy has initial, middle and final phases, but I will explain that to you later. It is also important to know that we will not just talk during the therapy. We will also do many exercises that focus on feeling and experiencing, because that helps you to understand things not only cognitively, but also emotionally. I will explain more about these exercises once we start doing them. I will also ask you to actively engage with what we do and practice between sessions, which will include homework assignments. This will help you to recognize and apply what you learn in therapy in your daily life.'

Appendix 2: Case conceptualization – Sandra

Brief description of the client

Sandra is a thirty-two-year-old woman who presents with anxiety symptoms, escalating arguments with her boyfriend, self-harm, mood swings and depressive episodes. She lives independently and has a social network that includes one significant friend.

She is in a relationship with a man who does not have a steady job and regularly uses drugs (often cannabis, sometimes ecstasy) and alcohol. His behaviour can change depending on the situation: sometimes he seems insecure and is sweet towards her, but he can also be distant and verbally aggressive, especially when under the influence of alcohol.

Sandra works twenty-four hours a week as a cleaner in people's homes.

She has low self-esteem, including doubts about her abilities. As a result of this insecurity, she can lose herself in avoiding social activities, which makes her feel lonely and depressed, or she can try to keep going by acting tougher than she feels, with the result that she feels exhausted and overwhelmed.

Current presenting problems

- mood swings;
- depressive episodes;
- self-harm;
- escalating arguments with boyfriend;
- feeling dependent.

Classification according to the DSM-5

There is a recurrent depressive disorder in partial remission, a generalized social anxiety disorder and a borderline personality disorder with paranoid, dependent and avoidant traits.

Temperament and biological factors

In childhood, Sandra used to be sensitive, temperamental and cheerful. Her sensitivity made her vulnerable to her father's anger and discontent.

Upbringing

Father's character and parenting style

Father is described as a dominant, aggressive man who, due to insecurity, was prone to drinking alcohol and could then become aggressive (*possibly leading to a lack of safe attachment to others; Mistrust/Abuse schema*). Father was himself abused by his own father, but never spoke about it. The consequences of that abuse were palpable in the home but not discussed – they included Father's distrust of others, and the angry tension he could radiate. He was harsh towards Sandra, her mother and her brother. Without alcohol, that harshness in his relationship with Sandra mainly consisted of name-calling and derogatory comments about her intelligence ('You can't do that', 'It's a waste of time trying to explain that to her') and her appearance ('My goodness, I hope you can still get a boyfriend with that face') (*lack of safe attachment to others, self-expression and competence; Emotional Deprivation, Defectiveness/Shame schemas*). When he was drunk, this verbal aggression became more intense and frequent, but he would also throw things around. When drunk, her father mainly hit Sandra's brother. He did hit Sandra herself a few times, but most of the time his aggression was directed at her brother, or her brother would stand up for Sandra and then get beaten up.

Mother's character and parenting style

Mother is not only gentle and sweet, but also a fearful and accommodating woman (*role model for the Subjugation schema and the Compliant Surrenderer mode*). Out of fear of her husband, Mother often kept her mouth shut and did not protect the children (*lack of safe attachment to others and the Emotional Deprivation schema*). After her husband's outbursts, she tried to restore calm and normality as quickly as possible. She would say things like, 'Oh, you know how he is' and 'You'd better keep your mouth shut, otherwise it will only get worse' (*Compliant Surrenderer and Detached Protector*).

Other relevant memories of influences during the client's childhood (e.g., influence of peers, traumatic events)

Sandra always felt lonely and different from peers (*lack of connection; Social Isolation / Alienation schema*). Her family was considered different from other families, and people were somewhat afraid of her father, which made it more difficult for Sandra to connect with peers.

During her childhood, Sandra not only often felt anxious and unsafe, and fearful of sudden danger (*Vulnerability to Harm or Illness schema*), but also insecure, lonely and incompetent; she could never do anything right and blamed this both on her abilities and on herself as a person (*Failure and Defectiveness / Shame schemas*). To escape the tensions of her family home, she often stayed out on the streets after school, where she learned to act tough.

She did well at school: she is of average to above-average intelligence, but as a result of her insecurity and the tensions at home, she only just managed to complete her vocational education.

Rules of life that the client has derived from the aforementioned childhood experiences

- I can't do it (I am incompetent).
- I am different from others.
- I am not good enough.
- Others are quick to get angry and punitive.
- If I have a different opinion, they will get angry.
- If I don't measure up, if I don't do well, they won't want to associate with me anymore.
- I am not allowed to make mistakes.
- I'd better keep my distance.
- I have to do what others expect of me so that they approve of me.

Deficits in fulfilling core emotional needs

- lack of safe attachment to others;
- lack of self-expression;
- lack of competence and autonomy;

- lack of spontaneity and play;
- lack of fairness;
- lack of realistic limits.

Of all the deficiencies in the fulfilment of emotional needs, the three most important are: 1) lack of safe attachment to others; 2) lack of self-expression; and 3) lack of competence and autonomy.

Relevant patterns (pitfalls)	Average score
1. Social Isolation/Alienation	4.2
2. Emotional Deprivation	4.8
3. Defectiveness/Shame	4.2
4. Failure	4.8
5. Mistrust/Abuse	3.4
6. Subjugation	4.8

Which situations or events can trigger which schemas (pitfalls)?

Situation		Schemas/pitfalls
1.	Conflict situations at work	Mistrust/Abuse Failure Subjugation Social Isolation/Alienation
2.	Making mistakes	Failure Defectiveness/Shame
3.	Making choices (e.g., which job to apply for)	Failure Subjugation

4.	Friend is angry or goes out	Mistrust/Abuse Subjugation Emotional Deprivation
5.	Viewing her own body	Defectiveness/Shame Social Isolation/Alienation

Coping strategies

Schema	Resignation (behaviour that leads to resignation to the schema)	Avoidance (behaviour that leads to avoidance of the schema)	Inversion (opposite behaviour, leading to inversion of the schema)
1. Social Isolation/ Alienation	She keeps to herself in company	At times, she withdraws and avoids social activities	Overly social behaviour, goes out a lot and meets up with friends frequently
2. Emotional Deprivation	Relationship with a man who does not offer her warm care and attention	Avoids contact with people in situations where she might feel unseen and unloved	Becomes angry when her boyfriend does not pay attention to her and demands care and attention
3. Defectiveness/ Shame	In company, she often expresses self-criticism; blames herself for things that go wrong	She avoids talking about intimate subjects for fear of not measuring up	She can express herself very assertively with friends and when going out, as if she feels no insecurity
4. Failure	She does not dare to tackle difficult tasks at work or performs below her level	She avoids applying for jobs for fear of being rejected	She tries to meet perfectionist standards

5. Mistrust/ Abuse	In relationships, she can be very jealous because she expects the other person to cheat on her	She avoids entering into a relationship because of the fear that the other person cannot be trusted	She may gullibly trust someone without protecting herself
6. Subjugation	She adapts her opinion to that of others	She does not express anger for fear that others will disapprove of her or respond with anger	She sometimes expresses herself very critically towards others, although rarely directly

Schema modes

Child modes

- **Vulnerable Child (Little Sandra):** She feels alone, fearful, unwanted and worthless. In this state, she asks for reassurance, seems insecure and afraid, and may cry when talking about how hard things are for her.
- **Angry Child (Angry Sandra):** As a child, Sandra always felt the injustice in her father's parenting style and the fact that her mother never protected her from it. She becomes very angry during arguments and can be very unreasonable and distrustful. In such an argument, she may hit the other person or herself, or threaten to harm herself to punish her boyfriend or make it clear how much he has hurt her. After such an outburst, she feels very guilty and bad about herself.
- **Happy Child (Happy, free Sandra):** This side of Sandra is not often visible. She does have a good sense of humour, and on rare occasions she can relax a little and make jokes. She is better able to let go of control with her friend Debbie, and they can get the giggles together.

Coping modes

- **Detached Protector (the Silent One):** In this state, Sandra seeks distraction from her feelings of loneliness by spending a lot of time outdoors and watching television when she is alone. This side is often active when Sandra feels lonely. In this state, she gives short answers, has little facial expression and quickly responds with irritation when asked further questions, which means that the Detached Protector can easily turn into a somewhat irritated Angry Protector.

- **Compliant Surrenderer (the Pleaser):** This side is only really visible once you get to know Sandra a little better. The Compliant Surrenderer is particularly present in her relationship with her boyfriend, especially during periods when he is using drugs or going out with friends. She then suppresses her own anger for fear that the other person will get angry and does what the other person wants, even if it is different from what she herself wants. In this state, she takes no initiative herself: the topic for the session must be determined by the therapist. Suggestions made by the other person are quickly accepted, even if she does not seem to fully agree with them.
- **Angry Protector (Tough Sandra):** Sandra can act tough and pretend that things don't affect her, as if talking about feelings is weak and stable relationships are for wimps and bourgeois types. This coping mechanism also manifests itself in periods of being very sociable, so that on the outside it is not apparent how lonely she feels and how afraid she is of failing and not measuring up. In this mode, she also tends to tell tough stories about exciting situations she has experienced, in which violence seems to be something tough rather than frightening or sad.

Inner critic mode

- **Punitive Critic:** The punitive messages in the form of her father's aggression, her mother's emotional deprivation and the unpleasant experiences she has had on the streets have been internalized into this Punitive Critic. When she makes mistakes, she not only feels insecure but also incompetent and bad about herself. In this Punitive Critic, her laughter takes on a somewhat scornful tone and she expresses herself in sarcastic terms: she condemns her difficulty in making choices as well as her feelings of loneliness.

Healthy mode

- **Healthy Adult (Big Sandra):** There is a Healthy Adult side to Sandra, which has led her to seek help and continue therapy, even though she often finds it very difficult and feels that she is not good enough and is not doing well enough in therapy. The Healthy Adult also contributes to her having managed to build up a reasonable social network, even though she does not dare to open up to her friends when it comes to intimate, emotional matters.

Appendix 3: Sandra's mode model

Mode model: Sandra

Presenting problems

Triggers

Arguments with partner, being criticized

The Silent One

Watching television, giving short answers. Avoidance of Defectiveness/Shame and Mistrust/Abuse schemas.

The Pleaser

Especially in romantic relationships, adapting herself to others.

Avoidance of Subjugation, Defectiveness/Shame and Emotional Deprivation schemas.

Tough Sandra

Acting as though nothing affects her, at times appearing very sociable. Mistrust/Abuse schema.

Big Sandra

Attending therapy sessions, sense of humour, perseverance, sensitive and intelligent.

Punitive Critic

Punitiveness and Unrelenting Standards schemas.

'You are worthless.'

Little Sandra

Feeling alone, unwanted, worthless.

Emotional Deprivation, Social Isolation/Alienation, Defectiveness/Shame, Mistrust/Abuse schemas.

Angry Sandra

Furious about injustice, threatening to harm herself.

Happy, Free Sandra

Sense of humour, having the giggles with a friend.

Appendix 4: Case conceptualization – Tim

Brief description of the client

Tim is a fifteen-year-old boy who lives with his mother and his half-sister (eight years old). His father has been out of his life since he was six and is currently in prison. Tim and his father have no contact. Tim has a group of friends consisting mainly of older boys, with whom he spends a lot of time on the streets. He regularly skips school. He has had run-ins with the police (theft, fights) and smokes cannabis with his friends every day.

Current presenting problems

- violent behaviour on the streets and towards his mother;
- smoking cannabis every day;
- truancy, not following rules;
- nonchalant attitude, as if nothing affects him.

Classification according to the DSM-5

- conduct disorder;
- cannabis abuse;
- parent–child relationship problems;
- cluster B personality disorder traits.

Temperament and biological factors

As a child, he was seen as the 'ringleader'. At the same time, he did not feel very comfortable around other people. His mother describes him as somewhat withdrawn, almost shy, in his interactions with others. He could have huge tantrums when things did not go his way.

Upbringing

Father's character and parenting style

His father was violent towards his mother and Tim. When Tim was six years old, his mother left his father with the help of a youth care agency. His father then stalked them for a while. His mother describes his father as an impatient, explosive man who regularly lost his temper. Afterwards, he always expressed regret and made an extra effort to be nice to them, which is why his mother stayed with him for so long. His father has been convicted of various violent crimes and is currently serving a prison sentence.

Mother's character and parenting style

Tim's mother had him at a young age (twenty) and tried to protect him during his early years, but was unable to stand up to her partner. The youth care agency warned that Tim was not safe at home as long as his mother stayed with his father. With help, his mother then left his father, taking Tim with her. She subsequently had several partners, and Tim's half-sister was born from one of those relationships. His mother works hard to earn enough money for the family, which means she is often away from home and has little insight into what Tim is doing.

The mother tries to set limits for Tim, but this leads to many arguments, during which Tim has been verbally and physically aggressive on several occasions. She then becomes afraid of Tim and no longer sets limits. However, they also share a close, positive bond.

Other relevant memories

Tim has been profoundly impacted by several events in his life: his experience of being held at the police station for a few hours; his father's detention; the arguments with his mother.

Rules for living

- Ultimately, you're on your own, so you might as well do it alone.
- Crying is weak.
- If you don't stand up for yourself or show that you're in charge, people will walk all over you.

Relevant emotional needs

Tim's early childhood was marked by a lack of safe attachment due to his father's violent behaviour and the breakdown in contact. In terms of autonomy, Tim was somewhat overburdened: he had to learn to perform everyday tasks at an early age because his mother had to work a lot. He also felt responsible for his mother and later for his half-sister. This also stood in the way of spontaneity and play, although his mother did try to do as many fun things as possible with him in her spare time. Because she wanted to keep things fun, there was a lack of fulfilment of the emotional need for realistic limits. In terms of the need for self-expression, being bullied had a negative impact, as did the many corrections by adults on his externalizing behaviour. There is a shortfall in the fulfilment of the need for fairness because he was given extra attention due to his hyperactive behaviour and was often blamed unjustly. With regard to self-coherence, little attention has been paid to the interpretation of the behaviour of others and his confusing feelings about it.

Of the above-mentioned deficiencies in the fulfilment of emotional needs, the needs for safe attachment to others and realistic limits are particularly relevant to Tim.

Which emotional needs have been met?

The emotional need for safe attachment was partially met by the warm contact with his mother and her involvement with him. The emotional need for autonomy and self-expression was also partially met by her: she gave him compliments and encouraged him to express himself during his childhood.

Relevant schemas (also mention hypotheses)	Average score
1. Abandonment/Instability	2.0
2. Mistrust/Abuse	2.0
3. Defectiveness/Shame	1.4
4. Emotional Deprivation	2.2
5. Insufficient Self-Control/Self-Discipline	2.6
6. Failure	2.8

Note: *Tim scores relatively low on all schemas on the schema questionnaire. The hypothesis is that he completed the list in an avoidant coping mode. Nevertheless, a few scores are above 2.5. After discussion, he recognizes himself in all of the above schemas.*

Which situations or events can trigger which schemas (pitfalls)?

Situation		Schemas/pitfalls
1.	Encountering a group of young people he does not know	Mistrust/Abuse Defectiveness/Shame
2.	Tim's father informs his probation officer that he would like to rebuild his relationship with Tim	Abandonment/Instability Mistrust/Abuse Emotional Deprivation
3.	The teacher at school informs Tim that a test week is planned soon	Insufficient Self-Control/Self-Discipline Failure
4.	Mother is angry with Tim and tells him that his behaviour is unacceptable	Abandonment/Instability Emotional Deprivation Defectiveness/Shame Insufficient Self-Control/Self-Discipline

Coping strategies

Schema	Resignation (behaviour that leads to resignation to the schema)	Avoidance (behaviour that leads to avoidance of the schema)	Inversion (opposite behaviour, leading to inversion of the schema)
1. Abandonment/ Instability	Being anxious and sad, expressing these feelings	Only engaging in superficial contact, nonchalant attitude	Bullying or intimidating others, breaking off friendships
2. Mistrust/ Abuse	Being angry about injustice, being vigilant in contact with others	Avoiding groups of young people he does not know	Trusting his 'mates' excessively, bullying or intimidating others
3. Defectiveness/ Shame	Putting himself down: 'You're useless, you can't do it anyway'	Avoiding new contacts, smoking cannabis to numb his feelings	Belittling others, bragging about himself

4. Emotional Deprivation	Saying that no one understands him, feeling lonely	Not sharing what is bothering him, not having in-depth conversations	Saying that he doesn't need anyone, that his friends understand him completely
5. Insufficient Self-Control/ Self-Discipline	Hanging around outside instead of studying for school, smoking cannabis	Skipping school; performing below his potential	Periods of (almost exaggerated) adherence to the rules of school and his mother
6. Failure	Performing below standard, thinking that everything he does will fail anyway	Truanting from school	Setting himself very high goals

Schema modes

Child modes

Vulnerable Child (Little Tim): Little Tim does not show himself very often, but sometimes comes to the fore when Tim says he is worried about his relationship with his mother. He is afraid that she will eventually kick him out and stop loving him.

Enraged Child (the Super Angry): Tim's Super Angry side becomes active when he feels he has been treated unfairly, for example, when a teacher sends him out of the classroom or when his mother confronts him about his behaviour. The Super Angry side then starts shouting and swearing, and sometimes throwing things around indiscriminately.

Undisciplined Child ('Screw it' side): The 'Screw it' side believes that others should not tell him what he can and cannot do. This side of Tim skips school when he does not feel like going, and hangs out on the streets, does not allow himself to be restricted and occasionally steals sweets or cans of soft drinks because he feels like it.

Happy Child (YOLO): Tim has a few friends with whom he can really have fun, who share his sense of humour and with whom he can laugh a lot. He also enjoys sport and drawing, although he doesn't always make time for it.

Coping modes

Angry Protector ('I don't care' side): He is somewhat sullen and indifferent, literally says that he 'doesn't care', makes little eye contact, does his own thing and sometimes skips school to avoid experiences of failure. The 'I don't care' side avoids contact with new people or only engages in superficial contact.

Detached Self-Soother (the Stoner): The Stoner smokes cannabis to feel better. He does this with friends, but also alone in the evening to help him sleep.

Bully and Attack mode (the Attacker): The Attacker can be bullying or intimidating, scaring others away, trying to pre-empt bullying behaviour from others, and using physical violence against peers (street fights) and against his mother (to 'overrule' her attempts to set limits).

Self-Aggrandizer (the Great One): The Great One comes to the fore when Tim feels insecure, especially in contact with peers. He then starts bragging, telling tall tales, acting tough or humiliating others.

Note: *There may also be a Perfectionistic Overcontroller (inversion of the Defectiveness / Shame and Failure schemas), but this is not prominent and is less linked to Tim's presenting problems. In order to limit the number of modes in his mode model, this has not been included here.*

Inner critic mode

Punitive Critic (the Moaner): Tim does not readily show this side, but says that it is in his head. The Moaner points out everything he does wrong and judges him for it: 'You can't do it, everything you do fails, you can't keep it up, you're a loser', etc.

Healthy mode

Healthy Adolescent (Calm Tim): Calm Tim thinks about his decisions before making them; he can reflect on what he feels, thinks and does; and he makes real contact with the people around him. Calm Tim comes to the fore when there is no tension at home, and during conversations with his neighbour.

Therapeutic relationship

In the first conversation, Tim has a very nonchalant attitude and says that he is only coming because his mother and his youth probation officer require him to. He barely makes eye contact. He slowly reveals a little more about the problems at home and how he experiences them. There is definitely a growing therapeutic connection, but it is also fragile; he can suddenly shut down again and deny that anything is bothering him, or he will start telling long-winded, tough stories about what he experiences on the streets.

Below is an example of how the interaction between the client's schemas and those of the therapist might look. Of course, the schemas are different for each therapist; it is important to think about how your client's schemas and modes can activate your own schemas and modes, and vice versa.

Therapist schemas

- Self-Sacrifice
- Unrelenting Standards/Hypercriticalness
- Emotional Deprivation

Interaction between therapist and client schemas

My Unrelenting Standards/Hypercriticalness schema can confirm Tim's Lack of Self-Control/Self-Discipline (and Failure) schema, and this could trigger my Self-Sacrifice schema, causing me to set too few limits to his behaviour. Or it could trigger my Unrelenting Standards/Hypercriticalness schema even further, causing me to give him too little encouragement and help in, for example, keeping appointments.

At the same time, my Self-Sacrifice schema could also have a positive effect on his Abandonment/Instability, Mistrust/Abuse and Defectiveness/Shame schemas, because it makes me put his interests first and go the extra mile for him. If I noticed that he appreciated that, it might also dampen my Unrelenting Standards/Hypercriticalness schema somewhat.

His avoidant and inversion coping with his schemas, such as Abandonment/Instability, Mistrust/Abuse and Defectiveness/Shame, may trigger my Emotional Deprivation schema. If I then respond with an avoidant coping response (distancing myself; my Detached Protector), this could reinforce his Abandonment/Instability schema, among other things.

Appendix 5: Case conceptualization model – Tim

Objectives:

- Learning to express my anger in a healthy way
- Improving the relationship with my mother by sharing my feelings and negotiating rules in a respectful manner

Basic emotional needs:

- **Safe attachment:** My father hit and stalked us. I was being bullied by peers in school.
- **Autonomy:** I had to take care of myself and had the feeling I had to also take care of my little sister.
- **Self-expression**: My father did not allow me to cry.
- **Spontaneity and play:** My mother tried doing fun things with me, but had little time and money.
- **Realistic limits:** No limits were set, or I did not comply.
- **Fairness:** Because of my hyperactive behaviour, people watched me more closely and often blamed me.
- **Self-coherence:** With so little support or explanation, I often felt confused about who I was and how the world fits together.

Positive Schemas:

- I stand up for myself
- I can take care of myself
- There are people who love me

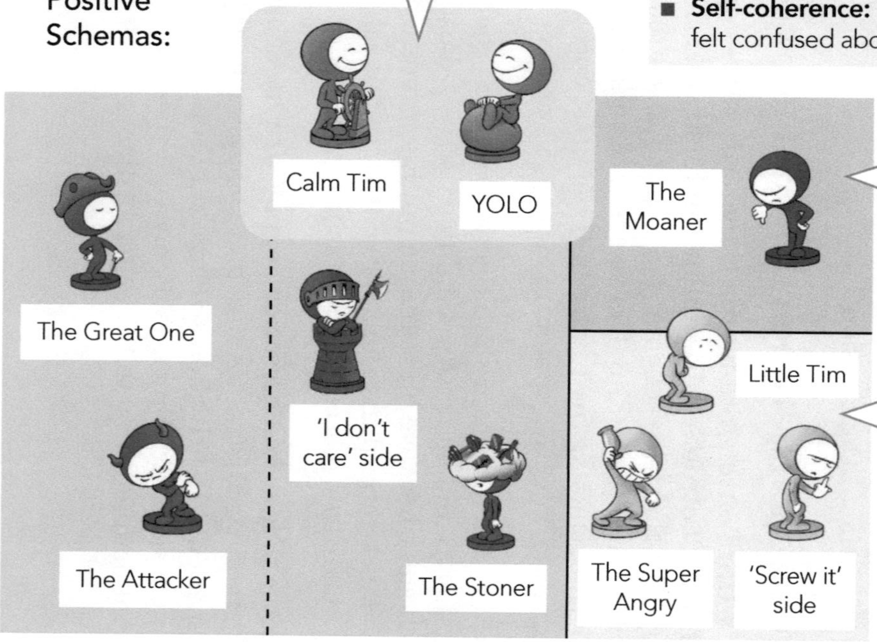

- You can't do it
- You're a loser, and you ruin everything

Schemas:

- I feel abandoned (Abandonment/Instability)
- I cannot trust anyone (Mistrust/Abuse)
- I fail (Failure)
- I'm not good enough (Defectiveness/Shame)
- I can't stick with difficult tasks (Insufficient Self-Control/Self-Discipline)

Appendix 6: Treatment plan – Tim

Therapy goals

- I want to understand where my anger comes from (Super Angry and Little Tim) and learn to express it in a healthy way (Calm Tim), so that I no longer get into trouble with the police because of my aggression (the Attacker).
- I want to improve my relationship with my mother by:
- sharing more of what is going on inside me (Little Tim and Calm Tim) instead of shutting her out ('I don't care' side) or putting myself above her (the Great One);
- negotiating rules with her in a respectful manner (Calm Tim) instead of getting very angry (Super Angry) or rebelling against them ('Screw It' side).

After completing the assessment phase, Tim agrees with the above goals. The therapist believes it is also important for Tim to stop using drugs, but Tim does not agree with this at the moment. The therapist therefore does not include it as a therapy goal (yet), but he does put it on the agenda in the treatment plan. Tim's inner critic side is also not yet included in the goals, because Tim often does not yet recognize it as a driver of his presenting problems. He will first need to gain insight into this during therapy.

Limited reparenting attitude

For Tim, the emotional needs of safe attachment to others and realistic limits are particularly important. It is therefore important to be predictable and reliable in the therapeutic relationship: to be a role model who not only offers security but also sets limits without being punitive.

Duration and session frequency

Given Tim's schemas in the domain of disconnection and rejection, it is important to be patient with regard to building the therapeutic relationship and the effects of treatment. Based on research into cluster B personality pathology, the duration of treatment is expected to be several years, but for adolescents, treatment lasting one to one-and-a-half years is more common (in the Netherlands, where Tim lives). Adolescents are still developing and also need space for important (developmental) tasks such as separating from their parents, forming their identity and making choices regarding education. Therapy can be a necessary temporary support in this process, but there must also be a clear end point in order to promote autonomy and competence. For Tim, one to one-and-a-half years already feels like an eternity. The therapist and Tim agree that they will evaluate the therapy every two months and that he can discuss any feelings of reluctance or discouragement at any time. This does not mean that the therapy will then be stopped immediately (the modes in which these feelings are expressed will be examined so that his underlying needs can be validated), but it does give Tim the feeling that he can have a say in it.

Ideally, the session frequency at the start of therapy would be twice a week, but because Tim is not open to this at the moment, they start with a frequency of once a week. The possibility of intensifying the therapy will be kept open and discussed repeatedly, at least during evaluation moments.

Involving significant others

Tim's mother will be actively involved in the therapy. Given Tim's age and the important role she can play in validating his emotional needs, separate sessions with her will also be planned to explore which of her own schemas and modes play a role in her interaction with Tim.

For more information about schema therapy with parents, see the book Schema Therapy for Children and Adolescents: A Practitioner's Guide *(Loose et al., 2020). It is important to work with parents to develop their own (mini) case conceptualization and implement interventions to address the schemas and modes that interfere with healthy interaction with their child. When working with adults, also consider involving significant others (e.g., a partner or close friend) in the treatment.*

Methods and techniques

Initial phase

Experiential techniques

In this first phase, Tim's Angry Protector will get in the way of working on his goals, so the main focus will be on reducing this mode so that more contact can be made with Little Tim. Empathic confrontation and chairwork will be used to give him insight into his Angry Protector and to negotiate with it. Chairwork will also be used to negotiate with other coping modes.

To make it clear that Little Tim is also present and has feelings and needs, an extra chair or stool will be placed in the room (even if he does not yet want to sit on it). The therapist will occasionally sit on it to 'charge' that chair with Little Tim's feelings and needs. When Tim finds it difficult to tolerate being cared for, the caring attitude and messages are directed at this chair instead of directly at him.

During sessions, the Super Angry gets the chance to rage, with limits being set when the anger becomes too uncontrolled (e.g., swearing or throwing things). When Tim indicates that he is not allowed to be angry or puts himself down after becoming angry, he is made aware of the activation of his inner critic mode, which can be combatted with chairwork. To make expressing anger more light-hearted and give it a more positive meaning, exercises are also done in which the therapist (as a model for expressing anger) and Tim express their anger in a creative way (forcefully flattening balls of clay, bouncing a ball as hard as possible or hitting a target with a small ball). Moments of anger and underlying vulnerable feelings will be used as an affect bridge in imagery rescripting, to rescript childhood memories (at least with regard to aggression by the father, and his history of bullying) with an emphasis on safe attachment to others.

Cognitive techniques

In each session, time is taken to consolidate experiences that do not fit with the schemas or dysfunctional thoughts by allowing Tim to consciously reflect on them. Mode sequences are created with him and his mother to clarify what happens during conflicts at home and on the street. This information is used to create a first version of a safety plan aimed at preventing aggressive behaviour. When smoking cannabis is discussed, motivational interviewing is used. Socratic dialogue is used to challenge statements made by his Angry Protector and other coping modes. Whenever Tim displays healthy behaviour, this is referred to as his Healthy side, so that Tim will become aware of what his Healthy side is about. In evaluations, the goals are assessed and adjusted where necessary.

Behavioural techniques

During the sessions, Tim practices sharing experiences and emotions, after which he is asked whether his expectations (e.g., 'No one listens to me anyway') have been met. Practice is also given in curbing the impulses of his Undisciplined Child, for example, by being clear about what is expected of him and letting him practice tolerating delayed gratification.

Middle phase

***Note:** If there is still no change in motivation to stop smoking cannabis, the therapist will provide more and more guidance, and limit setting may also be considered (depending on the extent to which drug use affects the therapeutic process and the feasibility of the goals).*

Experiential techniques

The techniques used in the initial phase are being repeated and extended, with Tim's Healthy side playing a greater role. In chairwork, he negotiates with his coping modes himself, and in imagery rescripting, his Healthy side is coached to validate the emotional needs of Little Tim in the image and to combat the antagonist. Rescripting will still mainly focus on validating the need for a safe attachment to others, but it is also important to be alert to other emotional needs such as self-expression and autonomy. In addition, explicit attention is paid to imagery rescripting aimed at validating the basic need for realistic limits: during rescripting, Tim will practice setting limits for the younger Tim in the image in memories in which he displayed uncontrolled and impulsive behaviour.

Tim will now have gained more insight into his inner critic mode, enabling him to play a role in combatting it himself using chairwork.

Cognitive techniques

Tim uses the safety plan actively and more independently (with support from his mother) and adapts it based on his experiences (what works and what doesn't). When creating mode sequences, the focus shifts from analysing and understanding the situation to actively looking at the underlying need and how Tim can meet it in a healthy way.

Tim's thoughts (e.g., 'No one can be trusted', 'People will ultimately let me down') are challenged using a historical test. The statements of his inner critic mode are tested with the continuum technique and the courtroom technique.

In evaluations, the therapy goals are assessed and adjusted where necessary.

Behavioural techniques

When his mother (unintentionally) gives critical messages that reinforce his inner critic mode, this is discussed with Tim and his mother together, encouraging Tim to express his feelings and needs.

In separate and joint sessions, Tim and his mother practice healthy responses to each other, such as: his mother clearly expressing her expectations and setting limits, remaining consistent, calm and reliable, and Tim indicating that he needs a time-out and then wants to continue the conversation afterwards.

Tim will actively practice ways to calm himself down when he is angry.

Final phase

Experiential techniques

In the final phase, the therapist will take an even more backseat role in the imagery rescripting and chairwork. In chairwork, the therapist plays the role of the coping modes or inner critic mode, while Tim practices how to deal with this from his Healthy side.

Future-oriented imagery exercises are used to practice dealing with schema-activating situations in the future.

The Vulnerable and Angry Child modes are encouraged to express their emotions regarding the approaching end of therapy and saying goodbye to the therapist.

Cognitive techniques

Tim is increasingly challenged to adjust his dysfunctional cognitions independently, for example, by the therapist asking questions such as: *That 'I don't care' side says this, but what do YOU actually think about it? Is what that side says correct?*

The upcoming end of therapy is repeatedly addressed, allowing space for adjusting any dysfunctional thoughts that may be triggered by this.

Behavioural techniques

It is agreed that if there has been a conflict between Tim and his mother, they will discuss this independently at home and tell the therapist during the next session how they resolved it.

Appendix 7: Relapse prevention plan

I can carry out the three steps of my Healthy Adult side:

- **Self-compassion:** Being kind to myself. Not pushing my feelings away but understanding them – it's understandable and OK that I feel this way right now.
- **Realistic thinking:** Check what I'm thinking, and what my different sides are whispering to me right now. Is that right?/Does that help?
- **Practical advice:** Advise myself on what I can best do right now. What do I really need right now (e.g., talk about it, grab my action plan, ensure a balance between things that give me energy and those that drain me, set boundaries)?

Combating my inner critic mode:

- Identifying self-criticism as my inner critic mode;
- Brush it aside or make fun of it; don't take what the inner critic mode says seriously;
- Reflect on my feelings; I'm allowed to feel what I feel!
- Focus on what is going well

General tips:

- share how I feel with others;
- keep moving, even when I don't feel like it!
- make a daily schedule;
- schedule time for myself;
- do things mindfully;
- write down my (worried) thoughts;
- sing or dance in the living room;
- go to bed on time.

I start worrying excessively to stay one step ahead of problems or to do better next time. I work very hard and want to do it perfectly.

I spend a lot of time scrolling on my phone or lose myself watching TV series on the sofa.

I blindly do what others want or expect of me and don't consider what I want. I adapt and try to please others/not be a burden.

I withdraw, I don't say what I think or feel. I switch off my feelings, but then I no longer feel any joy and become gloomy. I avoid contact with my friends or family.

'You're not good enough.'
'You need to try harder.'
'Everything is your responsibility.'

Signs of relapse:

I feel restless and insecure. I feel this in my stomach and in my throat. I also feel tension in my neck and shoulders. I see obstacles everywhere and feel ashamed of how I feel.

By the same authors:

Imagery Rescripting:
Theory and Practice

•

Chairwork:
Theory and Practice

•

Schema Therapy for Cluster C Personality Disorders:
Treating Dependent, Avoidant and Obsessive-
Compulsive Clients